DIE KUNST DES SPIEGEL

THE ART OF DER SPIEGEL

DIE KUNST DES SPIEGEL

*Titel-Illustrationen
aus fünf Jahrzehnten*

THE ART OF DER SPIEGEL

*Cover Illustrations
over Five Decades*

Herausgegeben von
Published by

Stefan Aust
Stefan Kiefer

teNeues

Published by teNeues Publishing Group

teNeues Book Division
Kaistraße 18
40221 Düsseldorf, Germany
Tel.: 0049-(0)211-99 45 97-0
Fax: 0049-(0)211-99 45 97-40

teNeues Publishing Company
16 West 22nd Street
New York, NY 10010, USA
Tel.: 001-212-627-9090
Fax: 001-212-627-9511

teNeues Publishing UK Ltd.
P.O. Box 402
West Byfleet
KT14 7ZF, Great Britain
Tel.: 0044-1932-40 35 09
Fax: 0044-1932-40 35 14

teNeues France S.A.R.L.
4, rue de Valence
75005 Paris, France
Tel.: 0033-1-5576-6205
Fax: 0033-1-5576-6419

www.teneues.com

ISBN 3-8327-9000-4

Printed in Germany

© 2004 teNeues Verlag GmbH + Co. KG, Kempen,
SPIEGEL-Verlag, Hamburg

Umschlag/Cover:
Thomas Bonnie/DER SPIEGEL
Typografie/Layout:
Thomas Bonnie, Reinhilde Wurst/DER SPIEGEL
Redaktion/Editor:
Hans-Ulrich Stoldt/DER SPIEGEL

Bibliographic information published by Die Deutsche
Bibliothek. Die Deutsche Bibliothek lists this
publication in the Deutsche Nationalbibliographie;
detailed bibliographic data is available in the Internet at
http://dnb.ddb.de

teNeues Publishing Group
Kempen
Düsseldorf
London
Madrid
New York
Paris

teNeues

Inhalt
Contents

STEFAN AUST: Die SPIEGEL-Titelbilder
The Covers of DER SPIEGEL **6**

STEFAN KIEFER: Die Kunst der Illustration **7**
The Art of Illustration **8**

WALTER GRASSKAMP: Alles im Rahmen **10**
Framed **12**

STEVEN HELLER: Titelgeschichten im SPIEGEL **14**
Cover Stories of DER SPIEGEL **18**

Interview mit/with EBERHARD WACHSMUTH:
„Ich wollte Bilder, die Geschichten erzählen" **22**
"I wanted pictures that told stories" **26**

Die Illustratoren
The Illustrators **31**

Register
Index **262**

Sponsoren
Sponsors **264**

Die SPIEGEL-Titelbilder
The Covers of DER SPIEGEL

S T E F A N   A U S T

Das Titelbild ist die wöchentlich aktuelle Visitenkarte des SPIEGEL – es soll das spontane Interesse des unvorbereiteten Betrachters wecken und das Titelthema schnell erfassbar visualisieren. Geschehen kann dies auf zweierlei Weise: direkt und unverschlüsselt, wie es bei politischen oder historischen Ereignissen oft sinnvoll scheint; oder illustrativ umgesetzt, was sich bei eher zeitlosen Geschichten anbietet, die über einen konkreten Anlass hinausblicken. Eine Zeichnung kann eher abstrahieren, überhöhen, verdichten, oder, wenn gewünscht, ein Thema ironisch brechen.

Hierbei helfen dem SPIEGEL seit vielen Jahrzehnten die weltweit besten Illustratoren, deren Arbeiten das Bild des SPIEGEL entscheidend mitgeprägt haben. Einige dieser gezeichneten Titelblätter haben international Aufsehen erregt, andere sind als grafische Meisterstücke im öffentlichen Gedächtnis verankert. In jedem Fall bilden der rote Rahmen des SPIEGEL und die Auftrags-Kunstwerke immer wieder eine überraschende und erhellende Einheit.

Diese Ausstellung würdigt erstmals die Künstler hinter den Arbeiten und präsentiert eine Auswahl der seit 1956 für den SPIEGEL entstandenen Original-Illustrationen als „Die Kunst des SPIEGEL". Dieses Mal aber nicht im roten Rahmen und nur für eine Woche, sondern – wie die Werke es eigentlich verdient haben – als Kunst an der Wand namhafter Museen und Galerien.

Stefan Aust ist Chefredakteur des SPIEGEL.

Each week, the cover of DER SPIEGEL serves as the magazine's current calling card, awakening the interest of the casual passer-by and bringing the subject of the cover story to visual life. This can be accomplished in two ways: in a direct, non-coded fashion, which is often the choice for important political or historical events; or in an illustrative fashion, which is appropriate for those timeless stories whose reach extends far beyond a concrete event. An illustration can lend a touch of abstraction, exaggeration, summation or, if need be, even irony.

Over the past few decades, DER SPIEGEL has called on the world's best illustrators for assistance, and their work has done much to shape the magazine's image. Some of these illustrated covers have earned international recognition, and others have gained a permanent place in readers' collective memories as graphical masterpieces. The cover's red frame and the artwork it surrounds form a surprising and illuminating entity week in and week out.

The goal of this exhibition is to honor the artists who have created these covers and present a selection of the original illustrations dating back to 1956 as "The Art of DER SPIEGEL." But this time, there is no red frame surrounding the illustrations or weekly expiration date stamped on them. Instead, the works are finally getting something they really deserve – recognition as art on the walls of well-known museums and galleries.

Stefan Aust is Editor in Chief of DER SPIEGEL.

Die Kunst der Illustration
The Art of Illustration

S TEFAN K IEFER

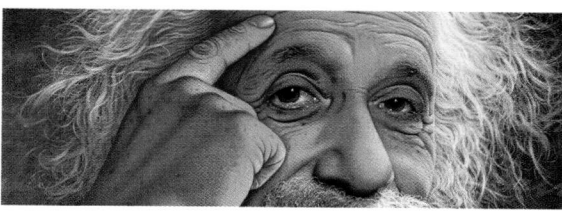

Der Illustrator ist ein weitgehend unbekanntes Wesen. Einzelkämpfer zumeist, lange Nächte in seinem Atelier über Auftragsarbeiten brütend, selten zufrieden mit dem Ergebnis seiner Mühen. Ist das Werk dann einmal abgeliefert, bleibt das bange Hoffen, ob es Gefallen findet und gar gedruckt wird.

Woche für Woche, und das seit bald fünfzig Jahren, bereitet die Titelredaktion des SPIEGEL den besten Illustratoren ebendiese schlaflosen Nächte. Im Spannungsfeld enger Vorgaben, hoher Ansprüche und nur weniger Tage Zeit sollen immer wieder originelle Titelblätter entstehen. Der SPIEGEL profitiert dabei vom besonderen Talent dieser „Miet"-Künstler, auftragsbezogen und unter Zeitdruck kreativ werden zu können. Und die Illustratoren lockt die Aussicht, millionenfach auf dem Cover unseres Magazins gedruckt zu werden.

Aus dieser Zusammenarbeit sind im Laufe der Jahrzehnte so viele außergewöhnliche Arbeiten entstanden, dass es an der Zeit war, sie in angesehenen Museen und Galerien zu zeigen. Denn hier zu Lande – im Gegensatz zu den USA – genießt die Illustration keinen besonders hohen Stellenwert, gilt bestenfalls als „Gebrauchsgrafik", keinesfalls jedoch als Kunst. Auch werden die Arbeiten der Illustratoren in der Regel nur einmal veröffentlicht und verschwinden dann in großen Schubladen. Aufträge mit hoher Resonanz sind selten, Titel-Illustrationsjobs wohl noch seltener. So ist es für den SPIEGEL in Deutschland auch immer schwieriger geworden, neben den wohlbekannten und häufig

gebuchten deutschen Top-Illustratoren auch andere, neue Talente zu finden. Fast die Hälfte der in dieser Ausstellung vertretenen Arbeiten stammen deshalb von Künstlern aus den USA. In den Vereinigten Staaten hat die Illustration seit Norman Rockwell eine höhere Reputation, einen viel größeren Markt und seit 100 Jahren auch eine Lobby: die „Society of Illustrators" mit Sitz in New York, wo „The Art of DER SPIEGEL" nach den deutschen Stationen zum Abschluss gezeigt wird.

„Die Kunst des SPIEGEL" möchte nur Original-Illustrationen ausstellen, mit wenigen Ausnahmen, bei denen es keine „Originale" im herkömmlichen Sinn geben kann: bei Werken von ausschließlich am Computer arbeitenden Künstlern. Hier zeigen wir hochwertige Digitaldrucke, in der Regel handsigniert. Veröffentlichte Arbeiten stellen wir dem gedruckten SPIEGEL-Titel gegenüber, darüber hinaus gibt es auch etliche unveröffentlichte. Insgesamt sind es fast 200 Werke. Wir konnten nicht alle jemals für den SPIEGEL-Titel angefertigten Illustrationen ausstellen, leider war auch manche Arbeit, die wir gern präsentiert hätten, nicht auffindbar. So ergaben selbst intensive Recherchen nichts über den Verbleib der Originale von Jean Mulatiers wunderbaren Politiker-Karikaturen zur Bundestagswahl 1976: Der Künstler konnte sich beim besten Willen nicht mehr erinnern, wohin er diese markanten Arbeiten verkauft hatte. Auch hätten wir sehr gern Tomi Ungerer, der fünf SPIEGEL-Titel geschaffen hat, mit seinen spitzfindigen Zeichnungen gezeigt, aber anderweitige Verpflichtungen ließen ihm keine Gelegenheit, rechtzeitig die Originale beizusteuern. In einem Fall aber wurde unsere Hartnäckigkeit belohnt: mit der allerersten, jemals für den SPIEGEL-Titel angefertigten Illustration aus dem Jahr 1956, dem Porträt des florentinischen Bürgermeisters La Pira, beeindruckend in Szene gesetzt vom Illustrations-Großmeister Boris Artzybasheff, der zu jener Zeit bereits regelmäßig für das „Time"-Magazin in New York arbeitete. So war es auch ein lang gehegter Wunsch meines Vorgängers Eberhard Wachsmuth, dem „Erfinder" des typischen SPIEGEL-Titels in den sechziger Jahren, gerade diesen – amerikanischen – Künstler für den SPIEGEL arbeiten zu lassen.

Hier schließt sich der Kreis: weist doch Wachsmuth im Gespräch (Seite 22) darauf hin, dass schon damals „die Kunst der Illustration hier weniger gepflegt wurde als in Amerika". Ich hoffe, unsere Ausstellung „Die Kunst des SPIEGEL" wird helfen, dieses zu ändern.

Danken möchte ich meinen Vorgängern als Ressortleiter der SPIEGEL-Titelbild-redaktion: Eberhard Wachsmuth, 30 Jahre Titelbildchef, ohne den der SPIEGEL heute sicher ganz anders aussähe; Rainer Wört-mann, der sehr viele Illustratoren für den SPIEGEL beschäftigte, sowie Thomas Bon-nie, von dem ich eine Menge lernen durfte und der diesen Katalog gestaltete. Diese Ausstellung wäre nicht zu Stande gekommen ohne die unermüdliche Ulla Morschhäuser, 19 Jahre lang, bis 1999, „Visualizerin" in der SPIEGEL-Titelredaktion, die über Monate die annähernd 200 Exponate herbeischaffte. Auch allen anderen SPIEGEL-Kollegen, die über ihre reguläre Arbeit beim SPIEGEL hinaus dieses Projekt ermöglichten, bleibt zu danken; aber ganz besonders allen Illustrato-ren, die mit ihren herausragenden Arbeiten auch weiterhin zur „Kunst des SPIEGEL" beitragen.

....
Stefan Kiefer ist Ressortleiter Titelbild des SPIEGEL.

Illustrators are largely faceless figures – lone rangers who spend long nights in their studio brooding over projects, rarely satisfied with the results. And once their piece has been delivered, they are filled with an anxious hope: Will the work be appreciated and will it be published?

Week in, week out, for nearly 50 years now, the cover editors of DER SPIEGEL have been the source of sleepless nights for some of the world's best illustrators. Caught between exact instructions, high demands and short deadlines, illustrators are asked to produce one outstanding cover illustration after the other. DER SPIEGEL profits from the special talent of these "rental" artists who accept an assignment and turn out their creative work under pressure. The illustrators, for their part, are lured by the prospect of having their work printed a million times on the cover of our magazine.

Over the decades, this cooperation has produced so many extraordinary pieces of art that the magazine's editors decided it was time to create an exhibition devoted to the illustrations and the people behind them. The result is "The Art of DER SPIEGEL," a display that will be shown in renowned museums and galleries. In contrast to the United States, Germany does not hold the art of illustration in very high regard. At best, it may be viewed as "run-of-the-mill graphics," but certainly not art. In most cases, an illustrator's work is published once and then disappears into the deep, dark reaches of a drawer somewhere. High-profile commissions that trigger a large response are rare; cover illustration jobs perhaps even rarer. This is why it is increasingly difficult for DER SPIEGEL to discover new talents to complement the group of well-known, frequently booked top illustrators in Germany. And it is why nearly half of the illustrators represented in this exhibition come from the USA. Since the days of Norman Rockwell, the United States has attached more significance to the art of illustration than Germany. They have a much bigger market for illustrations and, for the past 100 years, an illustrators' lobby: the Society of Illustrators in New York, where "The Art of DER SPIEGEL" will end its tour after being shown in Germany.

With very few exceptions, we show only original works. And those exceptions involve works where there can be no "originals" in the conventional sense: because the artists work exclusively on the computer. In such cases, we are exhibiting high-quality digital prints. We juxtapose the original pieces and the printed SPIEGEL cover, and also present a large number of unpublished illustrations. In all, the entire exhibit contains nearly 200 pieces of art. The works are displayed in chronological order based on the date that the artist's work first appeared in the magazine. This catalog is organized the same way. It would have been impossible for us to show all illustrations that have ever been created for the SPIEGEL cover. Unfortunately, some pieces that we would have liked to display could not be found. Even after an intense search, we were unable to track down the originals of the wonderful political caricatures that Jean Mulatier drew for the 1976 federal election. The artist simply could not remember where he had sold his striking illustrations. We also would have liked to have shown the works of Tomi Ungerer whose quirky drawings appeared on five SPIEGEL covers. But he had too many other commitments and could not provide us with the originals in time for this exhibition. In one case, though, the exhibition team was

rewarded for its tenacity: We will show the first illustration ever made for a SPIEGEL cover: the portrait of Florentine Mayor La Pira, an impressive painting by the American master of illustration, Russian-born Boris Artzybasheff, who was a regular contributor to "Time Magazine" in New York at that time. Indeed, it was a long-standing desire of my predecessor Eberhard Wachsmuth, the man who "invented" the typical SPIEGEL cover in the 1960s, to have this – American – artist work for DER SPIEGEL.

Now, we have come full circle: As Wachsmuth points out in his interview (page 26), "the art of illustration was less cultivated here than in the United States" even back then. I hope this exhibition, "The Art of DER SPIEGEL", will help change this attitude, and raise the level of esteem in Germany for this form of art.

As head of the SPIEGEL cover department, I would like to thank my predecessors: Eberhard Wachsmuth, Art Director for 30 years, without whom DER SPIEGEL would look very different today; Rainer Wörtmann, who recruited many illustrators on behalf of DER SPIEGEL; and Thomas Bonnie, who taught me a lot and who designed this catalog. This exhibition would not have been possible without the tireless Ulla Morschhäuser, who worked as "visualizer" in the SPIEGEL cover department for 19 years until 1999. She spent months conjuring up all 200 exhibits. I would also like to thank all SPIEGEL colleagues who took it upon themselves to support this project in addition to their normal workload. Above all, we must thank the illustrators whose extraordinary works continue to support "The Art of DER SPIEGEL."

Stefan Kiefer is Art Director/Cover Department of DER SPIEGEL.

Alles im Rahmen
Framed

Walter Grasskamp

Wovon träumen Popstars – tatsächlich nur von Sex & Drugs & Rock'n'Roll? Glaubt man dem Song „The Cover of the Rolling Stone" der amerikanischen Band Dr. Hook and the Medicine Show, dann träumen sie vor allem davon, auf das Titelbild der angesehensten Magazine zu kommen. Nachdem die kleine Satire vom ultimativen Pop-Ruhm („Wanna see my picture on the cover / Wanna buy five copies for my mother") an die Spitze der US-Hitparade gelangt war, zeigte die berühmte Zeitschrift ein Einsehen und setzte die schräge Truppe 1973 mit einer Illustration auf das vorauseilend angehimmelte Titelblatt des „Rolling Stone".

Zehn Jahre zuvor hatte es sich ein britischer Künstler noch einfacher gemacht: Der Pop-Pionier Richard Hamilton besorgte sich 1963 einen Layout-Block, mit dem das „Time Magazine" seine Cover-Gestalter ausstattete, und zeichnete kurzerhand sein Selbstporträt in den vorgedruckten roten Rahmen. In mehreren Varianten, auch als Druckgrafik, illustrierte diese eigenmächtige Selbstaufwertung, was offenbar auch manchem Künstler sehnlichster Wunsch ist.

Wenn es so vielen Menschen erstrebenswert scheint, einmal auf ein Magazin-Cover zu gelangen, wovon träumen dann Illustratoren, die solche Titelbilder gestalten dürfen, zum Beispiel im ebenfalls roten Rahmen des SPIEGEL? Mit ihren Illustrationen eines Tages in einem Kunstmuseum zu hängen, mit einem richtigen Holzrahmen statt dem grafischen des Magazintitels?

Das scheint von vornherein ausgeschlossen, denn im snobistischen Kunstbetrieb gilt selbst die beste Gebrauchsgrafik wenig, am allerwenigsten als Kunst. Und doch haben es 40 Titelblätter des SPIEGEL mit vier Original-Illustrationen von Hermann Degkwitz schon vor Jahren auf die berühmteste Weltausstellung moderner Kunst geschafft, auf die Documenta 5, die sich 1972 der „Befragung der Realität – Bildwelten heute" widmete.

Die Zeit war damals günstig, denn mit Pop Art und Fotorealismus hatte ein Impuls wieder an Aktualität gewonnen, der in der modernen Kunst zeitweise aus dem Blickfeld geraten war: Wie kann man die Welt anschaulich machen? Das war jahrhundertelang ein Hauptmotiv der Malerei gewesen; erst die abstrakte Kunst hatte es an Fotografie und Film delegiert, an Gattungen somit, die nicht museabel waren.

Vor allem aber waren es die Illustratoren, die von der Kunst die Aufgabe der bildhaften Veranschaulichung übernommen haben. In ihren Werken wird daher ein wichtiges Erbe bewahrt, nämlich, dass Kunst auch sein kann, was nicht den jeweils aktuellen Vorstellungen davon entspricht.

Das wurde beispielsweise deutlich, als 1986 Hans Ulrich Osterwalders Darstellung des Aids-Virus auf dem SPIEGEL-Titel erschien: Selbst wer nicht wusste, wie lange die strenge Naturwissenschaft die grafische Darstellung ihrer Forschungsobjekte der fotografischen vorgezogen hat, konnte hier die Überlegenheit der handwerklichen Mittel in der Veranschaulichung eines ebenso virulenten wie ungreifbaren Gegenstands erkennen.

Es ist diese Leistung der Veranschaulichung, mit der die Illustration eine Tradition der Kunstgeschichte fortsetzt: Wie ein Buchmaler des Mittelalters in seiner Minia-tur ein ganzes Weltbild symbolisieren konnte oder ein Renaissance-Zeichner die Natur im Detail einzufangen suchte, so sind zeitgenössische Illustratoren damit beschäftigt, das Sichtbare verständlich und das Unsichtbare anschaulich zu machen.

Dafür braucht es mehr als nur Handwerk, weil es eine Kunst ist, das Allgemeine im Detail bildhaft werden zu lassen. In diesem Buch gibt es zahlreiche Beispiele dafür, wie originell zeitgenössische Illustratoren schwierige und abstrakte Themen so veranschaulichen können, dass sie pointiert erscheinen, ohne sich in Karikaturen zu erschöpfen; raffiniert, ohne elitär zu sein; prägnant, ohne plakativ zu wirken, und gewitzt, ohne ein ernstes Thema zu verscherzen.

Wie schon der Documenta-Katalog anerkannte, ist das Titelbild des SPIEGEL zwischen Buchumschlag und Plakat angesiedelt. Aber die angelsächsische Redewendung „Don't judge a book by its cover" gilt für Nachrichtenmagazine nicht, im Gegenteil: Ein Magazin will nach seinem Umschlag beurteilt, das heißt gekauft werden. Das Titelbild muss deshalb optisch suggerieren, dass der Text hinter dem Umschlag sein Thema genauso kompakt und kompetent, angemessen und unterhaltsam behandelt wie die Illustration. Von ihr hängt also eine Menge ab.

SPIEGEL-Titel sind solche intellektuellen Lockbilder, die ihren Kaufanreiz am Kiosk in kurzer Zeit entfalten und danach eine Woche lang ansehnlich bleiben. Nur eine Woche? Viele von ihnen verdienen es zweifellos, länger angesehen zu werden. Sind nicht manche von ihnen sogar ins kollektive Gedächtnis gewandert, Degkwitz' vorzüglich düstere Kim-Philby-Entlarvung (1968) etwa, Artzybasheffs Tiefsee-Freud (1959), Dieter

Wiesmüllers Pulverfass-Idylle (1983), Jean-Pierre Kunkels Bush-Rambos (2002) oder Rafal Olbinskis elegantes Geigen-Ohr (2003), um nur einige Beispiele aus dem persönlichen musée imaginaire der SPIEGEL-Illustrationen zu nennen?

Und fallen nicht einige selbst aus dem SPIEGEL-Rahmen und wären es wert, einmal ohne diesen angeschaut zu werden? Vor allem sind sie es wert, in einem Betrachtungsrahmen gesehen zu werden, der ansonsten nur der Museumskunst vorbehalten bleibt: dem eines Gesamtwerks, eines Œuvres. Kann man die zeitgenössische Kunst nur aus komplizierten Werkzusammenhängen heraus verstehen, bleibt Illustratoren in der Regel aber genau dieses Privileg vorenthalten, dass man ihre Tagesarbeiten einmal im Kontext einer Werkgruppe oder sogar eines Lebenswerks betrachten kann und ihre Autorenschaft darüber namhaft wird.

Sollten Illustratoren tatsächlich von so etwas träumen, bringen sie dieses Buch und die dazugehörige Ausstellung der Erfüllung ein Stück näher. Freilich wird nie ihr eigenes Gesicht eines Tages auf dem SPIEGEL-Titel erscheinen. Aber vermutlich träumen sie davon auch nicht, wissen sie doch zu gut, was dabei alles angerichtet werden kann. Denn einige von ihnen haben Prominentenporträts so auf der Kippe von süffisanter Karikatur und detailverliebter Grafik angelegt, dass man den Betroffenen spontan einen kurzen Erholungsurlaub zugestehen würde. Deshalb wird nicht jeder Politiker unbedingt mit seinem Konterfei auf dem Titelbild des SPIEGEL landen wollen – aber doch wohl jeder Illustrator mit seinem Werk.

....
Walter Grasskamp ist Kunstkritiker, Professor für Kunstgeschichte an der Akademie der Bildenden Künste in München und Autor zahlreicher Bücher über Kunst, Design und Kulturpolitik.

What do pop stars dream about? Is the answer really sex & drugs & rock'n'roll? Not according to the song "The Cover of the Rolling Stone" by the American band Dr. Hook and the Medicine Show. It claims pop stars spend most of their time dreaming about getting onto the cover of the most renowned magazines. After the satire on the ultimate pop fame ("Wanna see my picture on the cover / Wanna buy five copies for my mother") made it to the top of the U. S. charts, the famous magazine changed its tune and in 1973 put an illustration of the motley crew on the coveted cover page of "Rolling Stone".

Ten years before, a British artist found an easier way to achieve the same goal. In 1963, the pop art pioneer Richard Hamilton got his hands on a layout block that "Time" magazine gave to its cover designers and sketched his self-portrait in the pre-printed red frame. In its several versions, including a print graphic, this unauthorized self-aggrandizement illustrated what is apparently the innermost desire of many artists.

If so many people think landing on the cover of a magazine is something worth striving for, what do the illustrators dream about who paint for these cover pages, for example for SPIEGEL's red frame? Do they hope to see their illustrations hanging on the walls of an art museum one day, where they will be shown in a real wood frame instead of the graphic frame of the magazine's cover?

That appears to be an impossible dream. In the snobbish art scene even the best graphic design isn't worth much, and it certainly isn't considered to be art. And yet 40 of SPIEGEL's cover pages with four original illustrations by Hermann Degkwitz made it to the most famous world exhibition in the world of modern art years ago. In 1972,

documenta 5 was dedicated to "Questioning Reality – Pictorial Worlds Today."

The time was ripe. Pop art and photo-realism pointed the modern art scene in a direction that before had at times disappeared from view: How can you illustrate the world? For centuries that was one, perhaps even the main motive of painting. Then abstract art came along and delegated this job to photography and film, and thus two genres that were not fit for museums.

Illustrators then became the main players to carry on the pictorial representation. Their works preserve an important legacy, namely that art can be something that does not fulfill the current expectations of what it should be.

That was made clear back in 1986 when Hans Ulrich Osterwalder's depiction of the AIDS virus appeared on the cover of DER SPIEGEL. Even those who were unaware of the inveterate preference of the natural sciences for graphic presentations – and not photographs – were able to discern the superiority of the technical means used to illustrate such a virulent and dangerous object. It is the power of illustration that continues a tradition of art history: As book illustrators in the Middle Ages were able to symbolize an entire world view in their miniatures, and as the Renaissance nature drawers attempted to capture the detail, modern illustrators attempt to make the -visible understandable and the invisible perceptible.

More than mere handicraft is required to achieve this, for it is an art to lend vividness to the general through the detail. This book contains several examples of how contemporary illustrators bring to life difficult and abstract themes in such a way as to make them appear to have a point without relying completely on the caricature, refined without being elitist, full without seeming plump, and funny without forfeiting a serious theme.

The documenta catalog rightly situated SPIEGEL's cover page somewhere between a book cover and a poster. But the old adage that you shouldn't judge a book by its cover doesn't apply to news magazines. On the contrary: A magazine wants to be judged by its cover, meaning it wants to be bought. The cover illustration must therefore convince potential readers that the story inside is just as compact, competent, appropriate and entertaining as the illustration. A lot depends on it.

SPIEGEL cover pages offer just this kind of intellectual bait. They unfold their buying incentive in a moment at the newsstand and then keep their composure for a full week. No more than a week? Many of them surely deserve to be looked at a bit longer. Haven't some of them even made their way into our collective unconscious, Degkwitz's terrifically bleak Kim Philby exposure (1968), Artzybasheff's deep sea Freud (1959), Dieter Wiesmüller's tinderbox idyll (1983), Jean-Pierre Kunkel's Bush as Rambo (2002) or Rafal Olbinski's elegant violin ear (2003), to name just a few examples from the personal musée imaginaire of SPIEGEL's illustrations?

And don't some of them deserve to be looked at in their own right for once? Above all it is worth putting them in a setting that is usually reserved for museum art: that of a retrospective, an oeuvre. If contemporary art is understood only as part of complicated works histories, illustrators are denied the privilege of being viewed and recognized in the context of a group of works or even a life work.

If illustrators do really dream about something like this, this book and the accompany-ing exhibition may bring them a bit closer to fulfilling that dream. Of course, their own faces will never make it onto the cover of DER SPIEGEL. But they probably wouldn't want them to, since they know too well what the drawbacks are. Some of their portraits of the rich and famous tread such a fine line between quick-witted caricature and meticulously detailed illustration that one would immediately send the person in question on a short trip to recover. That's why not every politician would necessarily want to end up on the cover of DER SPIEGEL with his portrait – but every illustrator with his work.

....
Walter Grasskamp is an art critic, professor of art history at the Munich Academy of Fine Arts and author of numerous books about art, design and cultural and educational policy.

Titelgeschichten im SPIEGEL
Cover Stories of DER SPIEGEL

Steven Heller

Noch erheiternder als der bedauernswerte Anblick des US-Präsidenten George W. Bush, wie er sich im Jahr 2003 an einer Brezel verschluckt, war das SPIEGEL-Titelbild, das kurz vor Beginn des zweiten Irak-Kriegs den US-Präsidenten als Rambo mit einer kleinen Brezel-Erkennungsmarke als Hinweis auf diesen denkwürdigen Moment zeigte. Es war nur ein kleines Detail in dieser Parodie eines Rambo-Kinoplakats, doch es erregte ein derartiges Aufsehen, dass sowohl das Weiße Haus als auch das US-Außenministerium sofort die SPIEGEL-Redaktion kontaktierten. Seitdem auf Video festgehalten wurde, wie der erste Präsident George Bush sich während eines Staatsdiners schmachvoll in den Schoß eines japanischen Diplomaten übergibt, sind die Imageberater im Weißen Haus bemüht, den Zugang der Medien zu Fotos von der Nahrungsaufnahme und anderen eventuell peinlichen Bildern einzuschränken.

Überraschenderweise empfanden die Staatsbeamten das SPIEGEL-Titelbild jedoch keineswegs als beleidigend. Ganz im Gegenteil: Die Angehörigen der US-Botschaft zeigten sich belustigt und baten um weitere Exemplare der Zeitschrift, um sie an Freunde zu verteilen. Mitarbeiter im Stab des Präsidenten forderten sogar Poster des Titelbildes an, um sie in ihren Büros im Weißen Haus aufzuhängen. Es ist das Paradoxe an politischem Witz und Karikaturen, dass Sarkasmus und derbe Kritik als schmeichelhaft ausgelegt werden können.

Zwar feixten die Europäer angesichts der Karikierung des Präsidenten und seiner Kriegsberater als kraftstrotzende, waffenschwenkende Ninja-Krieger in Vorbereitung des lange angedrohten Präventivschlags gegen den Irak. Doch die Bush-Regierung gefiel sich in einer eigenen Auslegung dieses Bildes kraftstrotzender, waffenschwenkender Ninja-Krieger, um Saddam Hussein, die Geißel des Nahen Ostens, effektvoll zu vernichten. Offensichtlich liegt der feine Unterschied zwischen Spott und Schmeichelei im Auge des Betrachters. Dieser SPIEGEL-Titel ist eine der denkwürdigsten politischen Satiren in einer langen Reihe von gezeichneten und gemalten Titelbildern aus fünf Jahrzehnten.

Die erste Titelbildillustration des SPIEGEL, ein Porträt des florentinischen Bürgermeisters Giorgio La Pira, wurde im April 1956 veröffentlicht (Seite 32). Sie wurde gemalt von Boris Artzybasheff (auch bekannt für seine herausragenden Titelbilder für das Magazin „Time" in den vierziger und fünfziger Jahren). Die Federführung als Art Director hatte Eberhard Wachsmuth, der fast 30 Jahre für das Design des SPIEGEL zuständig war. Durch die Verbindung von Hyperrealismus und Renaissance-Anmutung gelang es der Illustration, den Kern der Persönlichkeit des Bürgermeisters in seiner heimatlichen Umgebung einzufangen. Ein Foto hätte vielleicht das Ziel der einfachen Darstellung erreicht, nicht jedoch die nur durch eine Zeichnung mögliche emotionale Dimension. Die Illustration zeigte auch eine Hintergrundszenerie, die mit fotografischen Mitteln unmöglich in einem einzigen Bild hätte dargestellt werden können. Seither hat der 1947 gegründete SPIEGEL stets auf die talentiertesten Illustratoren und Karikaturisten der Welt zurückgegriffen. Bedauerlicherweise gehört das Magazin zu den letzten Verteidigern dieses speziellen Genres der Titelbildkunst.

Bis zum Zweiten Weltkrieg dominierte der Fotojournalismus in den Zeitschriften, Mitte der Fünfziger jedoch waren es Illustrationen, die auf vielen Titelseiten der beliebtesten wöchentlichen Nachrichtenmagazine erschienen. Die Kunst wurde rasch zu einer wichtigen visuellen Stütze der Magazine und Zeitungen. Redakteure und Art Directoren verließen sich auf die scharfsinnigen Interpretationen von Künstlern, um inhaltlich komplexe Themen dort zu konkretisieren (und zu vereinfachen), wo objektive Fotografie an ihre Grenzen stieß. Im besten Fall imitierten diese visuellen Kommentare nicht Text oder Realität, sondern zwangen den Betrachter im Rahmen anspruchsvoller Denkspiele dazu, Symbole und Allegorien zu entziffern, die versteckte Botschaften kommunizierten. Auf dieselbe Weise haben die SPIEGEL-Titel Persönlichkeiten, Ereignisse und Ideen in Ikonen des Moments umgewandelt.

Doch die thematische Illustration erwies sich als kurzlebig und war rasch überholt. Die Zeichenkunst von Artzybasheff mag noch so vollendet gewesen sein – wer erinnert sich heute noch an den florentinischen Bürgermeister oder unzählige andere Ereignisse und Persönlichkeiten, die keine Bedeutung mehr haben? Je enger eine Illustration auf eine bestimmte Person oder ein bestimmtes Ereignis der Zeitgeschichte bezogen ist, umso weniger dauerhaft ist sie. Die Titelbildillustration eines Magazins dient zuallererst einem bestimmten Zweck, limitiert durch die Veröffentlichungsdauer. Wie soll dann eine Illustration über dieses Datum hinaus noch einen künstlerischen Wert bewahren?

Die erste Prüfung der künstlerischen Bedeutung ist die Zeit. Wenn eine Illustration noch nach fünf, zehn oder zwanzig Jahren eine Botschaft oder Emotion vermittelt, die über ihren ursprünglichen Zweck hinausgeht – wenn sie sich also durch ihre inhärenten grafischen oder konzeptionellen Qualitäten auszeichnet –, hat sie ein starkes Fundament, auf dem sie dauerhaft stehen kann. Dies ist natürlich selten. Veränderte Gegebenheiten beeinträchtigen das künstlerische Überleben einer Illustration erheblich. So wird die Rambo-Bush-Parodie, wenn man sich ihrer denn überhaupt erinnern sollte, als Kritik der überzogenen Ängste fehlgeleiteter Kriegsgegner dienen, falls der Irak-Krieg und die Besetzung des Landes durch die USA zu Demokratie und politischer Stabilität für das irakische Volk führen sollten. Umgekehrt würde diese Titelillustration als Ikone der Anmaßungen und des blindwütigen Draufgängertums des US-Präsidenten im Angesicht europäischer Missbilligung dienen, falls die Ziele des Irak-Kriegs (also die Herstellung eines demokratischen Systems) nicht erreicht werden. Erst die Zeit wird zeigen, welche dieser Interpretationen sich durchsetzt.

Die Erfahrungen der letzten Jahre belegen, dass sehr wenige Zeitschriftentitel das Maß an Tiefe erreichen, das beispielsweise Picassos „Guernica" aufweist, vor allem, weil Kritiker, Geschichtswissenschaftler und die Leserschaft die Illustration als solche für eine niedere Kunstform halten. Es ist durchaus denkbar, dass „Guernica", wenn Picasso es zunächst als Titelbildillustration für eine Zeitschrift veröffentlicht hätte, nie in die Sammlung der großen modernen Kunst des 20. Jahrhunderts aufgenommen worden wäre. Stattdessen ist das Gemälde das meistgefeierte aller künstlerischen Zeugnisse gegen den Krieg – das zudem häufig und auf respektvolle Weise auf Zeitschriftentiteln parodiert wird.

Gelegentlich jedoch überdauert eine Illustration die Verfallszeit der Zeitschrift, auf deren Titel sie erschienen ist. Doch selbst die herausragendsten Zeitschriftentitel erreichen nicht den Status der höchsten Kunst. Die Titelbilder, die Norman Rockwell in den dreißiger, vierziger und fünfziger Jahren für die „Saturday Evening Post" zeichnete, erwiesen sich als weniger umwälzend als die Tropfleinwände von Jackson Pollock. Viele von ihnen wurden jedoch von Anhängern als Einblicke in ein ideales oder nostalgisches Amerika hoch geschätzt. Und auch Jahrzehnte nach Rockwells Tod erfreuen sie sich unverminderter Beliebtheit. Im besten Fall sind Zeitschriftenillustrationen wegweisende historische Dokumente. Aber als Meilensteine im Bereich der Kultur werden sie kaum wahrgenommen. Letztlich ist diese hierarchische Unterscheidung jedoch unwichtig. Unabhängig von ihrem zu Grunde liegenden Zweck muss die redaktionelle Kunst auf der Grundlage ihres inhärenten Verdienstes (ihrer Schönheit oder der in ihr sich ausdrückenden Intelligenz) bewertet werden sowie auf Grund der Reaktion, die sie im Betrachter hervorruft. Schließlich ist eine Zeitschrift ein wahrhaftes Museum der Straße – das zudem weitaus zugänglicher ist als manche der angesehensten Museen der Welt.

Dennoch gehen wenige redaktionelle Illustratoren weiter als ein paar Schritte über die bestehenden Grenzen der künstlerischen Konventionen hinaus – nicht einmal die so genannten Experimentalisten. Stattdessen entwickeln die besten Illustratoren einen eigenen Stil, mit dessen Hilfe sie die Zeit, in der sie leben, festhalten und wiedergeben.

Das ist durchaus eine ehrenwerte künstlerische Berufung. Daher muss die Illustration, insbesondere die Illustration von Zeitschriftentiteln, daran gemessen werden, wie ihr dieses komplizierte Unterfangen gelingt. Die wahre Schwierigkeit dabei ist es, Klischees zu vermeiden und bekanntes grafisches Vokabular mit Intelligenz und Einfallsreichtum in frische Bildersprache zu verwandeln.

Verschiedene Avantgardebewegungen des 20. Jahrhunderts – wie Symbolismus, neue Objektivität, magischer Realismus und Surrealismus – haben die Illustrationen der SPIEGEL-Titel beeinflusst. Einige von ihnen sind einzigartige Amalgame eines oder aller Ansätze, die einen innovativen zeitgenössischen Stil schaffen. Die Methoden sind unterschiedlich – vom detaillierten Realismus eines Braldt Bralds bis zur Comic-Kurzschrift eines Guy Billout –, aber allen SPIEGEL-Titeln gemein ist ein konzeptionell-erzählerischer Kern. Alle Titelbildillustrationen erzählen Geschichten, manchmal auf mehreren Ebenen. Kunst um der Kunst willen oder Stil um des Stils willen wird nicht akzeptiert, denn das oberste Ziel ist die Vermittlung des so genannten Aha-Effekts. „Aha-Ideen" sind jene Konzepte, die intelligent genug sind, um anspruchsvoll zu sein, aber dennoch so eingängig, dass der durchschnittliche Leser sie verstehen kann. „Ein brillant illustriertes Titelbild spricht eigentlich für sich selbst durch ein starkes visuelles Konzept, aber durch die Verbindung mit einer intelligenten, überraschenden Titelzeile gewinnt es noch an Bedeutung", meint der Art Director des SPIEGEL-Titels, Stefan Kiefer.

Die Titel des SPIEGEL sind mit provokanten Zeilen bestückt – die Kombination von Text und Bild ist die Essenz der Massenkommunikation. Die Titelzeile „Radikal-Kur gegen Arbeitslosigkeit" erklärt das alarmierende Bild des deutschen Adlers von Rob Brooks, der in einem Menschenmeer versinkt (Seite 237), mit der Zeile „Der göttliche Funke" versteht man Robert Giustis beeindruckenden Kommentar zur Schöpfung (Seite 176). Und „Was fühlen Tiere?" ergänzt das bewegend friedliche Königreich der Tiere Wilson McLeans (Seite 259).

Angesichts der heutigen Überschwemmung mit Massenmedien ist es schwierig, Aufmerksamkeit zu erzeugen. In den letzten Jahren haben selbst seriöse Zeitschriften immer mehr auf sensationsträchtige Bilder zurückgegriffen, um die Öffentlichkeit anzusprechen. Nicht jedoch die SPIEGEL-Titel, die mit Kunstfertigkeit und Geist die Aufmerksamkeit des intelligenten Lesers auf sich ziehen.

Oft sind die denkwürdigsten Titel auch die mutigsten – solche, die durch eine extreme Darstellung auch beleidigen können. Michael M. Prechtls „Liebe und Verbrechen" (Seite 67) ist eine herausragende Montage gewichtiger Ikonen des 20. Jahrhunderts, die den Holocaust, das Christentum und die Erotik verkörpern. Dieses unglaublich vielschichtige „Porträt" des Marquis de Sade könnte für sich neben jedem anderen Kunstwerk stehen, das die Moral und die Sitten der Gesellschaft kritisiert, indem es diese mit Hilfe gesellschaftlicher Tabus kommentiert. Die intellektuelle Kraft dieser Illustration ist immens, gleich ob sie als Kunst an der Wand hängt oder sich auf einer Zeitschriftenseite befindet. Zweifellos waren einige SPIEGEL-Leser nicht begeistert von dieser Illustration. Ob etwas beleidigend oder tiefsinnig wirkt, liegt eben im Auge des Betrachters. Doch da das Magazin seine Leser daran gewöhnt hat, Titelillustrationen zu schätzen und zu erwar-

ten, ist Prechtls Werk nicht ungewöhnlich. Der wahre Beitrag des SPIEGEL zum Zeitschriftendesign, der Illustration und der Kunst im Allgemeinen ist seine Bereitschaft, ein grafisches Vokabular aufzubauen, das Menschen dazu bringt, sich kritisch mit der Welt zu beschäftigen.

Laut Stefan Kiefer war ein besonders wirkungsvoller SPIEGEL-Titel – zumindest gemessen am Ausmaß der öffentlichen Reaktion und der höchsten Verkaufszahl in dem Jahr – die Illustration „Die verwöhnten Kleinen" von Chris Payne (Seite 227). Ohne die Anstandsregeln zu verletzen, sprach die Illustration durch ihre subtile Subversion Herz und Verstand der Leser an. In dieser markanten Illustration fing Payne die wahre Natur vieler Eltern-Kind-Beziehungen ein – das ungezügelte Verlangen der egozentrischen Kinder, ihre Eltern zu versklaven. Die Erniedrigung, dargestellt durch eine eigenartig sinnliche Frau – die typische Mutter (das einstmals sexuelle, nun aber domestizierte Wesen) –, die sich gehorsam beugt, um die Schnürbänder ihrer arroganten kleinen Göre zu binden, spricht Bände über die Psychologie dieser verbreiteten Beziehung. Doch die Zeichnung ist nicht nur lustig. In ihrer Ausführung ist sie seltsam erotisch, was das Unbehagen des Betrachters nur noch verstärkt. Die Illustration wirkt auf vielen Ebenen und spricht doch ein Thema an, das alle verstehen können.

Doch nicht alle Provokationen erfahren eine derart positive Resonanz. Laut Kiefer war einer der weniger beliebten Titel die von Nancy Stahl gezeichnete Version des Manneken Pis (Seite 191) als Aushängeschild für die Europäische Union. Vielleicht kann selbst die bekannteste urinierende Statue der Welt nicht wirklich wirksam zur Kritik des neuen Europa genutzt werden. Ungeachtet, ob dies nun die toll-kühne oder mutige Seite der Bebilderungs-politik des SPIEGEL reflektiert, war es auf alle Fälle eine unvergesslich symbolische, wenn auch unpopuläre Darstellung.

Zeitschriftentitel kommen und gehen – stellen Sie sich nur vor, wie viele Titel allein der SPIEGEL seit 1956 veröffent-licht hat! Ohne diese eindrucksvolle Aus-stellung und den dazugehörigen Katalog wäre jede dieser Illustrationen wohl dazu bestimmt, in Vergessenheit zu geraten. Eine so umfangreiche Sammlung an Kunst-werken vor dem kulturellen Kompost zu bewahren, mag künstlerisch nicht so wich-tig erscheinen wie die Bewahrung einer antiken Statue oder eines Renaissance-gemäldes. Doch auch sie sind Schätze einer großen Epoche – des Zeitalters der mecha-nischen Reproduktion – und daher ebenso bedeutsam. Dass ein Kunstwerk hundert- und tausendfach reproduziert wird, be-deutet noch längst nicht, dass es von der Nachwelt nicht mehr beachtet werden muss. Die Tatsache, dass es in so großer Zahl verteilt wird, sollte seine Bedeutung eigentlich vergrößern. Für jeweils eine Woche wurde jedes dieser Bilder immerhin als bedeutend genug angesehen, um auf dem Titel eines der wichtigsten europäi-schen Magazine abgebildet zu sein. Dieser Katalog verleiht dem Vergänglichen Dauer und dem Flüchtigen Bestand. Er zeigt außerdem auf eindrucksvolle Weise, wie brillant die SPIEGEL-Künstler ihre jewei-ligen Titelgeschichten erzählten.

....

Steven Heller, Art Director der „New York Times Book Review", gilt in den Vereinigten Staaten als der bedeutendste Experte der Geschichte des Grafik-Designs. Er ist außerdem Dozent, Designer und Autor von mehr als 90 Büchern über Illustration, satirische Kunst, Grafik-Design und Popkultur.

....

More amusing than George W. Bush's unfor-tunate pretzel choking mishap in 2003 was the SPIEGEL cover published on the eve of the second Iraqi war that depicted the Ameri-can President wearing a commemorative pretzel necklace. It was but one small detail in a larger parody of a Rambo-like movie poster yet it caused such a stir that both the White House and State Department imme-diately contacted the SPIEGEL editors. Ever since the first President Bush was caught on video ignominiously vomiting into a Japanese diplomat's lap during a state dinner, the White House spin doctors have tried to re-strict media access to eating and other poten-tially embarrassing pictures.

Surprisingly, however, government officials were not offended by this illustration. On the contrary, the American embassy staff was giddy. They simply wanted additional copies of the magazine to distribute to friends, and the President's aides requested enlargements to display in their White House offices. Such is the paradox of political humor and carica-ture that sarcasm and criticism can be con-strued as complementary.

While many in Europe and some in the United States were indeed enjoying this lam-poon of George W. Bush and his war coun-selors dressed like muscle-bound, Ninja-fighting, weapon-wielding super-heroes poised to launch their much threatened pre-emptive invasion of Iraq, the Bush admin-istration savored the image because they proudly saw themselves as muscle-bound, Ninja-fighting, weapon-wielding super-heroes poised to crush the scourge of the Middle East, Saddam Hussein. Obviously the fine line between mockery and adulation is in the eye of the beholder. Nonetheless this SPIEGEL cover is one of its most memor-able political satires in a long line of drawn and painted illustrated covers that spans 50 years.

The first such illustrated SPIEGEL cover, a portrait of Florentine mayor Giorgio La Pira, was published in April 1956 (page 32), painted by Boris Artzybasheff (also known for his prodigious execution of American "Time" magazine covers during the 40s and 50s), and art directed by Eberhard Wachsmuth (who oversaw the magazine's design for nearly 30 years). A marriage of hyperrealism and renaissance craft, it captured the essence of the mayor in his native environment. A photograph might have accomplished the basic representational goal, but the art provided an emotional dimension that was otherwise unattainable – it also included background scenery that would have been impossible to capture in a single image using straight photography. Since then DER SPIEGEL, founded in 1947, has consistently employed the world's most talented illustrators and caricaturists. Sadly, today it is one of the last bastions for this special genre of cover art.

But in the mid-fifties, illustration was common on covers of many of the world's most popular newsweeklies, and conceptual editorial art soon became a visual mainstay. Editors and art directors relied on artists' keen interpretations to make concrete (and also simplify) complex editorial themes where objective photography proved impossible. Illustration also supplemented literal representation and triggered reader interaction with the magazines' core content. At best this visual commentary and illustration did not mimic text or imitate reality, rather as sophisticated brain-teasers it forced viewers to decipher symbols and allegories that communicated discrete messages. In this way SPIEGEL covers have transformed personalities, events, and ideas into icons of the moment.

Yet topical illustration is ephemeral and quickly made obsolete over a short period of time. Despite Artzybasheff's consummate artistry, who remembers the Florentine mayor or the countless other personalities and events that no longer matter? Since magazine cover illustration is first and foremost utilitarian, it functions for a specific purpose that is proscribed by a limited shelf-life. So what does it take for an illustration to pass the proverbial test of time?

The first qualifying trial must be time itself. If after five, ten, or twenty years the illustration communicates a message or emotion that transcends its original purpose – if it can be appreciated for its inherent graphic or conceptual qualities – then it may have strong legs on which to stand forever. Of course, this is rare. Turns of events severely diminish historical viability. If, for example, the Iraqi war and occupation bring democracy and stability to the people of Iraq then the Bush-as-Rambo parody will, if remembered at all, serve as a criticism of the alarmist fears instilled by misguided anti-war opponents. Conversely, if the goals of the Iraqi war are not accomplished (i.e. creating a democratic Iraq), then this cover could possibly commemorate Bush's hybris and recklessness in the face of European disapproval – only time will tell.

Recent history reveals that very few magazine covers actually reach the level profundity of, say, Picasso's "Guernica", in large part because critics, historians, and the audience believe illustration is inherently a lesser art. If Picasso had initially published "Guernica" as a magazine cover, it may very well have been rejected from the pantheon of twentieth century modern art. Instead it is the most celebrated of all artistic testaments against war.

Sometimes an editorial illustration might outlast its shelf-life, but even the most exemplary magazine covers will not be designated as high art. Norman Rockwell's covers for "The Saturday Evening Post" from the 30s through the 50s were not as transforming as Jackson Pollock's drip canvases. Yet many were cherished by fans as windows on an ideal or nostalgic view of America; and they remain popular decades after Rockwell's death. Regardless of rational and despite intended function, editorial art must be judged on intrinsic merits (beauty or intelligence) and on what intensity of response the specific work triggers in the viewer. A magazine is, after all, a veritable museum of the street – indeed more accessible than some of the world's most respected museums.

Still, few editorial illustrators, even so-called experimentalists, push the boundaries of artistic convention more than a few paces beyond the status quo. Instead the best illustrators develop distinct styles that they use to both freeze and chronicle the times in which they live, which in it's own right is a worthy artistic calling. Therefore, illustration, and particularly magazine cover art, must be judged by how effectively it achieves this very difficult goal. The real difficulty is to avoid clichés and transform common graphic vocabularies into fresh imagery by virtue of intelligence and imagination.

SPIEGEL illustrations are influenced by various twentieth century avant-garde movements, including symbolism, the new objectivity, magic realism, and surrealism. Quite a few are unique amalgams of one or all approaches that result in innovative contemporary graphic styles. Methods and mannerisms may vary from the detailed realism of Braldt Bralds to the comic shorthand of Guy Billout, but common to all SPIEGEL covers is a core conceptual narrative. The portraits, caricatures and representational vignettes tell stories, sometimes on multiple levels. Art for art sake or style for style sake is routinely rejected because conveying the so-called ah-ha idea is the paramount mission. Ah-ha ideas are those concepts smart enough to be sophisticated yet accessible enough to be deciphered by the average viewer. "A brilliantly illustrated cover actually speaks for itself because of the strong visual concept, but in combination with a smart, surprising headline it even gains in importance," says SPIEGEL art director Stefan Kiefer.

SPIEGEL covers are laden with provocative headlines – the combination of text and image is the essence of mass communication. Headlines augment Rob Brooks' startling German eagle sinking in a sea of humanity (page 237). Words underscore Robert Giusti's stunning commentary on creationism (page 176). And a declarative text compliments Wilson McLean's touching peaceable animal kingdom (page 259). Each opens more entry-points to involve the reader. With today's mass media glut, attracting attention is no easy task and in recent years even serious news magazines have come to rely on sensational imagery to attract an audience. SPIEGEL covers, however, never pander but through artistry and wit capture the intelligent eye.

The most memorable covers are also often the most courageous – those that push certain extremes that may offend. Michael M. Prechtl's "Love and crime" (Page 67) is an exquisitely rendered montage of charged twentieth century icons referencing the Holocaust, Christianity, and eroticism that transcend the bounds of mere illustration. This incredibly layered "portrait" of the Marquis de Sade could stand alongside any other artwork that criticizes morals and mores of society in so far as it uses the societal taboos to comment on them. Yet doubtless some readers of DER SPIEGEL were not entirely sanguine about the depiction. What is offensive or profound is also in the eye of the beholder. But since the magazine has conditioned its readers to appreciate and anticipate illustrated covers Prechtl's work is not an anomaly. In fact, the real contribution DER SPIEGEL has made to magazine design, illustration, and art in general is its willingness to build graphic vocabularies that force people to engage and criticize the world.

The most effective cover, according to Stefan Kiefer – at least one that generated high popular response (and in fact sold the most copies of that year) – was Chris Payne's "The spoiled brats" illustration (page 227). Although it did not break the back of propriety, it definitely captured the hearts and minds of the readers through its subtle subversion. In this striking illustration Payne captured the truth behind many parent/child relationships – the unmitigated gall of the young to be totally self-centered and force parents to be their willing slaves. The humiliation conveyed by a curiously sensual woman – the quintessential mother (the one-time sexual but now domesticated being) – bending submissively down to tie her arrogant little brat's sneakers speaks volumes about the psychology of this common relationship. But the drawing is not simply funny; its execution is oddly erotic, which adds to the apprehension one feels when viewing the image. It works on multiple levels yet speaks to one theme that everyone can understand. But not all provocation earns such positive accolades. Kiefer notes that one

of the more unpopular covers was Nancy Stahl's version of Brussel's Manneken Piss (page 191) as a poster-child for the European Union. Perhaps even the most famous urinating statute in the world simply cannot be efficiently used to criticize the new Europe. For whatever reason the readers felt it seemed to overstep the bounds of acceptability. Whether it showed the foolhardy or the courageous side of the SPIEGEL illustration policy, even though it was unpopular it was still an unforgettable symbolic depiction.

Magazine covers come and go. Imagine how many have been published since 1956 on DER SPIEGEL alone. By definition each was destined for oblivion if not for this stunning exhibition and catalog. Saving such an extensive body of artifacts from becoming cultural mulch may not seem as artistically important as preserving a statue from antiquity or a painting from the Renaissance, but relatively speaking these are treasures from a major epoch – the age of mechanical reproduction – and therefore as significant. Just because a work of art is reproduced in the hundreds of thousands does not mean it should be ignored by posterity. That it is distributed in such huge numbers should actually elevate its status. For at least one week each of these images was deemed important enough to be on the cover of a major national magazine. This catalog allows the ephemeral to be permanent and the fleeting to be treasured. It also convincingly illustrates just how brilliantly SPIEGEL artists narrated their respective cover stories.

Steven Heller, Art Director of the "New York Times Book Review", is considered as foremost authority in the United States on the history of graphic design. Besides being a practicing educator, he is also designer and author of more than 90 books on illustration, satiric art, graphic design and popular culture.

„Ich wollte Bilder, die Geschichten erzählen"
"I wanted pictures that told stories"

INTERVIEW MIT/WITH EBERHARD WACHSMUTH

Eberhard Wachsmuth, 84, hat acht Semester an der Berliner Hochschule der Künste studiert. Nach dem Krieg zeichnete er politische Karikaturen, erst beim „Insulaner" in Berlin, ab 1948 für die amerikanisch geführte „Neue Zeitung" in München, die 1953 eingestellt wurde. Im Januar 1954 wurde Wachsmuth Bildredakteur des SPIEGEL. Fast 30 Jahre lang war er – bis auf ein Zwischenspiel bei der Illustrierten „Quick" – für den SPIEGEL tätig und in diesen Jahren auch verantwortlich für das Titelbild.

SPIEGEL: *Herr Wachsmuth, was zog Sie, einen Karikaturisten, in den fünfziger Jahren zu einem wortgewaltigen Magazin wie dem SPIEGEL?*

Wachsmuth: Der SPIEGEL und seine Macher hatten längst einen besonderen Ruf; so hieß es in München, das seien ein paar Verrückte in Hannover, die über alles schimpften; lange würde sich das Magazin ohnehin nicht halten. Das klang schon einmal interessant. Ich suchte einen Job, kannte den Journalismus inzwischen ganz gut, und der SPIEGEL, der übrigens gerade nach Hamburg umgezogen war, sah sich zu dieser Zeit nach einem Mitarbeiter um, der die Innenbebilderung und die Gestaltung des Titelbildes übernehmen sollte. Beschlossen – und mit einem Cognac-Verschnitt begossen – wurde meine Einstellung im Dezember 1953.

SPIEGEL: *Das Erscheinungsbild des SPIEGEL, das Sie später neu erfinden sollten, war damals auf eine prägnante Art einheitlich. Jede Woche wurde ein eindrucksvolles Porträtfoto präsentiert, stets blickte ein anderer bedeutender Kopf vom Cover herab: Politiker wie Winston Churchill, Schriftsteller wie Thomas Mann, dann wieder Unternehmer, Sportler oder Schauspielgrößen wie Greta Garbo. Warum löste man sich schließlich von diesem Prinzip, eine Physiognomie der Woche zu präsentieren?*

Wachsmuth: Die Zeiten und Themen änderten sich, also musste sich auch die Bebilderung verändern. Erst einmal betrafen die Neuerungen nur Details, etwa die Schrift, dann die Rahmung. Jede Woche ein Gesicht auf den Titel zu heben – dieses Gestaltungsprinzip war allerdings so etwas wie eine Trademark, an die man sich nicht herantraute. Die Porträts wurden in der Regel vom Hausfotografen Max Ehlert aufgenommen und waren von hervorragender Qualität. Warum sollte man, so hieß es, an diesem Markenzeichen etwas ändern? Ich hielt diese Ausschließlichkeit aber für eine Einbahnstraße.

SPIEGEL: *Warum?*

Wachsmuth: Weil sie kaum Vielfalt zuließ. Die fotografische Nahsicht auf eine Person ist ja nach wie vor eine wichtige, aber nicht die einzige Herangehensweise. Warum sollte man nicht auch einen Gegenstand zeigen können? Außerdem gewannen Themen an Bedeutung, die sich nur noch schwer auf eine einzige Person zuspitzen ließen, in denen es zum Beispiel um gesellschaftliche Entwicklungen ging. Ich hatte etwas ganz anderes im Sinn: die gezeichnete Illustration.

SPIEGEL: *Das dürfte damals ein kühnes Ansinnen gewesen sein. Denn schließlich hatte sich die Fotografie längst als das modernere Medium etabliert.*

Wachsmuth: Wirklich? Fotos, insbesondere Fotoporträts, sah man überall, sie prägten auch die Titelblätter damaliger Illustrierten, auch wenn da meistens Starlets abgebildet wurden. Ein gezeichnetes Bild aber kann, wenn es gut gemacht ist, mehr sagen als eine Fotografie. Es kann zuspitzen, überhöhen, verschärfen, auch abstraktere Zusammenhänge pointiert darstellen, es liefert also womöglich das stärkere Bild. Natürlich ist eine Illustration nicht bei jedem Thema das angemessene Gestaltungsmittel. Doch ich sah das Titelblatt des SPIEGEL mehr als Zeichnung, weniger als Foto.

SPIEGEL: *Was fingen Sie mit dieser Erkenntnis an?*

Wachsmuth: Ich skizzierte lauter Vorschläge, Anschauungsmaterial, mit dem ich die Chefredaktion überzeugen wollte. Als zum Beispiel 1954 die Ankündigung einer Biografie über den legendären britischen Offizier Lawrence von Arabien Furore machte und wir einen Titelbeitrag dazu planten, zeichnete ich einen verwegenen Lawrence. Das Blatt zeigte ich – erfolglos – bei der Chefredaktion vor. Immerhin brachten mir solche Vorstöße den Spitznamen „gelernter Kunststudent" ein; den hat Rudolf Augstein erfunden. Allmählich nahmen dann aber die Vorbehalte ab. Wir tasteten uns mit einer Art Mischform an die Illustration heran.

SPIEGEL: *Wie sah das aus?*

Wachsmuth: Wir kombinierten Fotografie und Illustration. Im Vordergrund des Titelbilds wurde nach wie vor eine Porträtfotografie gezeigt. Der Hintergrund war fortan meine – grafisch dominierte – Spielwiese. Dort ergänzte ich Zeichnungen oder Ausschnitte aus anderen Fotos. So mogelte ich das erzählerische Element aufs Titelblatt. Einen Schlagerkomponisten montierten wir vor seine Noten, Agatha Christie vor eine Art Tapete aus den Titelseiten ihrer Bücher. Über das Gesicht von James Joyce druckten wir, das war dann schon 1961, ein handschriftlich ausgefülltes rotes Formular. Das war die entscheidende Wende zum gestalteten Titelbild. Wir haben nie aufgehört, mit der Grafik und der Fotografie zu experimentieren: Im Fotolabor des SPIEGEL wurden – oft auch in Nachtarbeit, weil stets die Zeit knapp war – schon sehr früh grafische Umsetzungen entwickelt, die für andere erst denk- und machbar waren, als der Computer zur Standardausstattung gehörte.

SPIEGEL: *Zurück ins Jahr 1956: Damals erschien – das war eine Sensation und für Sie womöglich ein Triumph – eine Illustration, und zwar im noch gar nicht so selbstverständlichen Farbdruck. Die Zeichnung stammte von Boris Artzybasheff, einem russischen Illustrator, der in New York lebte. Warum musste der SPIEGEL so weit in die Ferne schweifen?*

Wachsmuth: Weil dieser Mann einer der besten Illustratoren war. Darauf, dass wir ihn gewinnen konnten, war ich stolz. Schon bevor ich beim SPIEGEL begann, bewunderte ich die Arbeiten von Artzybasheff, der unter anderem Titel für das amerikanische Nachrichtenmagazin „Time" zeichnete. Ich war von seinen Bildern – insbesondere seinem überspitzten Realismus und seinem treffenden Surrealismus – beeindruckt und pries seine Begabung immer wieder an. Es wurde also eigens eine Dienstreise nach New York unternommen, leider nicht von mir. Für uns hat Artzybasheff damals den italienischen Kommunalpolitiker und florentinischen Bürgermeister Giorgio La Pira porträtiert.

SPIEGEL: *Ein Jahr später, 1957, folgte das Bildnis von Franz Josef Strauß, der damals seit einigen Monaten als Verteidigungsminister im Amt war. Neben seinem Kopf vollzieht sich in mehreren Schritten die Metamorphose einer Kopfbedeckung: Ein typisch bayerischer, federgeschmückter Hut mutiert zum Stahlhelm. Von wem stammte die Idee?*

Wachsmuth: Von Artzybasheff selbst. Er hatte das Talent, die Aussage eines Textes in ein unmissverständliches, witziges Bild umzusetzen. Das war es, was ich wollte: die Geschichte in einem Bild andeuten, so die Neugier wecken. Und Artzybasheff hatte den brisanten Inhalt der Geschichte, die von Deutschlands Plänen zur Aufrüstung handelte, ebenso wie die Physiognomie von Strauß verblüffend gut erfasst.

SPIEGEL: *Der SPIEGEL mag für seine Unabhängigkeit und seine unverblümte Berichterstattung längst bekannt gewesen sein. Sich an so prominenter Stelle wie dem Titelblatt eine klare*

Respektlosigkeit gegenüber einem Regierungsmit-glied zu erlauben – das müsste im braven Nach-kriegsdeutschland Proteste ausgelöst haben. Gab es wütende Reaktionen auf die Satire?

Wachsmuth: Keine, an die ich mich erinnern kann. Der SPIEGEL war nun einmal tatsächlich bekannt dafür, in seinen Texten nicht übertrieben höflich mit Funktionsträgern umzugehen. Wir näherten uns dieser Tugend auch mit dem Titelbild an.

SPIEGEL: *Warum blieb das gezeichnete Titelbild noch eine ganze Weile eine Ausnahme-erscheinung?*

Wachsmuth: Der wichtigste Grund war wohl: Wir konnten nicht jede Woche Artzybasheff beauftragen. Und in Deutschland gab es noch keine vergleichbaren Zeichner, Leute, mit denen wir eine Zusammenarbeit gewagt hätten. Hier wurde die Kunst der Illustration weniger gepflegt als in Amerika. Das ist übrigens noch heute so. Also mussten wir uns begabte Leute heranziehen. Das dauerte natürlich. Aber es hat sich gelohnt. Leute wie Hermann Degkwitz – er ist da nur ein Beispiel – gehören zu den Besten ihres Fachs. Diese Illustrationen sind handwerklich so perfekt wie Gemälde.

SPIEGEL: *Und äußerst bissig dazu. Zur Titelzeile „Maos letztes Gefecht" hat Degkwitz 1967 den Gründer, Führer und Knechter der Volksrepublik China mit einer Schlinge um den Hals ge-schmückt, und die bestand aus einem widerlichen Drachen, der sich selbst ins Hinterteil beißt. Der mächtige Verleger Axel Springer schlängelte sich auf einem Degkwitz-Titelbild 1968 ziemlich dicht über dem Straßenpflaster entlang – sein Körper, dem eines Wurmes ähnlich, bestand aus lauter Springer-Publikationen. Wurden Sie, nachdem das gestalterische Korsett der frühen Jahre gesprengt war, übermütig?*

Wachsmuth: Keine Sorge. Auf uns passte die Chefredaktion auf, insbesondere Augstein,*

der stets die endgültige Auswahl aus unterschiedlichen Titelentwürfen traf.

SPIEGEL: *Wie lauteten die typischen Vorgaben für Zeichner wie Degkwitz oder Ursula Arriens, die auch immer wieder Titelblätter illustrierte?*

Wachsmuth: Natürlich sprachen wir Termine ab, gaben auch gestalterische Anregungen. Aber es war uns genauso wichtig, dass jeder dieser brillanten Zeichner seine eigene, unverwechselbare Handschrift pflegte; also mischten wir uns nicht zu sehr ein. In einer Zeit, in der Illustrationen noch nicht als künstlerische Ausdrucksformen anerkannt waren, haben wir diese Zeichnungen schon als wertvolle Unikate gesehen. Deshalb wurden diese Blätter auch signiert.

SPIEGEL: *Sie haben, immer mal wieder, mit bildenden Künstlern zusammengearbeitet, etwa mit Marc Chagall oder Bernard Buffet. Konnte das gut gehen?*

Wachsmuth: Manchmal sogar zu gut. Der französische Maler Bernard Buffet, der in den fünfziger Jahren extrem erfolgreich war, hat für uns ein eindrucksvolles Selbstporträt angefertigt. Einige Jahre später kam die Chefredaktion auf die Idee, ihn mit einem Porträt von Kanzler Ludwig Erhard zu beauftragen. Ausgerechnet! Bei Buffet sahen alle Gestalten aus wie knochige Hungerleider, und dann sollte er den rundgesichtigen Erhard porträtieren?

SPIEGEL: *An einem der berühmtesten deutschen Künstler sind Sie 1979 gescheitert: an Joseph Beuys. Das Titelbild, so wie er es gestaltet hatte, wurde abgelehnt.*

Wachsmuth: Es war, um mit unseren Worten zu sprechen, nicht titelfähig. Das war ein einziges Durcheinander. Der Anlass war eine Titelgeschichte über ihn. Unberechenbar war übrigens auch Horst Janssen. Er war ein begnadeter Zeichner und leider auch ein freier Künstler im wahren Sinne des Wortes, einer, der sich an keine Kette, auch nicht an die unserige, binden ließ. Absprachen interessierten ihn nicht. Zum Glück konnten wir den Zeichner Michael Mathias Prechtl für eine regelmäßige Zusammenarbeit gewinnen …

SPIEGEL: *… der zuvor schon für die „New York Times" gezeichnet hatte und für den SPIEGEL den Papst als moderne Hexe auf dem Hirtenstab herumfliegen ließ.*

Wachsmuth: Prechtl hatte einen bemerkenswert feinen Strich und ein ungeheures satirisches Talent. Wir hatten es inzwischen geschafft, eine Bildsprache zu erfinden, die Abwechslung, wöchentliche Überraschung und Unverwechselbarkeit vereinte. Die Illustration war dabei so etwas wie ein Highlight, das wir regelmäßig einsetzten.

SPIEGEL: *Ihre Arbeit als Titelbildchef wurde belohnt, mit Auszeichnungen, aber auch mit der Zuwendung der Kunstszene. Die Kasseler Kunstschau Documenta von 1972 bat darum, eine Auswahl von Titelbildern des SPIEGEL ausstellen zu dürfen: Gezeigt wurden außer den veröffentlichten Blättern auch die jeweiligen ungedruckten Alternativen. Hatte Sie die Anfrage erstaunt?*

Wachsmuth: Ja, und noch mehr hat mich dann das Interesse des Publikums verblüfft. Dass es üblicherweise jede Woche etwa zehn Entwürfe für ein Titelbild gab, dass so viel Energie und Aufwand in ein Cover gesteckt wurde – das war den meisten Lesern neu, und es hat sie fasziniert. Die Besucher der Documenta nutzten die Möglichkeit, nachträglich über das jeweils beste Blatt mitzuentscheiden. Sie konnten Wahlzettel ausfüllen und diese in eine Urne stecken. Heraus kam, dass – wenn es nach dem Publikum gegangen wäre – die von uns ausgewählten Blätter stets durchgefallen wären. Die Documenta-Gäste hätten sich jedenfalls stets anders entschieden als wir.

SPIEGEL: *Eine Schmach?*

Wachsmuth: Nein, ein großer Anreiz. Wer hätte denn gedacht, dass sich so viele Menschen am liebsten in unsere Titelgestaltung eingemischt hätten? Das ist doch wunderbar. Wir Grafiker empfanden das Interesse als Bestätigung dafür, wie ernst der Leser das Erscheinungsbild nimmt. Der Chefredaktion war das natürlich auch vorher schon klar, aber nun war es ihr eben noch klarer.

SPIEGEL: *Weltberühmt wurde 1977 eine Titelbildgestaltung zum Thema Italien: Den Titel „Urlaubsland Italien" garnierten Sie mit einem provokanten Foto: Auf einem Teller haben Sie zwischen Spaghetti eine Pistole appetitlich angerichtet.*

Wachsmuth: Die Stimmung in Italien kochte daraufhin hoch. Ein italienisches Blatt bildete als Antwort eine Handgranate in einem Haufen Sauerkraut ab. Es war wohl das erste Mal, dass ein Magazin mit einem Titelbild beinahe diplomatische Verstimmungen auslöste. Selbst Augstein bekam das auf einer Italien-Reise zu spüren.

SPIEGEL: *Sie haben sich viele Jahre lang für die Illustration eingesetzt. Hatten Sie, ein Zeichner, nie den Ehrgeiz, eigene Illustrationen zu veröffentlichen?*

Wachsmuth: Habe ich ja, heimlich. In den sechziger Jahren wurde – unter Pseudonym – eine meiner Illustrationen als Titelblatt des SPIEGEL gedruckt. Bis heute weiß niemand, dass ich hinter diesem Bild stecke. Seit fast 20 Jahren nicht mehr im Amt, habe ich immer noch ein sehr großes Interesse an dem, was auf dem Titel passiert, und ich kann zum Glück sagen: Der SPIEGEL-Titel heute ist so gestaltet, wie ich es auch machen würde.

Interview: Ulrike Knöfel,
Redakteurin im Kulturressort des SPIEGEL

Eberhard Wachsmuth, 84, studied at the Berlin Academy of Fine Arts for eight semesters. After World War II, he became a political cartoonist, starting at the "Insulaner" in Berlin and moving in 1948 to the American-run, Munich-based "Neue Zeitung", which closed in 1953. Wachsmuth became picture editor at DER SPIEGEL in January 1954. He spent nearly 30 years at the newsmagazine with the exception of a stint he did at the magazine "Quick". At DER SPIEGEL, he was also responsible for the magazine's cover.

SPIEGEL: *Mr. Wachsmuth, what drew you, a cartoonist, to the word-filled world of a magazine like DER SPIEGEL back in the 1950s?*

Wachsmuth: DER SPIEGEL and its editors already had a special reputation. In Munich, people considered them to be a group of crazy journalists in Hanover who just complained about everything. And they assumed the magazine wouldn't last long. That sounded interesting. I was looking for a job, had gotten a good feel for journalism in my previous work and DER SPIEGEL, which had just moved to Hamburg, needed somebody to handle the inside pictures and cover design. The deal was sealed in December 1953 and toasted with a shot of cheap cognac.

SPIEGEL: *Back then, the look of DER SPIEGEL, which you were to redevelop later on, was distinctly uniform. Every week, the cover bore a striking portrait photo of some important person: Winston Churchill, writers like Thomas Mann, business executives, athletes or movie stars like Greta Garbo. Why was this approach of showing an interesting person, this face of the week, eventually discarded?*

Wachsmuth: Times and subjects change. The images must change with them. The changes focused on the details at first, like the picture cropping and the frame. But the design principle of putting a face on the cover each week had become a trademark. And we were reluctant to toy with it. The portrait photos were usually taken by staff photographer Max Ehlert and were excellent. The staff asked itself: Why should any changes be made in the trademark cover? But I considered this exclusive approach to be a dead end.

SPIEGEL: *Why?*

Wachsmuth: Because it gave you no leeway. A close-up of a person is one important technique but it is not the only one. Why shouldn't you be able to show an object? As time went on, other issues moved to the forefront, and it was difficult to use one single person to illustrate them. Changes in society are one example. I had something totally different in mind: the drawn illustration.

SPIEGEL: *That must have been a bold way of thinking back then. After all, photography was already firmly established as the more modern medium by then.*

Wachsmuth: Really? Photos, particularly portrait pictures, were everywhere. They were all over the covers of the celebrity magazines, even if they generally showed starlets. A drawing, if done well, actually can say more than a photograph. It can magnify, exaggerate or sharpen a subject, even abstract issues. It can give you the more powerful image. Of course, an illustration is not the best form of communication for every subject. But my vision of the SPIEGEL cover was more of an illustration than a photograph.

SPIEGEL: *What approach did you take?*

Wachsmuth: I drew some sketches that I could use to build my case with the editors in chief. Back in 1954, plans to publish a biography about the legendary British officer Lawrence of Arabia created quite a stir, and we decided to do a cover story. I drew a picture of a swashbuckling Lawrence and then showed it to the editor-in-chief. The idea went nowhere. Thanks to my drawings, though, I became known as the "learned art student." Rudolf Augstein bestowed that nickname on me. But as time passed, the objections faded away, and we gingerly moved toward the use of illustrations by introducing a mixed form.

SPIEGEL: *What did that look like?*

Wachsmuth: We combined photos and illustrations. As always, we had a portrait shot on the cover's foreground. But I used my own graphically dominated style to design the background. I would add drawings or cutouts from other pictures. This is how I managed to get a narrative element onto the cover. We put a songwriter in front of his notes and Agatha Christie in front of a tapestry of her book covers. In 1961, we even put a hand-written red document over the face of James Joyce. That was the turning point for the cover design. But we never quit experimenting with the graphics and photographs. In the photo lab at DER SPIEGEL – often at night because there was never a lot of time – we developed forms of graphics that others could envision and create only after the computer became standard equipment.

SPIEGEL: *Let's return to 1956 for a second. Back then, you published one illustration – and it was even in color – that really must have caused a sensation and been a triumph for you. The drawing was done by Boris Artzybasheff, a Russian living in New York. Why did DER SPIEGEL have to journey so far to find an artist?*

Wachsmuth: Because this man was one of the best illustrators around. And I was really proud of our hiring him. I had admired the work of Artzybasheff even before I started working at DER SPIEGEL. He had done covers for such American newsmagazines as "Time". I was really impressed by his pointed realism and dead-on surrealism. I made a point of always praising his talent. To arrange the job, someone had to make a business trip to New York. Unfortunately, I wasn't the one who got to go. Artzybasheff did a portrait of the local Italian politician and Florentine Mayor Giorgio La Pira for us.

SPIEGEL: *A year later, in 1957, he did a picture of Franz Josef Strauß, who was defense minister. The illustration shows his head and a form of headwear that, in several steps, evolves from a typical Bavaria hat with a feather to a military helmet. Who came up with this idea?*

Wachsmuth: Artzybasheff did. He could turn the message of the words into an unambiguous, witty picture. That was just what I was looking for: Using an image to arouse interest in the story. And Artzybasheff had the amazing ability to capture both the explosive content of the story, which was about Germany's rearmament plans, and the face of Strauß – even though he lived on a different continent and probably didn't even know this politician.

SPIEGEL: *DER SPIEGEL is well known for its independence and its hard-nosed reporting. Using the cover to show such clear disrespect for a member of the government must have upset many people in well-behaved postwar Germany. Did this satire generate a lot of angry reaction?*

Wachsmuth: There was none as far as I can remember. DER SPIEGEL was already known as a publication that was not very polite in its writing about high-ranking people. With this cover, we were adopting this style as well.

SPIEGEL: *Why did the illustrated cover remain an exception to the rule for quite a while?*

Wachsmuth: The most important reason was: We couldn't hire Artzybasheff each week. And there weren't any comparable artists in Germany, people with whom we wanted to work. Here, there was much less emphasis on the art of illustration than in the United States. That is still the case today. As a result, we had to develop a pool of talented people. That took time, of course. And, perhaps, you could say that I was a difficult employer because I draw, too. But the effort paid off. People like Hermann Degkwitz – he's just one example – are among the best in the profession. The drawings are as technically perfect as paintings.

SPIEGEL: *And cutting, too. For the 1967 cover titled "Mao's last battle", Degkwitz outfitted the founder, leader and slave driver of the People's Republic of China with a necklace made of a horrible dragon that was biting its tail. One of Degkwitz's covers in 1968 showed the powerful German publisher Axel Springer slithering over the asphalt – his worm-like body is made up of Springer publications. After breaking free of the tight-fitting design corset of the early years, weren't you going a bit too far?*

Wachsmuth: Not at all. The editors in chief, particularly Augstein, always kept an eye on us, and he had final say about the various proposed cover designs.

SPIEGEL: *What sort of instructions did you give artists like Degkwitz or Ursula Arriens, who did many of the covers?*

Wachsmuth: Of course, we talked about the deadline and made a few design suggestions. But it was important that each of these brilliant illustrators would be able to employ his or her own unique style. For that reason, we didn't do a lot of meddling. In a time when illustrations weren't considered to be a form of artistic expression, we considered them to be valuable, one-of-a-kind works. That's why we had the pictures signed.

SPIEGEL: *You also worked from time to time with artists like Marc Chagall or Bernard Buffet. Did that really work out?*

Wachsmuth: Sometimes too well, actually. The French painter Bernard Buffet who was extremely successful in the 1950s did an impressive self-portrait for us. A few years later, the editors in chief came up with the idea of having him do a portrait of Chancellor Ludwig Erhard. Of all people! Everybody in Buffet's work looks very bony, as if they were starved. And he was supposed to do a portrait of the well-fed Erhard?

SPIEGEL: *It didn't work out with one of Germany's most famous artists in 1979 – Joseph Beuys. The cover that he designed was rejected.*

Wachsmuth: It wasn't "fit for the cover," to use one of our own expressions. It was just total chaos, and it was supposed to illustrate a cover story about him. Horst Janssen was also unpredictable. He was a gifted drawer but an independent artist in the true sense of the word. He was someone who would wear nobody's leash, including ours. Deadlines were the last thing on his mind. He had assignments, but they produced nothing we could print. Fortunately, we got the illustrator Michael Mathias Prechtl to do regular assignments.

SPIEGEL: *He was the one who had done illustrations for the "New York Times". And for DER SPIEGEL, he even turned the pope into* *a modern-day witch riding around on a shepherd's staff.*

Wachsmuth: Prechtl had a remarkably fine stroke and immense satirical talent. Over time, we developed a language of images that brought together variety, weekly surprises and uniqueness. The illustration became a highlight that we regularly used.

SPIEGEL: *Your work as cover editor received awards and was even recognized by the art community. In 1972, the Kassel art show Documenta asked for permission to display a selection of SPIEGEL covers. The exhibition showed not only the published versions but also unpublished alternatives. Were you surprised by the request?*

Wachsmuth: Yes, and I was even more amazed by the interest shown by the visitors. Most of the readers didn't know that there were usually about ten different proposed designs for the cover each week, and that so much time and energy went into a cover. It fascinated them. The visitors at the Documenta took advantage of the opportunity to select the best cover from all of the proposed designs. They filled out ballots and dropped them into a box. The result was that if the public had had its way the covers that we selected would have been tossed aside. People attending the Documenta always made a different selection than the one we made.

SPIEGEL: *An embarrassment?*

Wachsmuth: No, a real stimulant. Who would have thought that so many readers would like to have a say in the design of our cover? That's really great. We graphic artists see this interest as confirming the importance that the readers attach to the cover. This was already clear to the editors in chief, but afterward it became even more clear.

SPIEGEL: *One of your 1977 covers created a sensation around the world. You garnished the cover titled "Vacation land Italy" with a provocative image: You placed a savory pistol in the middle of spaghetti.*

Wachsmuth: That really did steam the Italians. One Italian publication responded to our cover with an illustration of a hand grenade lying in sauerkraut. It was probably the first time that a magazine's cover nearly triggered a diplomatic dispute. Even Augstein felt it during a trip he made to Italy.

SPIEGEL: *Over the years, you fought for illustrations. Didn't the illustrator in you want to publish his own work?*

Wachsmuth: Of course, secretly. In the 1960s, one of my illustrations was used as a SPIEGEL cover – under a pseudonym. Even today, nobody knows that it is my work. Even though I have not been art director for nearly 20 years, I'm still very interested in what is published there. And I'm glad to say: SPIEGEL covers today are designed just the way I would do them.

....

Interview: Ulrike Knöfel,
editor with the culture department of DER SPIEGEL

Die Illustratoren
The Artists

BORIS ARTZYBASHEFF 32

BERNARD BUFFET 36

HERMANN DEGKWITZ 38

VICCO VON BÜLOW/LORIOT 50

URSULA ARRIENS 52

HANS-GEORG RAUCH 60

MICHAEL M. PRECHTL 62

JEAN SOLÉ 70

TILMAN MICHALSKI 72

HORST HAITZINGER 78

DIETER WIESMÜLLER 80

ALFONS KIEFER 92

MATHIAS WASKE 102

RITA MÜHLBAUER 104

PETER SCHÖSSOW 106

FRIEDRICH DE BOER 110

H. U. OSTERWALDER 112

DEWA WAWORKA 114

PETER KRÄMER 124

MARIE MARCKS 128

KINUKO CRAFT 132

UWE BRANDI 134

DIETRICH EBERT 136

NILS FLIEGNER 138

SILKE BACHMANN 140

LUDVIK GLAZER-NAUDÉ 142

TOM JÜTZ 150

BRALDT BRALDS 152

MARK ENTWISLE 158

TIM O'BRIEN 162

KAZUHIKO SANO 168

MARVIN MATTELSON 170

GUY BILLOUT 174

ROBERT GIUSTI 176

DUBOSARSKIJ & VINOGRADOV 180

DYNAMIC DUO 182

NANCY STAHL 186

JEAN-PIERRE KUNKEL 192

RAFAL OLBINSKI 202

WERNER BANDEL 212

ROBERT RODRIGUEZ 214

JOHN MACDONALD 218

GREGORY BRIDGES 222

CHRIS F. PAYNE 226

HANNES BINDER 232

ROBERTO PARADA 234

ROB BROOKS 236

MICHAEL PLEESZ 238

JOHN HARWOOD 240

SANDRA SHAP 242

MICHAEL DEAS 244

DANIEL ADEL 246

THOMAS FLUHARTY 248

ROBERT HUNT 250

GARY KELLEY 252

LIZ LOMAX 254

JOHN MARTIN 256

WILSON MCLEAN 258

MARCO VENTURA 260

SPIEGEL-Titel 16/1956
Närrische Streiche der
Barmherzigkeit

*Der Bürgermeister von
Florenz, Giorgio la Pira, ist
Mitglied des linken Flügels
der christdemokratischen
italienischen Regierungs-
partei. Wegen seines sozialen
Engagements kann sich der
fromme und pfiffige Politiker auch gegen die starken
Kommunisten profilieren.*

SPIEGEL cover 16/1956
**The wit and wisdom
of compassion**

*Florentine Mayor Giorgio
la Pira is a member
of the left wing of Italy's
governing Christian
Democratic Party. Thanks
to his social commitment,
the pious and sharp
politician can hold his
own even against the strong
communists.*

BORIS ARTZYBASHEFF

Für seinen Sohn Boris hatte der russische Schriftsteller Michail Artzybasheff kurz vor Ausbruch des Ersten Weltkriegs nur eine Empfehlung: „Verlass Russland, verdirb nicht meinen guten Ruf, und ändere deinen Namen!" Boris Artzybasheff, 1899 in der Ukraine geboren, befolgte den Rat seines Vaters in einem Punkt nicht – er behielt seinen Namen und wurde unter diesem als Illustrator weltberühmt. Nachdem er sich 1919 in New York niedergelassen hatte, arbeitete Artzybasheff zunächst als Designer für Bierflaschen und Arzneimittel. Später illustrierte er mehr als 40 Bücher, von denen er einige selbst schrieb und herausgab. Werbeaufträge und Titelillustrationen für verschiedene Zeitschriften folgten. Dem „Time Magazine" lieferte er innerhalb von 24 Jahren über 200 Porträts und Gemälde. Während des Zweiten Weltkriegs beriet der Zeichner, Illustrator und Karikaturist das amerikanische Außenministerium in psychologischer Kriegsführung. Boris Artzybasheff starb 1965.

Shortly before World War I began, Russian writer Michail Artzybasheff had only one recommendation for his son Boris: "Leave Russia, don't tarnish my good reputation, and change your name!" Boris Artzybasheff, who was born in the Ukraine in 1899, followed all but one piece of his father's advice – he kept the name and with it became a world-renowned illustrator. After he settled in New York in 1919, Boris Artzybasheff initially worked as a designer of labels for beer bottles and drug containers. He later illustrated more than 40 books, including some that he himself wrote and published. Advertising commissions and cover illustrations followed, including commissions for more than 200 portraits and illustrations for

"Time" magazine over the course of 24 years. During World War II, the graphic designer, illustrator and cartoonist served as a consultant in psychological warfare for the U.S. State Department. Boris Artzybasheff died in 1965.

SPIEGEL-Titel 1/1957
Kopf aus dem Sand

Mit 41 Jahren ist Verteidigungsminister Franz-Josef Strauß jüngstes Mitglied der Bundesregierung. Durch seine forsche und unkonventionelle Art beeindruckt der CSU-Politiker die Nato-Partner.

SPIEGEL cover 1/1957
Pulling his head
out of the sand

At the age of 41, Defense Minister Franz-Josef Strauss is the youngest member of the national cabinet. With his snappy and unconventional manner, this member of Bavaria's Christian Social Union has made an impression on West Germany's NATO partners.

COURTESY OF THE SYRACUSE UNIVERSITY ART COLLECTION, USA

SPIEGEL-Titel 51/1959
Die Seele ist ein Eisberg

Der Wiener Nervenarzt Sigmund Freud ist berühmt, seine Arbeit aber wurde bislang nur verhalten zur Kenntnis genommen. Jetzt, 20 Jahre nach seinem Tod, gibt es im deutschsprachigen Raum eine Freud-Renaissance.

SPIEGEL cover 51/1959
The soul is an iceberg

Sigmund Freud, the neurologist from Vienna, is world-renowned, but his work has so far received relatively little attention. Now, 20 years after his death, Freud is experiencing a renaissance in the German-speaking areas.

BERNARD BUFFET

As an 18-year-old, Bernard Buffet exhibited his first painting in 1946 at the Galérie Beaux-Arts in Paris. He had begun his training at the art school "Ecole Nationale Supérieure des Beaux-Arts" three years earlier. From 1952 to 1975, Bernard Buffet presented his work in annual exhibitions. Before creating the portrait of Chancellor Ludwig Erhard, the father of West Germany's economic miracle, in 1963 for DER SPIEGEL, Bernard Buffet completed a portrait of the French president Charles de Gaulle for the U.S. magazine "Time" in 1958. In response to objections expressed by "Time" editors, Buffet retorted: "I've drawn him the way my eyes see him. If others see him differently, then they should draw him differently." Referring to the Erhard portrait he did for DER SPIEGEL, Buffet commented: "Je l'ai embelli" ("I made him more beautiful"). Bernard Buffet died in Tourtour in 1999.

Als 18-Jähriger stellte Bernard Buffet 1946 ein erstes Gemälde in der Pariser Kunstgalerie aus. Drei Jahre zuvor hatte er seine Ausbildung an der dortigen Kunsthochschule begonnen. Von 1952 bis 1975 präsentierte Buffet seine Werke in jährlichen Themenausstellungen. Bevor er 1963 Bundeskanzler Ludwig Erhard, den Vater des deutschen Wirtschaftswunders, für den SPIEGEL porträtierte, hatte er bereits 1958 den französischen Staatspräsidenten Charles de Gaulle für das amerikanische Magazin „Time" gezeichnet. Einwendungen der „Time"-Redaktion gegen seine Arbeit wies er damals mit dem Hinweis zurück: „Ich habe ihn gezeichnet, wie mein Auge ihn sieht. Wenn andere ihn anders sehen, sollen sie ihn anders zeichnen." Zum Erhard-Porträt für den SPIEGEL bemerkte er: „Je l'ai embelli" („Ich habe ihn verschönt").
Bernard Buffet starb 1999 in Tourtour.

SPIEGEL-Titel 42/1963
Kanzler Erhard

*Nach 14 Jahren Regent-
schaft von Konrad Adenauer
ist der CDU-Politiker
Ludwig Erhard neuer
Kanzler der Bundesrepublik.
Sein Regierungsstil
unterscheidet sich erheblich
von dem seines Vorgängers.*

SPIEGEL cover 42/1963
Chancellor Erhard

*After 14 years under
Konrad Adenauer,
West Germany has a new
chancellor: Ludwig Erhard,
also a Christian Democrat.
His style of governing
differs significantly from
that of his predecessor.*

HERMANN DEGKWITZ

1972 waren meine Arbeiten mit vielen anderen SPIEGEL-Titeln auf der Documenta in Kassel ausgestellt. 1974 wurde ich als Dozent für Illustration an die Hochschule für Künste in Bremen berufen."

A life summary:

"I, Hermann Degkwitz, was born on Aug. 29, 1921, in Munich as the second son of a very well-known pediatrician. My mother came from an artistic family. Painting and drawing were encouraged in our home just as much as the occupation with all forms of art was. I trained as a freelance painter at the Academy of Fine Arts in Hamburg from 1938 to 1941. After the war, I earned my living as a political cartoonist for daily newspapers throughout West Germany until the start of the 1970s, when Conny Ahlers brought me in contact with DER SPIEGEL and Eberhardt Wachsmuth.

After years of trying, my first SPIEGEL cover appeared in 1967, followed by many more cover illustrations for the magazine over the next 28 years.

In 1972, my work was exhibited together with numerous other SPIEGEL covers at the Documenta in Kassel. Two years later, I was appointed lecturer for illustration at the Academy of Fine Arts in Bremen".

Der Lauf des Lebens:

„Hermann Degkwitz, geboren am 29. August 1921 in München als zweiter Sohn eines damals sehr bekannten Kinderarztes. Meine Mutter stammte aus einer kunstsinnigen Familie. Eigenes Malen und Zeichnen wurde zu Hause ebenso gefördert wie die Beschäftigung mit allen Künsten.

An der Hansischen Hochschule für Bildende Künste am Lerchenfeld in Hamburg hatte ich von 1938 bis 1941 eine Ausbildung als freier Maler.

Nach dem Krieg verdiente ich mein Geld als politischer Karikaturist für Tageszeitungen in ganz Westdeutschland. Bis mich Anfang der sechziger Jahre Conny Ahlers mit dem SPIEGEL und Eberhardt Wachsmuth zusammenbrachte. Nach langjährigen Versuchen war es dann 1967 so weit, dass mein erster SPIEGEL-Titel erschien, dem dann 28 Jahre lang viele weitere folgten.

SPIEGEL-Titel 5/1967
Maos letztes Gefecht

*Seit einem Jahr tobt in
China die Kulturrevolution,
jetzt kämpfen Maos
Kommunisten auch gegen
Funktionäre der eigenen
Partei: Das Reich der Mitte
steht am Rande eines
Bürgerkriegs.*

SPIEGEL cover 5/1967
Mao's last battle

*A cultural revolution
has been raging in China
for a year. Mao's commu-
nists are battling their own
party functionaries. China
is on the brink of civil war.*

SPIEGEL-Titel 14/1967
Charles de Gaulle

*Präsident Charles de Gaulle
verliert an Zustimmung
im Land. Sozialisten
und Kommunisten werden
immer stärker.*

SPIEGEL cover 14/1967
Charles de Gaulle

*French President Charles
de Gaulle is losing support
at home. Socialists and
communists are gaining
strength.*

SPIEGEL-Titel 22/1967
CDU-Parteitag

*Die CDU um Bundeskanz-
ler Kurt Kiesinger sorgt
sich um ihre Zukunft – wer
soll die Partei künftig
führen?*

SPIEGEL cover 22/1967
CDU party convention

*The CDU under Chancellor
Kurt Kiesinger is growing
concerned about the party's
future – who should lead the
party in the years ahead?*

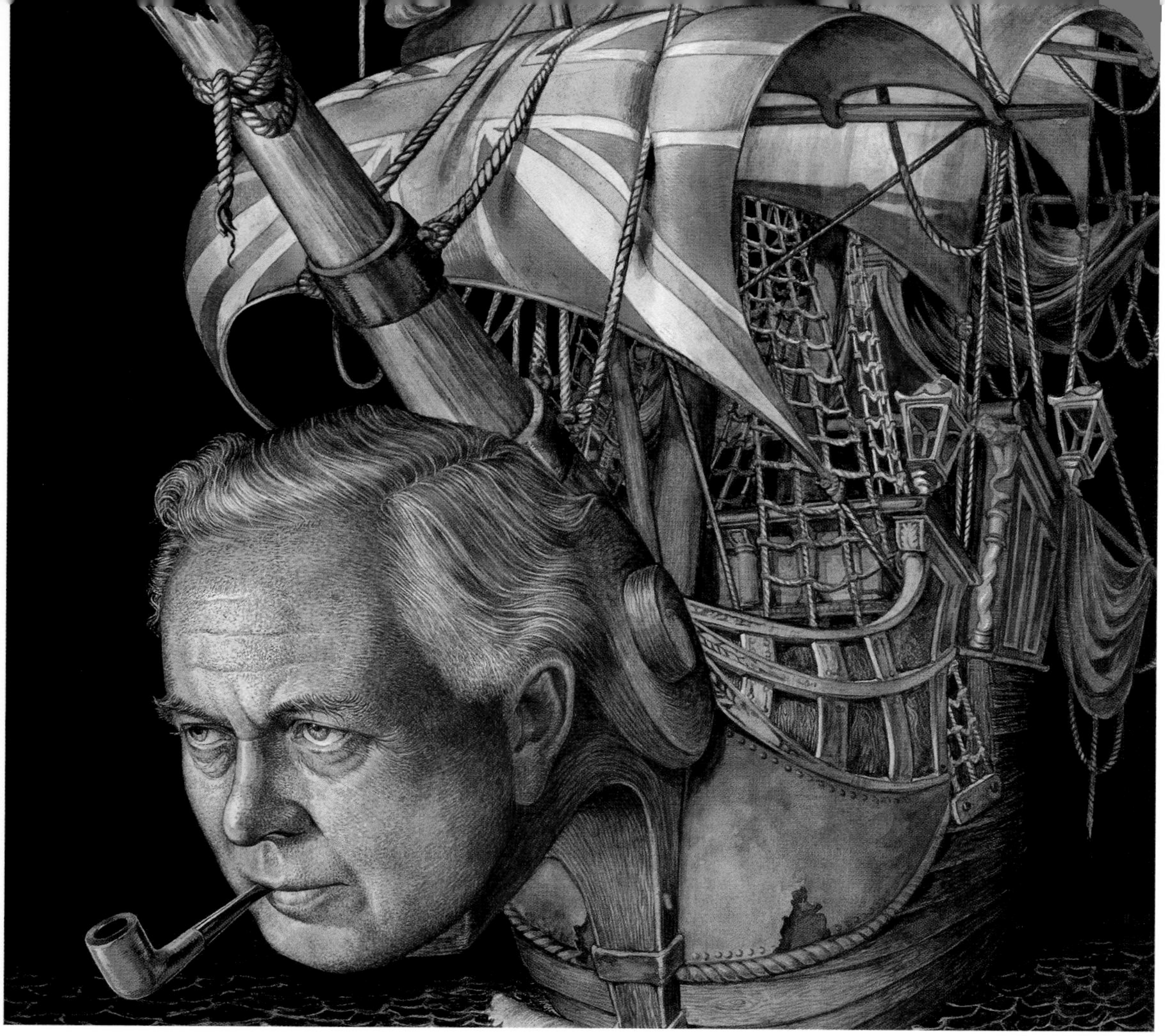

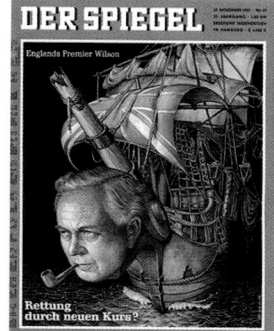

SPIEGEL-Titel 49/1967
Rettung durch neuen
Kurs?

*Labour-Premier Harold
Wilson wertet das
britische Pfund um mehr
als 14 Prozent ab und hofft
so, aus der Schuldenfalle
zu kommen.*

SPIEGEL cover 49/1967
Charting a new course

*By devaluing the British
pound by more than
14 percent, Labor Prime
Minister Harold Wilson
hopes to free Britain from
the debt trap.*

SPIEGEL-Titel 5/1968
Moskaus größter Spion

*Der Engländer Kim Philby
arbeitete beim britischen
Geheimdienst und war seit
den dreißiger Jahren Spion
für die Sowjetunion.*

SPIEGEL cover 5/1968
Moscow's best spy

*Englishman Kim Philby
worked for the British Secret
Service. He has also been
a spy for the Soviet Union
since the 1930s.*

41

SPIEGEL-Titel 18/1968
Karl Marx

*150 Jahre nach seiner
Geburt kehrt Karl Marx in
seine westdeutsche Heimat
zurück: Vielerorts finden
Kongresse und Diskussions-
veranstaltungen statt –
und die demonstrierende
Jugend trägt auf den
Straßen sein Bild.*

SPIEGEL cover 18/1968
Karl Marx

*Karl Marx is returning
to his West German home
150 years after his birth.
Conferences and round-table
discussions are taking place
everywhere – demonstrating
youths are also taking
him to the streets.*

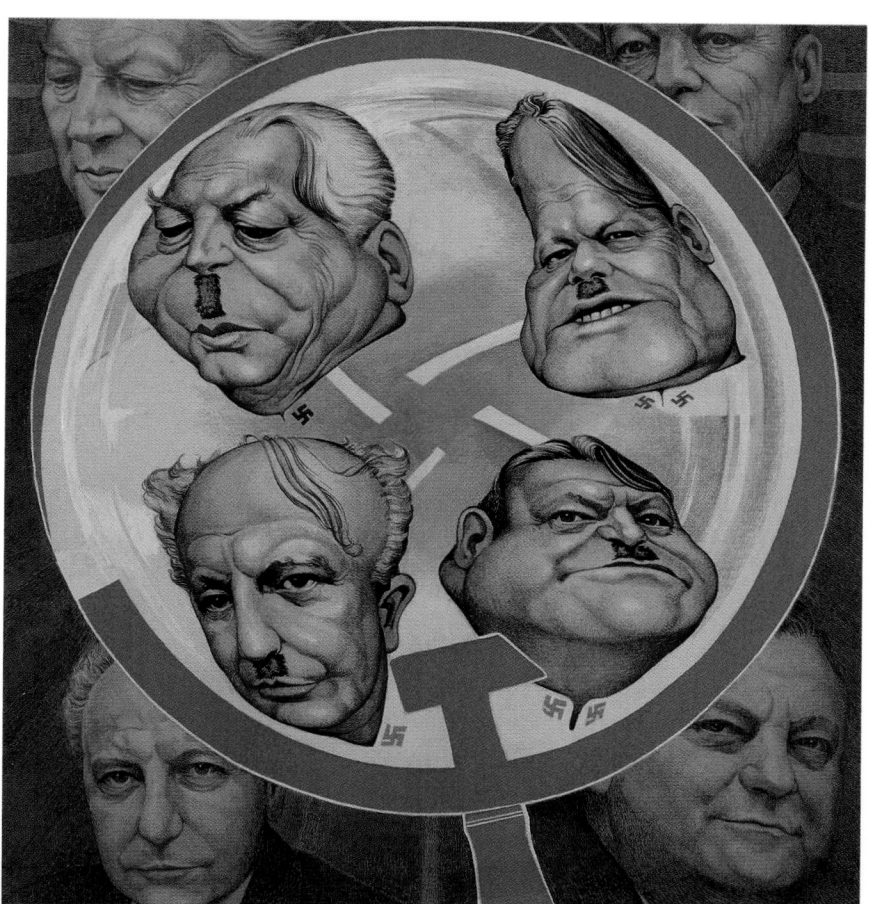

SPIEGEL-Titel 1/1969
Moskaus Bild
der Deutschen

*Die Deutschen sind in den
Augen vieler Sowjetbürger
die größten Störenfriede:
Militarismus und
Revanchismus gefährdeten
den Weltfrieden.*

SPIEGEL cover 1/1969
Moscow's view
of Germany

*In the eyes of many Soviet
citizens, Germans are
the biggest troublemakers.
Germans' militarism
and revanchism are said
to threaten world peace.*

SPIEGEL-Titel 18/1969
Papst in Bedrängnis

In der katholischen Kirche regt sich Widerstand gegen die päpstliche Autorität. Paul VI. warnt vor einem neuen Schisma.

SPIEGEL cover 18/1969
Pope in peril

Opposition to the Pope's authority is growing within the Catholic Church. Paul VI warns that a new schism may be brewing.

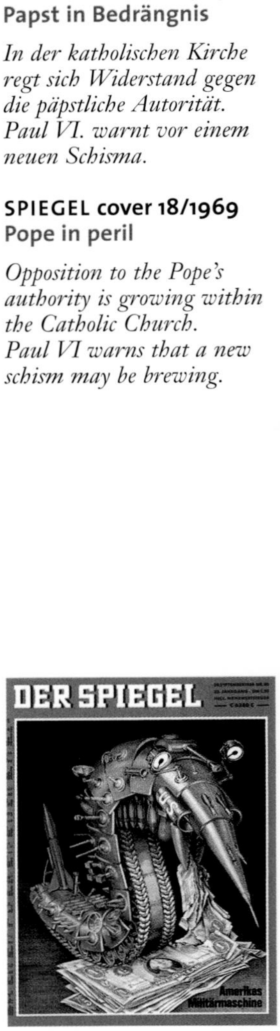

SPIEGEL-Titel 40/1969
Amerikas
Militärmaschine

Die USA geben jährlich fast die Hälfte ihres Staatshaushalts für Militär und Rüstung aus.

SPIEGEL cover 40/1969
The U.S. military machine

The United States spend almost half of its budget each year on the military and defense.

SPIEGEL-Titel 20/1971
Die DDR nach Ulbricht

*Staats- und Parteichef
Walter Ulbricht hat 1961
den Bau der Mauer
organisiert. Jetzt endet seine
Ära. Wohin steuert die
DDR unter dem neuen
SED-Chef Erich Honecker?*

SPIEGEL cover 20/1971
East Germany after
Ulbricht

*State and party head
Walter Ulbricht organized
the building of the Berlin
Wall in 1961. Now that
he has stepped down, what
course will East Germany
take under its new leader,
Erich Honecker?*

SPIEGEL-Titel 11/1974
China

*Steht China vor einer
neuen Kulturrevolution?
Der Kampf um die Mao-
Nachfolge ist entbrannt.*

SPIEGEL cover 11/1974
China

*Is China on the verge of
a new cultural revolution?
A fight over Mao's successor
has broken out.*

Kanzler in der Krise (unveröffentlicht 1973)

Im fünften Kanzler-Jahr ist Willy Brandt an die Grenzen seiner Führungs- kunst geraten: Die Ost- politik stagniert, und das Programm der inneren Reformen kommt kaum voran.

Chancellor in a crisis (unpublished 1973)

In his fifth year as chancellor, Willy Brandt has nearly exhausted his leadership skills. His policy regarding the Soviet bloc has reached an impasse, and his program of domestic reforms has slowed to a crawl.

SPIEGEL-Titel 48/1985
Der Höhenflug von Genf

*Nach einem Gipfeltreffen
in Genf demonstrieren
Michail Gorbatschow und
Ronald Reagan Optimismus.
Weltweit gibt es Hoffnung
auf Entspannung zwischen
den beiden Supermächten
USA und UdSSR.*

SPIEGEL cover 48/1985
Aloft at Geneva

*After their summit
meeting in Geneva,
Mikhail Gorbachev and
Ronald Reagan are
displaying optimism.
Hope for a détente between
the two superpowers
is growing worldwide.*

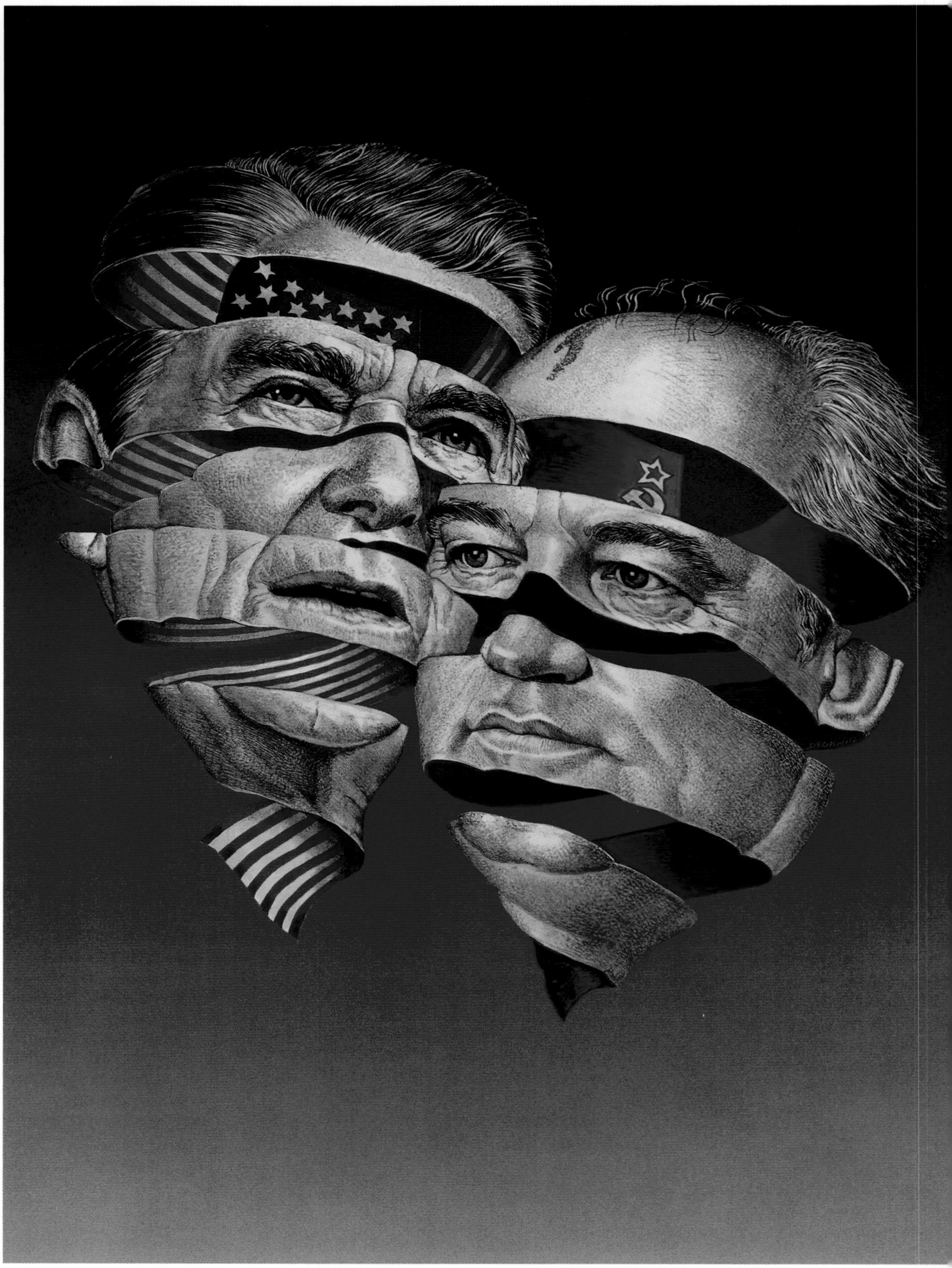

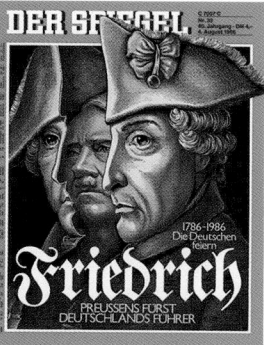

SPIEGEL-Titel 32/1986
Friedrich

*Die Deutschen in Ost und
West feiern den 200. Todes-
tag des Preußenkönigs
Friedrich II. Die Wider-
sprüche zwischen seiner
aufklärerischen Philosophie
und seinen militärischen
Ambitionen stehen dabei
im Mittelpunkt.*

SPIEGEL cover 32/1986
Frederick

*Prussia's Frederick the
Great died 200 years
ago. The contradictions
between his Enlightenment
philosophy and his military
ambitions take center
stage as Germans in the
East and West mark the
event.*

**SPIEGEL-Titel 40/1976
Wahl-Krampf um ein
Wort**

*Mit der Parole „Freiheit
oder Sozialismus" geht
die CDU/CSU in den
Bundestagswahlkampf.
Wirkliche Probleme werden
nicht thematisiert.*

**SPIEGEL cover 40/1976
The cramped campaign**

*The CDU/CSU enters
the federal election campaign
with the motto "freedom
or socialism." But the
real problems are not being
addressed.*

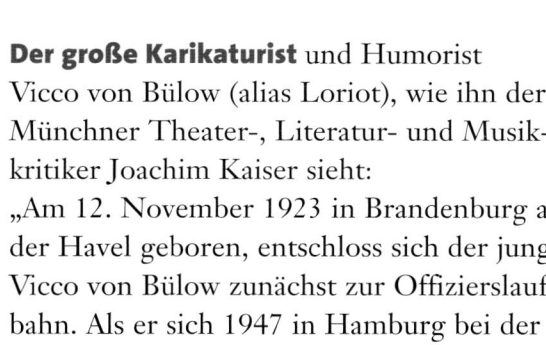

VICCO VON BÜLOW/LORIOT

Der große Karikaturist und Humorist Vicco von Bülow (alias Loriot), wie ihn der Münchner Theater-, Literatur- und Musik-kritiker Joachim Kaiser sieht:

„Am 12. November 1923 in Brandenburg an der Havel geboren, entschloss sich der junge Vicco von Bülow zunächst zur Offizierslauf-bahn. Als er sich 1947 in Hamburg bei der Kunstakademie einschrieb, da verfertigte er, um des finanziellen Zubrots willen, auch Karikaturen. Es waren, neben zahlreichen eiskalt-witzig betexteten und gezeichneten Karikaturbüchern, hauptsächlich seine Fern-sehsendungen, die ihn zum viel bestaunten Exemplar dafür werden ließen, wie witzig Deutsche sein können.

Loriots Komik hat mit Disziplin zu tun, mit meisterhafter Brillanz sowie mit einer genau vermessenen symmetrischen Welt. Er ist Deutschlands erfolgreichster und nobelster Humorist. Sein Ruhm, seine phantastische Popularität sprechen nicht nur für ihn, son-dern bedeuten eine tröstliche Rechtfertigung des viel gelästerten Publikumsgeschmacks.“

The great cartoonist and humorist Vicco von Bülow (alias Loriot), as described by Joachim Kaiser, the Munich theater, litera-ture and music critic:

"Born in Brandenburg on the Havel River on Nov. 12, 1923, the young Vicco von Bülow initially set off for a career as an offi-cer. In 1947, he entered the Art Academy in Hamburg. During that time, he earned some extra money with caricatures. Aside from numerous books of stone-cold funny carica-tures, it was above all his television programs that made him become the much-admired representative of just how funny German humor can be.

Loriot's humor has to do with discipline, with masterly brilliance as well as with a pre-cisely measured, symmetrical world. He is Germany's most successful and most noble comedian. His fame and his fantastic popu-larity not only speak in his favor, but also provide a comforting justification of much maligned public taste."

URSULA ARRIENS

Afterward, Ursula Arriens worked as an illustrator and fashion illustrator in Italy – with a strong preference for tempera and colored pencils. From 1978 to 1988, she worked exclusively as a cover designer for DER SPIEGEL.

Das Skizzenbuch ihrer Mutter, die selbst eine begabte Zeichnerin war, und die umfangreiche Kunstbibliothek im Elternhaus weckten bei Ursula Arriens das Interesse an der künstlerischen Arbeit. Ihre Ausbildung absolvierte die in São Paulo, Brasilien, geborene Grafikerin an der Landeskunstschule Hamburg. Anschließend arbeitete Ursula Arriens als Illustratorin und Modezeichnerin in Italien – bevorzugt mit Tempera und Farbstift. Von 1978 bis 1988 war sie als Titelzeichnerin exklusiv für den SPIEGEL tätig.

Ursula Arriens' interest in art was awakened by the sketchbook of her mother, a talented illustrator in her own right, and the extensive art library her parents maintained at home. The graphic artist, who was born in São Paulo, Brazil, received her training at the State Art School in Hamburg, Germany.

SPIEGEL-Titel 10/1978
Sieg der Roten?

*Kommunisten und
Sozialisten könnten bei den
bevorstehenden Wahlen
in Frankreich die Mehrheit
erringen. Beide Parteien
planen drastische Eingriffe
in die Wirtschaft. Über
die Milliarden-Kosten ihrer
Programme sind sie aber
tief zerstritten.*

SPIEGEL cover 10/1978
Victory for the Reds?

*The communists and
socialists could capture the
majority in France's
upcoming elections. Both
parties are planning
to intervene heavily in the
economy. But they are
deeply divided over the huge
costs of their programs.*

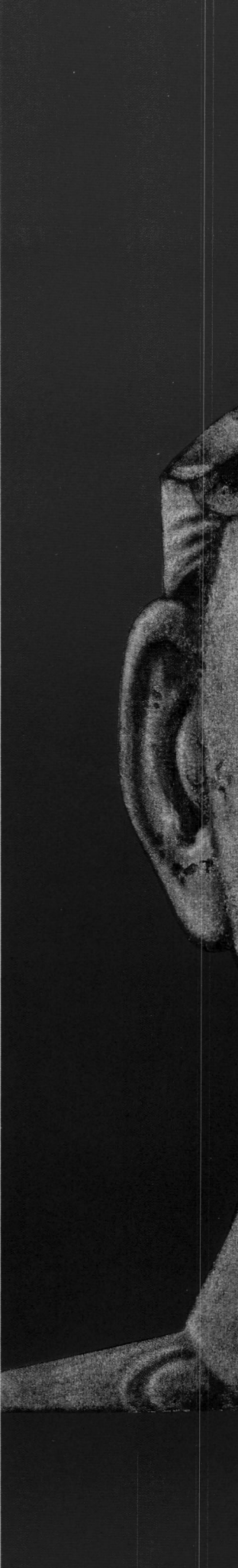

SPIEGEL-Titel 46/1979
Chaos im Iran

*Neun Monate nach der
Machtübernahme durch
Ajatollah Chomeini liegt die
islamische Republik Iran
wirtschaftlich und politisch
am Boden.*

SPIEGEL cover 46/1979
Chaos in Iran

*Nine months after
Ayatollah Khomeini took
power, the Islamic Republic
of Iran has hit rock
bottom – politically and
economically.*

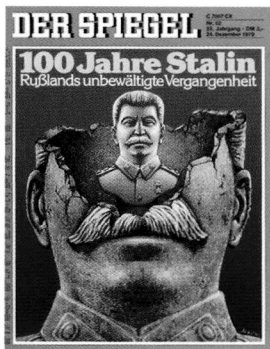

SPIEGEL-Titel 52/1979
100 Jahre Stalin

Auch ein Vierteljahrhundert nach seinem Tod ist Josef Stalin in der Sowjetunion gegenwärtig. Vielen Russen gilt er nicht als Massenmörder und Despot, sondern als Sieger über Hitler. Der Stalinismus bleibt unbewältigt.

SPIEGEL cover 52/1979
100 years of Stalin

Twenty-five years after his death, Josef Stalin is very much alive in the Soviet Union. Many Russians view him not as a mass murderer and despot, but as the victor over Hitler. Stalinism has yet to be scrutinized.

SPIEGEL-Titel 36/1980
Kommunismus
reparabel?

*Streikende Werftarbeiter
in Danzig haben dem
kommunistischen Regime
große Zugeständnisse
abgetrotzt. Künftig soll es
freie Gewerkschaften geben.*

SPIEGEL cover 36/1980
Can communism
be repaired?

*Striking dock workers in
Gdansk have won major
concessions from the communist regime. Free unions are
to be allowed in the future.*

SPIEGEL-Titel 22/1981
Kanzlers letzter Einsatz

*Im Kampf um die
Nachrüstung hat Kanzler
Helmut Schmidt mit
Rücktritt gedroht, im
Bundeshaushalt klaffen
große Löcher – die
Ära Schmidt geht zu Ende.*

SPIEGEL cover 22/1981
Chancellor's last mission

*In the battle over
rearmament, Chancellor
Helmut Schmidt has
threatened to resign. Huge
holes are also developing
in the federal budget – the
end of the Schmidt era is
drawing near.*

SPIEGEL-Titel 13/1984
Thatcher gegen Europa

*Im Streit um Beitrags-
und Ausgleichszahlungen
stürzt die unnachgiebige
Haltung der britischen
Premierministerin
Margaret Thatcher die
Europäische Gemeinschaft
in ihre bisher schwerste
Krise. Thatcher fordert
eisern: „Ich will mein Geld
zurück."*

SPIEGEL cover 13/1984
Thatcher vs. Europe

*In the feud over contribu-
tions and compensation
payments, the unyielding
position taken by British
Prime Minister Margaret
Thatcher has triggered
the worst crisis so far in the
history of the European
Community. Thatcher, the
Iron Lady, is demanding:
"I want my money back."*

SPIEGEL-Titel 6/1983
Wer ist der Dr. Vogel?

Als Kanzlerkandidat der SPD tritt Hans-Jochen Vogel bei der Bundestagswahl 1983 gegen Amtsinhaber Helmut Kohl an.

SPIEGEL cover 6/1983
Who is Dr. Vogel?

Hans-Jochen Vogel is challenging incumbent chancellor Helmut Kohl as the Social Democratic Party's candidate in the 1983 parliamentary election.

**Herbert Wehner
(unveröffentlicht 1983)**

*Der langjährige SPD-
Fraktionsvorsitzende
Herbert Wehner tritt
76-jährig von der
politischen Bühne ab.*

**Herbert Wehner
(unpublished 1983)**

*The long-time SPD
parliamentary group leader
Herbert Wehner is
making his final exit from
the political stage at
the age of 76.*

SPIEGEL-Titel 16/1980
Castro's Cuba:
Muster ohne Wert

*Trotz erheblicher Unter-
stützung durch Moskau
steht Kuba vor dem
wirtschaftlichen Ruin.
Tausende wollen aus
dem sozialistischen Inselreich
Fidel Castros fliehen.*

SPIEGEL cover 16/1980
Castro's Cuba:
a worthless prototype

*Despite Moscow's massive
support, Cuba is an
economic mess. Thousands
of people want to flee
from Fidel Castro's socialist
island paradise.*

HANS-GEORG RAUCH

Nach dem Militärdienst bei der Bundeswehr 1958 bis1959 hatte Hans Georg Rauch, so sagte er, „die geistige Ausbildung zum Karikaturisten abgeschlossen". 1961 bis 1963 studierte der 1939 in Berlin geborene Rauch an der Hochschule für Bildende Künste in Hamburg. Von 1965 an war er Mitarbeiter zahlreicher europäischer und amerikanischer Zeitschriften wie „Look", SPIEGEL, „Observer", „New York Times", „Stern" und „Zeit". 1987 wurde Hans Georg Rauch „Cartoonist of the Year", stellte seine Bilder in Montreal und Kanada aus. Er engagierte sich in der Friedensbewegung und in Initiativen zur Unterstützung politisch Verfolgter. Gleichzeitig begann Rauch mit farbigen Landschaftszeichnungen. Sein Werke zeigte der Künstler auf zahlreichen internationalen und nationalen Ausstellungen. Hans-Georg Rauch starb 1993 in seinem Haus in Worpswede.

Hans-Georg Rauch served in the West German military from 1958 to 1959, and when he was through, he said he "had completed his mental training to become a caricaturist." Rauch, who was born in 1939 in Berlin, studied at the Hamburg College for Fine Arts from 1961 to 1963. In 1965, he began working for numerous European and American magazines, including "Look", DER SPIEGEL, "Observer", "New York Times", "Stern" and "Zeit". In 1987, Hans-Georg Rauch was named Cartoonist of the Year, and his work was displayed in exhibits in Canada, including Montreal. He took an active role in the peace movement and in efforts to support the politically persecuted. At the same time, he began drawing colorful landscapes. His work has been shown at many international and national exhibitions. Hans-Georg Rauch died in his house in Worpswede in 1993.

SPIEGEL-Titel 46/1980
Der Papst in Luthers Land

Erstmals besucht ein Papst das Land Martin Luthers. Die Protestanten hoffen auf ein besseres Verhältnis zwischen evangelischer und katholischer Kirche.

SPIEGEL cover 46/1980
The pope in Luther's country

For the first time, a Pope is visiting the country of Martin Luther. The Protestants hope for a better relationship between the Protestant and Catholic churches.

MICHAEL M. PRECHTL

Geboren wurde Michael M. Prechtl 1926 in Amberg. Seit 1956 war er als freiberuflicher Maler und Grafiker tätig. Prechtl starb 2003 in Nürnberg.
1986 beschrieb der bedeutendste Illustrator Deutschlands und weltweit geschätzte Künstler den Lauf seines Lebens:

„Vor sechzig Jahren geboren,
Kind gewesen,
zur Schule gegangen,
viel gelesen,
mehr gezeichnet,
weit gewandert,
keine Anstrengungen gemacht,
dem Führerbefehl zu folgen,
hart wie Kruppstahl, zäh wie Leder,
flink wie ein Windhund zu werden;
in den Krieg gemußt,
in Gefangenschaft geraten,
an Ruhr erkrankt;
im Sägewerk Holz geschnitten,
im Bergwerk Ölschiefer gebrochen,
in der Raffinerie Asche geschaufelt;
von Skorbut schwach geworden,
auf dem Land Rüben gehackt,
Heu gewendet, Dünger gestreut;
Gräben gegraben,
Salz verladen,
Bäume gefällt;
an Distrophie erkrankt,
Schriften geschrieben;
vom Lager entfernt,
in Dunkelhaft gesessen,
heimgekehrt;
als Röhrengießer gearbeitet,
zur Akademie gegangen,
in der Hoffnung, Kunst lernen zu können.
Vor dreißig Jahren angefangen,
als freier Künstler
Kunst lernend auszuüben;
geheiratet;

viel gezeichnet,
mehr gelesen,
mit Ölfarben gemalt,
Holzschnitte geschaffen,
Lithographien gedruckt;
Plakate entworfen;
Vater geworden;
Wände bemalt,
photographiert,
für Keramik gearbeitet,
für Zeitungen gezeichnet,
Bücher illustriert;
in die Kulturpolitik eingemischt,
Aufsätze geschrieben,
Kataloge redigiert;
eine Oper ausgestattet;
Vorträge gehalten;
Landschaften erlebt,
Tiere gesehen,
Menschen dargestellt,
Leute abgebildet;

die Versuche,
diese Welt, dieses Leben in Kunst zu fassen,
begreifbar zu machen,
dauern an."

Michael M. Prechtl was born in Amberg,
southern Germany, in 1926, and worked as
a freelance painter and illustrator from 1956.
Prechtl died in Nuremberg in 2003.
Prechtl, Germany's most significant illustrator and a globally renowned artist, described
the course of his life in 1986:

"Born 60 years ago,
been a child,
went to school,
read much,
drew more,
walked far,
made no effort
to follow the Führer's orders
to become as hard as Krupp steel, as tough
as leather, as fast as a greyhound;
sent to war,
went into captivity,
fell sick with dysentery,
cut wood in a saw mill,
broke oil shale in a mine,
scooped slag in a refinery,
weakened by scurvy,
chopped up turnips in the country,
turned over the hay, spread fertilizer;
dug ditches,
loaded salt,
felled trees,
got sick with dystrophy,
wrote documents;
ran away from the camp,
detained in darkness,
returned home;
worked as a pipe molder,
attended the academy

in hopes of being able to learn art.
Started 30 years ago
to learn art on the job as a freelance artist;
got married,
drew much,
read more,
painted with oil colors,
created woodcarvings,
printed lithography,
designed posters,
became a father;
painted walls,
took photographs,
worked for ceramics,
drew for newspapers,
illustrated books,
meddled in cultural policy,
wrote essays,
edited catalogs,
outfitted an opera,
gave lectures,
experienced landscapes,
saw animals,
presented human beings,
drew people;
the attempts to make this world, this life
tangible, comprehensible through art go on."

SPIEGEL-Titel 24/1981
Täter Hitler/Denker Nietzsche

Das Interesse an Friedrich Nietzsche ist neu erwacht. War der Philosoph, der das Wort vom Übermenschen prägte, Adolf Hitlers Wegbereiter?

SPIEGEL cover 24/1981
Nietzsche – the brain behind Hitler?

Interest in Friedrich Nietzsche has been newly awakened. Did the philosopher, who coined the expression "Über-mensch," pave the way for Adolf Hitler?

SPIEGEL-Titel 52/1984
Zweifel an Freud

*Die Zahl der Kritiker
an Sigmund Freuds
Psychoanalyse wächst.
Hirnforscher, Biologen
und Psychologen rütteln
am Denkmal des
Wiener Nervenarztes.*

SPIEGEL cover 52/1984
Doubting Freud

*The number of critics
of Sigmund Freud's
psychoanalysis is swelling.
Brain researchers, biologists
and psychologists are
questioning the monumental
legacy of the neurologist
from Vienna.*

SPIEGEL-Titel 14/1986
Bayern-König Ludwig II.

Vor 100 Jahren ertrank Ludwig II. auf geheimnisvolle Weise im Starnberger See. Millionen Menschen pilgern inzwischen nach Neuschwanstein und den anderen Prachtschlössern des „Märchenkönigs".

SPIEGEL cover 14/1986
Ludwig II, King of Bavaria

Ludwig II drowned 100 years ago under mysterious circumstances in Lake Starnberg, near Munich. Millions now make the pilgrimage to Neuschwanstein and the other pompous castles of the "fairy-tale king."

SPIEGEL-Titel 23/1990
Liebe und Verbrechen

Zum 250. Geburtstag des Marquis' de Sade erlebt der Klassiker der bizarren Erotik eine Renaissance: Seine Werke werden neu aufgelegt.

SPIEGEL cover 23/1990
Love and crime

Marquis de Sade, the author of bizarre erotic classics, is experiencing a renaissance on the occasion of his 250th birthday: His works are being republished.

SPIEGEL-Titel 49/1997
Denk ich
an Deutschland ...

*Sein berühmtestes Gedicht
ist die „Loreley", das
„Wintermärchen" seine
wohl bekannteste Schrift.
Vor 200 Jahren starb
der deutsche Dichter
Heinrich Heine.*

SPIEGEL cover 49/1997
If I think of Germany ...

*The "Loreley" is his most
famous poem, "Deutschland:
A Winter's Tale" his most
well-known piece of prose.
The poet Heinrich Heine
died 100 years ago.*

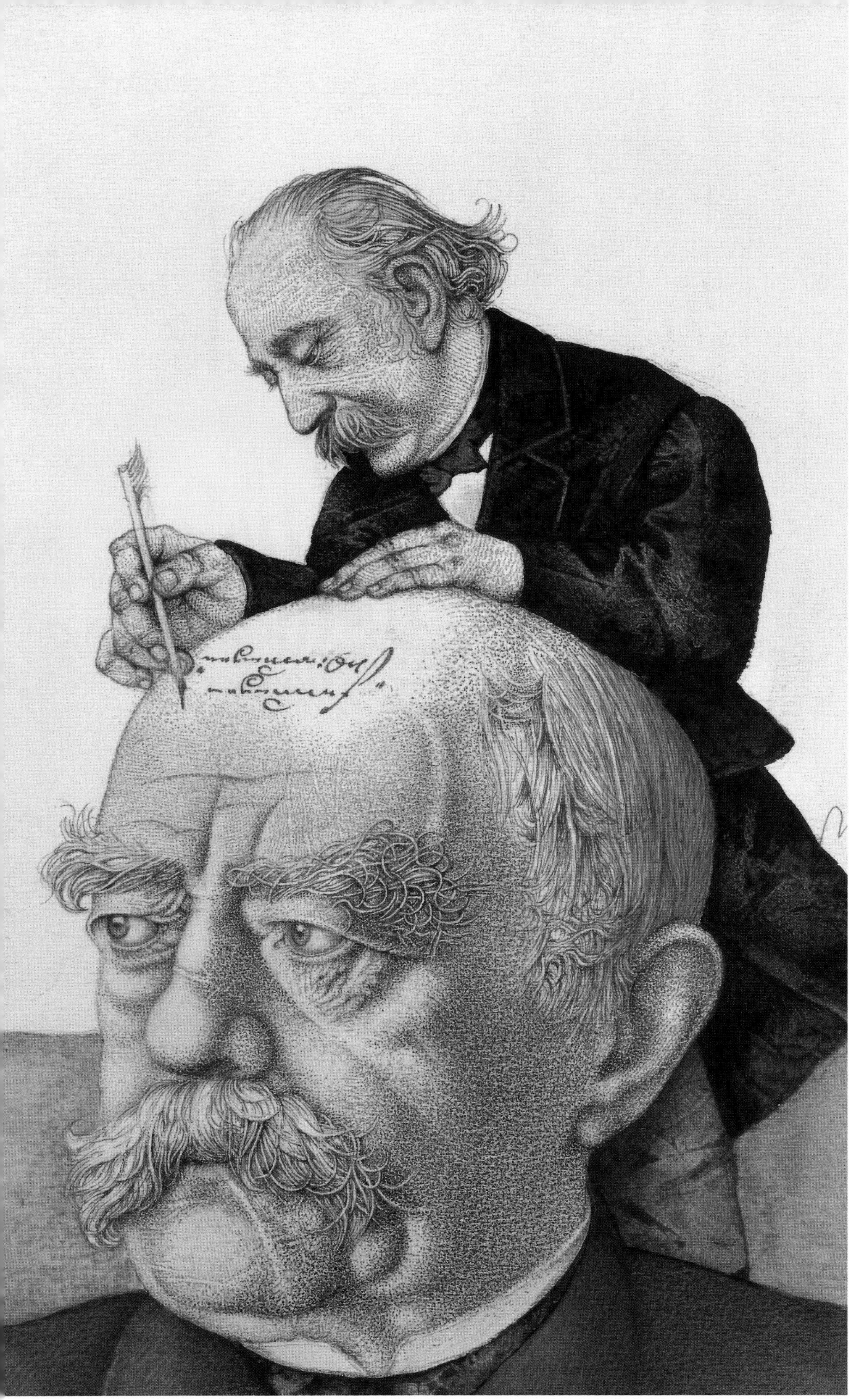

SPIEGEL-Titel 28/1998
Der Dichter und der Schwefelgelbe

Reichsgründer Otto von Bismarck und Romancier Theodor Fontane lebten zur gleichen Zeit – begegnet sind sich die beiden berühmten Preußen nie. Vor hundert Jahren starben sie.

SPIEGEL cover 28/1998
The poet and the politician

Otto von Bismarck, the founder of the German Reich, and novelist Theodor Fontane lived during the same period – but the two famous Prussians never met. Both died 100 years ago.

SPIEGEL-Titel 41/1981
Revolution
im Sowjet-Block

*In einem beispiellosen
Kraftakt hat die polnische
Gewerkschaft Solidarność
der herrschenden Staats-
partei einen Teil der Macht
abgerungen. Moskau ist
alarmiert.*

SPIEGEL cover 41/1981
Revolution
in the Soviet bloc

*In an unprecedented display
of political strength, the
Polish union "Solidarity"
has grabbed a portion of
power from the ruling state
party. Moscow is alarmed.*

JEAN SOLÉ

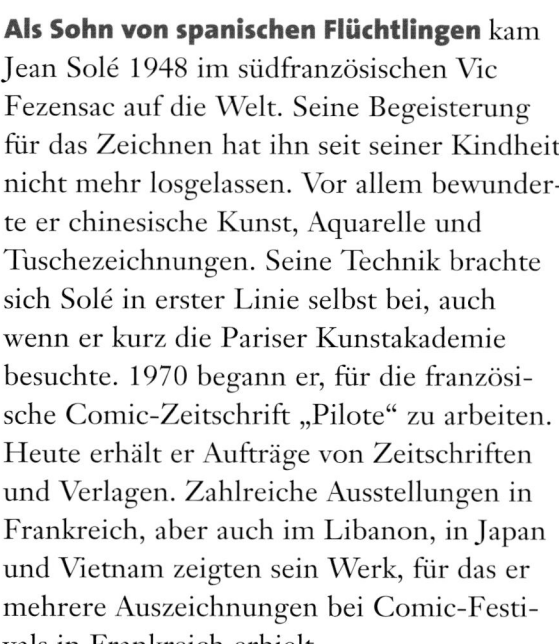

Als Sohn von spanischen Flüchtlingen kam Jean Solé 1948 im südfranzösischen Vic Fezensac auf die Welt. Seine Begeisterung für das Zeichnen hat ihn seit seiner Kindheit nicht mehr losgelassen. Vor allem bewunderte er chinesische Kunst, Aquarelle und Tuschezeichnungen. Seine Technik brachte sich Solé in erster Linie selbst bei, auch wenn er kurz die Pariser Kunstakademie besuchte. 1970 begann er, für die französische Comic-Zeitschrift „Pilote" zu arbeiten. Heute erhält er Aufträge von Zeitschriften und Verlagen. Zahlreiche Ausstellungen in Frankreich, aber auch im Libanon, in Japan und Vietnam zeigten sein Werk, für das er mehrere Auszeichnungen bei Comic-Festivals in Frankreich erhielt.

The son of Spanish refugees, Jean Solé was born in Vic Fezensac in southern France in 1948. His enthusiasm for drawing took hold during his childhood. He is a particular fan of Chinese art, watercolors and ink drawing. Jean Solé primarily taught himself to draw (even though he did attend the Paris Academy of Art for a short time). In 1970, he began working for the French comic magazine Pilote. Today, he does projects for magazines and publishing companies. His work has been shown at numerous exhibitions in France as well as in Lebanon, Japan and Vietnam. He has also received many honors at comic festivals in France.

SPIEGEL-Titel 3/1982
Die Angst der Deutschen

*Wirtschaftskrise, Umwelt-
zerstörung, Demonstratio-
nen, Hausbesetzungen und
Krawalle auf der Straße –
Angst, Griesgram und
Depressionen suchen die
Deutschen heim. Es herrscht
Endzeitstimmung.*

SPIEGEL cover 3/1982
German angst

*Economic crisis, environ-
mental damage, demonstra-
tions, house occupations
and street riots – angst,
belly-aching and depression
are haunting the Germans.
It is a time of gloom
and doom.*

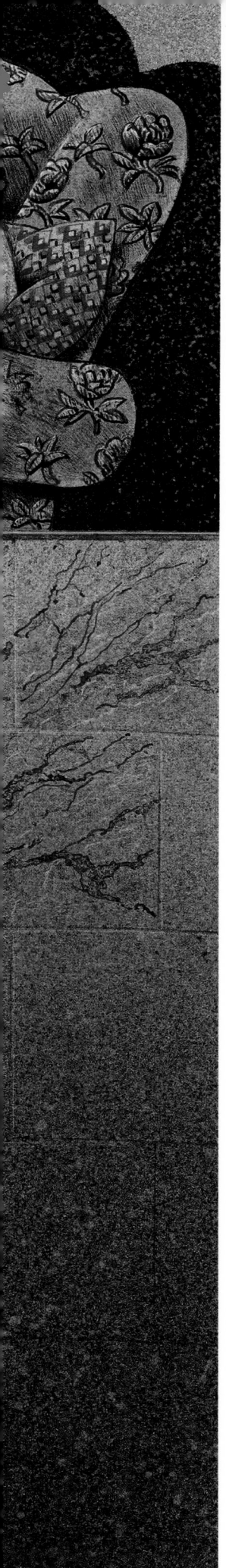

TILMAN MICHALSKI

Zeichentechniken mit schnell trocknenden Farben bevorzugt der 1941 in München geborene Tilman Michalski. Von 1961 bis 1968 besuchte er die Kunstakademie und die Akademie für das Grafische Gewerbe in München. Als entscheidend für seine Karriere als selbständiger Illustrator betrachtet Tilman Michalski eine zehnjährige Tätigkeit in verschiedenen Werbeagenturen. Seit 1978 arbeitet er in eigener Regie für verschiedene Buch- und Zeitschriftenverlage. Einige seiner Werke erhielten Auszeichnungen, unter anderem vom Art Directors Club Deutschland. Prämiert wurden auch drei SPIEGEL-Titel: „Vereint, aber fremd" (1990), „Beamte weg?" (1991) und „Deutsche gegen Deutsche" (1992).

The preferred technique of Tilman Michalski, who was born in Munich, Germany, in 1941, is drawing with fast-drying colors. Between 1961 and 1968, Tilman Michalski attended the Academy of Fine Arts and the Academy for Applied Arts in Munich. He says a milestone in his career as a freelance illustrator was the 10 year period he spent working for different advertising agencies. Tilman Michalski has been working on his own for different book and magazine publishers since 1978. Some of his pieces have won prizes, including an award from the German Art Directors Club. He also received awards for three SPIEGEL covers: "Strangers, united" (1990), "Out with the civil servants?" (1991) and "Germans vs. Germans" (1992).

SPIEGEL-Titel 39/1990
Vereint, aber fremd

Nach dem Freudentaumel zur Grenzöffnung zwischen der Bundesrepublik und der DDR kehrt Ernüchterung ein. Jetzt reden Ost- und Westdeutsche vor allem aneinander vorbei.

SPIEGEL cover 39/1990
Strangers, united

Germany has sobered up from the euphoria that accompanied the opening of the border between West Germany and East Germany. Now Germans on both sides are mostly talking over each other's heads.

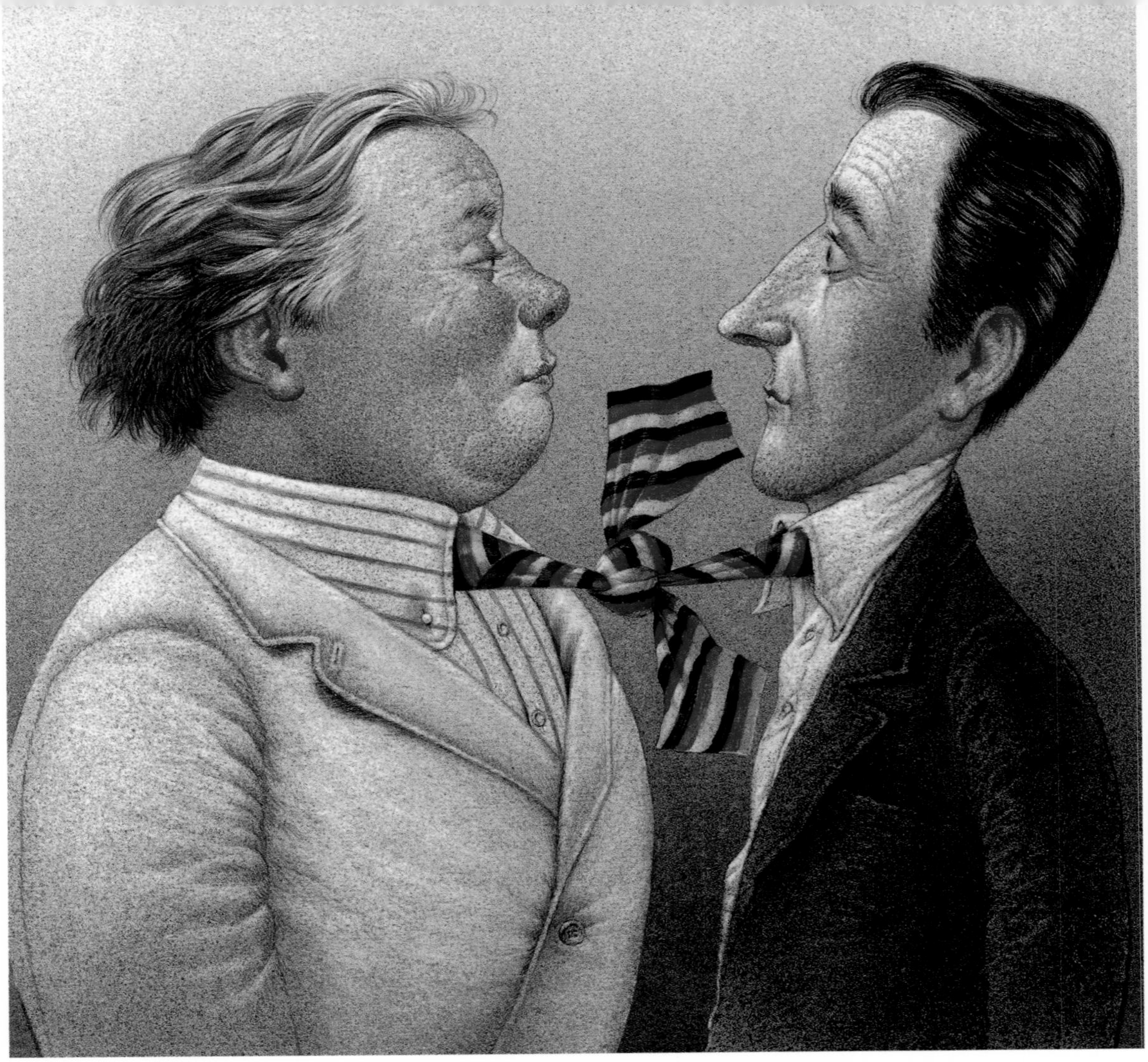

SPIEGEL-Titel 34/1992
Deutsche
gegen Deutsche

Tiefe Depression im Osten und Gleichgültigkeit im Westen haben das Glücks-gefühl der deutschen Einheit längst verdrängt. Die Mauer in den Köpfen wächst.

SPIEGEL cover 34/1992
Germans vs. Germans

Deep depression in the east and complacency in the west replaced elation over German unity long ago. The wall in people's minds is rising.

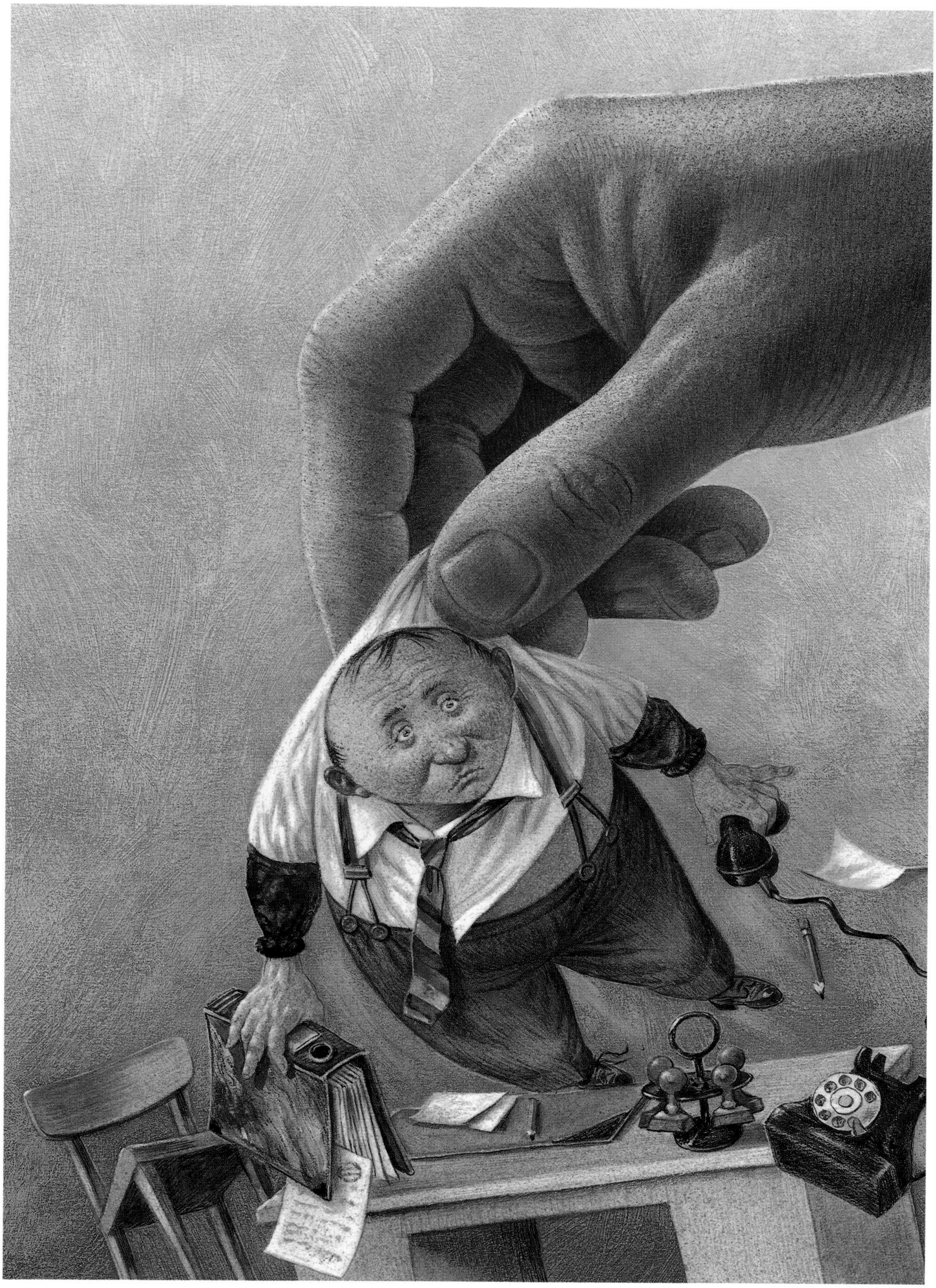

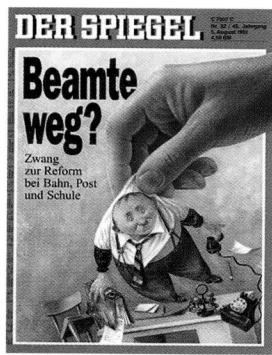

SPIEGEL-Titel 32/1991
Beamte weg?

*Bei Bahn und Post drohen
neue Milliardendefizite,
doch das öffentliche
Dienstrecht behindert
die Sanierung. In der
Politik wird jetzt ein für
viele unerhörter Ruf laut:
Das Beamtentum gehöre
abgeschafft!*

SPIEGEL cover 32/1991
Out with the servants?

*New multi-billion deficits
threaten German railroad
and postal operations,
but civil service work
contracts stand in the way
of restructuring.
Increasingly, politicians
are risking an unheard-of
demand: Germany's
special form of civil service
should be scrapped!*

Weltmacht Deutschland (unveröffentlicht 1993)

Von seinen Nachbarn argwöhnisch beäugt, wird das vereinigte Deutschland zum gewichtigen Machtfaktor in der internationalen Politik.

World power Germany (unpublished 1993)

Eyed suspiciously by its neighbors, unified Germany is becoming a heavyweight in international power politics.

Vogel oder Kohl?
(unveröffentlicht 1983)

*Welche Chancen hat
SPD-Kanzlerkandidat
Hans-Jochen Vogel bei
der Bundestagswahl im
März gegen Amtsinhaber
Helmut Kohl?*

Vogel or Kohl?
(unpublished 1983)

*What are the chances that
the Social Democratic
Party's chancellor candidate,
Hans-Jochen Vogel, can oust
incumbent Helmut Kohl
in the March parliamentary
election?*

HORST HAITZINGER

Looking back, Horst Haitzinger says he decided to become an artist because he was "hopeless" in most subjects at school but did have a knack for drawing. Haitzinger was born in Eferding, Austria, in 1939 and attended the School of Applied Arts in Linz, Austria, and the Academy of Fine Arts in Munich, Germany. He prefers watercolors and India ink. As a freelance illustrator, he published his first political cartoons in the German satire magazine "Simplicissimus" in 1958. Haitzinger started drawing cartoons for daily newspapers in 1960. And he began to do a weekly page for the German celebrity magazine "Bunte" in 1982. Horst Haitzinger has received the Ludwig Thoma Medal, the Swabian Arts Award and the Thomas Nast Medal. He lives in Munich.

Für die künstlerische Laufbahn habe er sich entschieden, weil er in fast jedem anderen Schulfach „eine Niete" gewesen sei, wohl aber sein Zeichentalent erkannt habe, sagt Horst Haitzinger. 1939 in Eferding, Österreich, geboren, erhielt er seine Ausbildung an der Kunstgewerbeschule Linz und an der Kunstakademie München. Haitzinger arbeitet am liebsten mit Aquarell und Tusche. 1958 erschienen erste politische Karikaturen im „Simplicissimus", dessen freier Mitarbeiter Haitzinger wurde. Seit 1960 zeichnet er tägliche Karikaturen für die Tagespresse und von 1982 an wöchentlich eine Seite für die „Bunte". Horst Haitziger wurde unter anderem mit der Ludwig-Thoma-Medaille, dem Schwabinger Kunstpreis und mit der Thomas-Nast-Medaille ausgezeichnet. Er lebt in München.

SPIEGEL-Titel 12/1983
**Was ist dran
am Aufschwung?**

*Nach dem Wahlsieg der
konservativ-liberalen
Koalition unter Bundes-
kanzler Helmut Kohl
rechnen jetzt viele mit
einem wirtschaftlichen
Aufschwung. Der Arbeits-
markt dürfte davon
kaum profitieren.*

SPIEGEL cover 12/1983
**How high will
the upswing go?**

*Now that the coalition
of Chancellor Helmut Kohl
has won the election, many
are predicting that the
economy will take off.
The job market, though,
is unlikely to profit much.*

SPIEGEL-Titel 22/1983
Überall ist Seveso

Nach monatelangem Suchen sind 41 Seveso-Fässer mit Dioxin gefunden worden. Doch die Affäre um das Gift ist längst noch nicht aufgeklärt.

SPIEGEL cover 22/1983
Seveso is everywhere

After months of searching, 41 Seveso barrels with dioxin have been found. But the poison scandal is far from cleaned up.

DIETER WIESMÜLLER

Bis zu seinem fünften Geburtstag wohnte Dieter Wiesmüller in einem Bahnhofsgebäude. Also zeichnete er, was er sah: Lokomotiven und Züge. 1950 in Rotenburg geboren, zog Wiesmüller 1955 mit der Familie nach Hamburg. Während der Schulzeit wird das Zeichnen für ihn zur Hauptbeschäftigung. Von 1969 bis 1973 studierte er Grafik, Malerei und Illustration an der Fachhochschule in Hamburg. Bereits ein Jahr später arbeitete Wiesmüller selbständig für mehrere Zeitschriften und illustrierte Buchtitel für diverse Verlage. Dabei bevorzugt er Tempera und Aquarelltechniken. Außerdem gestaltete er Bildergeschichten für ARD und ZDF. Dieter Wiesmüller lebt in Hamburg.

Until his fifth birthday, Dieter Wiesmüller lived in a railroad station. So he drew what he saw: locomotives and trains. Born in Rotenburg, Germany, in 1950, Wiesmüller and his family moved to Hamburg in 1955. While at school, drawing became his main pastime. He studied graphic design, painting and illustration at the Technical College in Hamburg between 1969 and 1973. A year later, Wiesmüller was working as a freelancer for magazines and designing book covers for publishing. He prefers tempera and watercolor techniques. He has also illustrated picture stories for Germany's public television broadcasters ARD and ZDF. Dieter Wiesmüller lives in Hamburg.

FRANK SCHUMANN/DER SPIEGEL

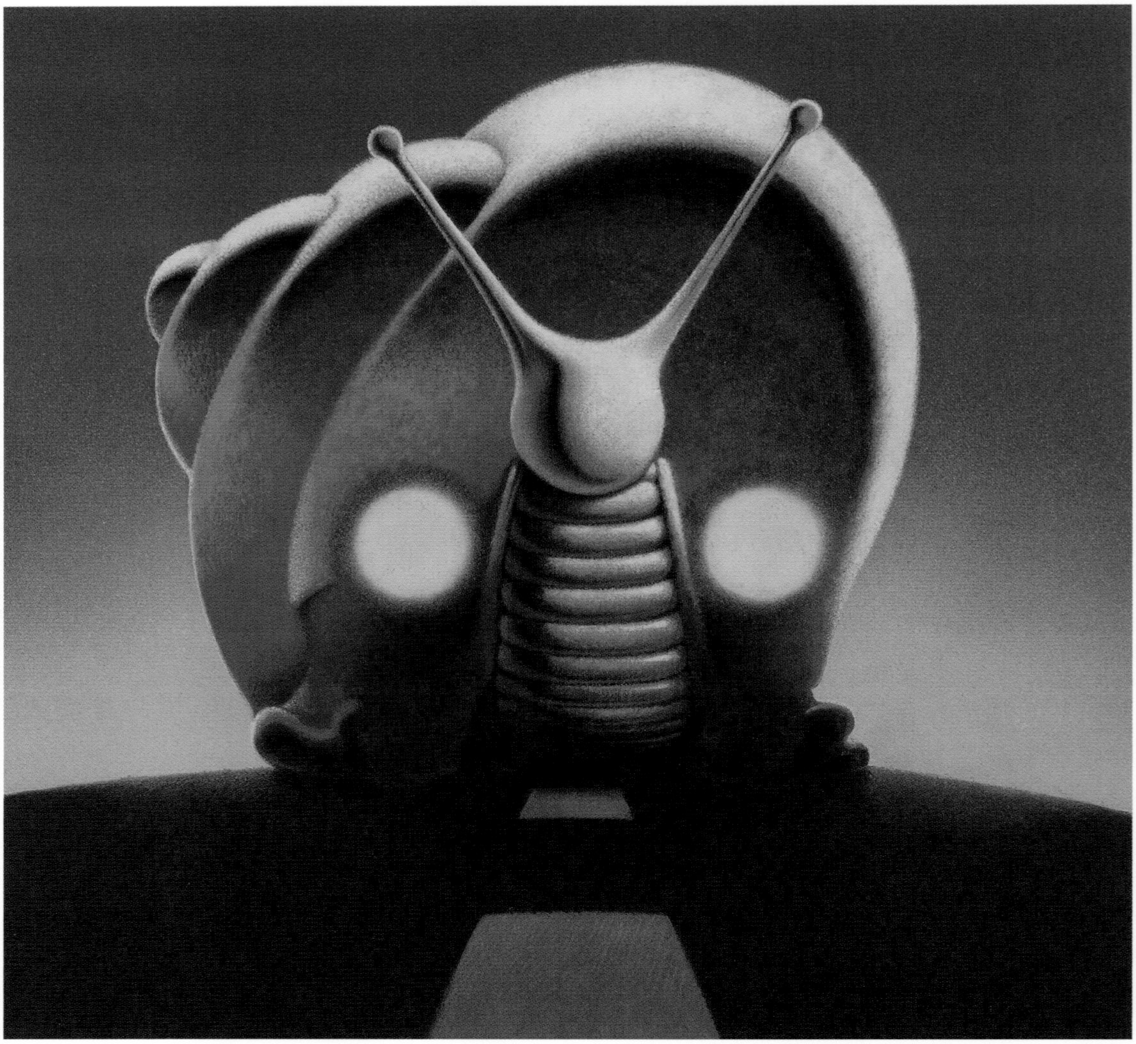

SPIEGEL-Titel 41/1984
Tempo 100

*Hilft Tempo 100 dem
Waldsterben Einhalt zu
gebieten?*

SPIEGEL cover 41/1984
100 km/h speed limit

*Would a speed limit
of 100 km/h help prevent
forests from dying?*

SPIEGEL-Titel 20/1991
Reizthema Abtreibung

*Der Streit um eine
Verschärfung des Abtrei-
bungsparagrafen 218
eskaliert. Die Bonner
Regierungskoalition aus
CDU/CSU und FDP
könnte daran zerbrechen.*

SPIEGEL cover 20/1991
The controversy
of abortion

*The dispute over a
tightening of Germany's
abortion paragraph 218
is escalating. The governing
coalition of CDU/CSU
and FDP could break up
over it.*

SPIEGEL-Titel 36/1991
Ein Weltreich zerbricht

*Auf den Trümmern der
Sowjetunion will Boris
Jelzin eine Wirtschafts-
gemeinschaft selbständiger
Staaten ohne starke
Zentralgewalt errichten.*

SPIEGEL cover 36/1991
A global empire
falls apart

*From the ruins of the
Soviet Union, Boris Yeltsin
hopes to create an economic
community of independent
states without a strong
central power.*

SPIEGEL-Titel 17/1993
Deutsche in den Krieg?

*Somalia ist erst der Anfang:
Die Bonner Regierung
will Bundeswehrsoldaten
weltweit für den Frieden
streiten lassen.*

SPIEGEL cover 17/1993
Germans at war?

*Somalia marks just the
beginning: The German
government wants
to send German troops
on peacekeeping missions
around the world.*

SPIEGEL-Titel 29/2000
Wer kriegt was?

*In einem Verhandlungs-
marathon erkämpften
Kanzler Schröder und
Finanzminister Eichel eine
Bundesratsmehrheit für
ihre Steuerreform. Der erste
große Erfolg von Rot-Grün
versetzt die Wirtschaft
in Aufbruchstimmung.*

SPIEGEL cover 29/2000
Who gets what?

*In marathon negotiations,
Chancellor Gerhard
Schröder and Finance
Minister Hans Eichel
have eked a majority in
favor of their tax reform in
the Bundesrat chamber
of state representatives.
The SPD-Green coalition's
first major success sets off
a wave of euphoria among
the business community.*

**Anschlag auf TWA-Jumbo
(unveröffentlicht 1996)**

*Beim Absturz eines
amerikanischen Verkehrs-
flugzeugs über dem
Atlantik vor New York
sterben 230 Menschen.*

**Attack on TWA jumbo
(unpublished 1996)**

*A total of 230 people die
in the crash of a
U. S. passenger jet over
the Atlantic outside of
New York.*

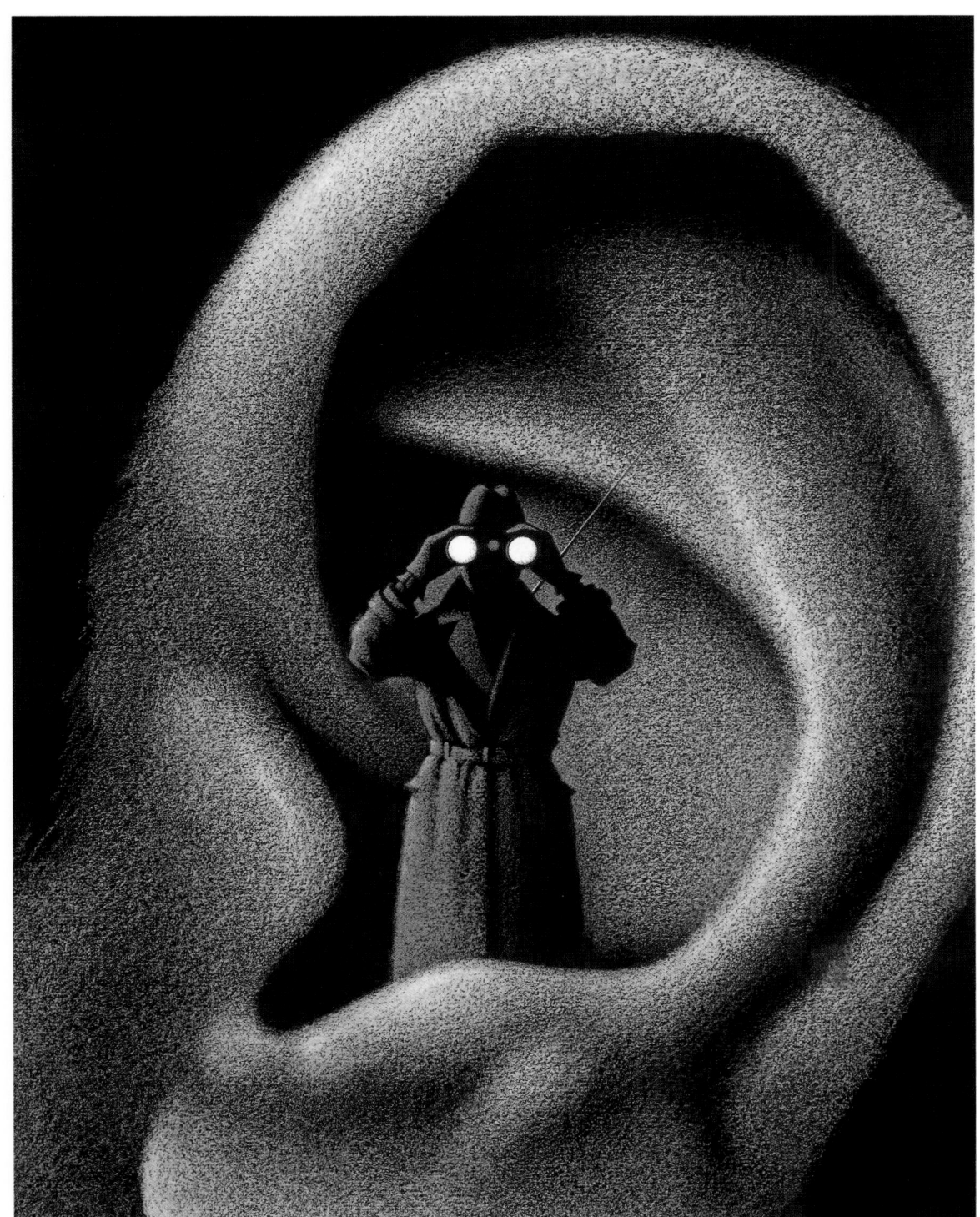

**Lauschangriff
(unveröffentlicht 1990)**

*Die konservativ-liberale
Bonner Regierungskoalition
streitet über Pläne, Abhör-
maßnahmen künftig leichter
und umfassender einsetzen
zu können.*

**Bugging operation
(unpublished 1990)**

*The coalition government
in Bonn is arguing over
plans that would clear the
way for far-reaching
eavesdropping operations in
the future.*

**Olympische Spiele
(unveröffentlicht 1993)**

*Sydney veranstaltet die
Olympischen Spiele im Jahr
2000. Die Mitbewerberstadt
Berlin trägt Trauer.*

**Olympic Games
(unpublished 1993)**

*Sydney will host the
Olympic Games in 2000,
and rival Berlin is grieving.*

**Russland läuft Amok
(unveröffentlicht 1996)**

*In Tschetschenien eskaliert
der Krieg Russlands gegen
die Aufständischen.*

**Russia runs amok
(unpublished 1996)**

*The Russian war against
the rebels in Chechnya
is escalating.*

ALFONS KIEFER

the art director of a Munich advertising agency. Since 1981, Kiefer has been working as a freelance illustrator in Munich. He received an award from the German Art Directors Club for his illustration of the "Stern" book "Der Mörder" (The Murderer) in 1985. Kiefer designs movie posters (Highlander II), CD covers (the Beatles Anthology) and magazine covers.

Sein erstes Titelbild für den SPIEGEL erschien 1983. Alfons Kiefer, 1953 im Saarland geboren, schloss 1979 sein Studium an der Fachhochschule Trier mit dem Schwerpunkt Illustration ab und wurde anschließend Art Director in einer Münchner Werbeagentur. Seit 1981 arbeitet Kiefer als freier Illustrator in München. 1985 erhielt er eine Auszeichnung des Art Directors Club Deutschland für die Illustration zum „Stern"-Roman „Der Mörder". Kiefer gestaltet Filmplakate (Highlander II) und CD-Cover (Beatles-Anthologie) sowie Titel-Illustrationen für Zeitschriften und Magazine.

His first SPIEGEL cover appeared in 1983. Alfons Kiefer, born in the state of Saarland in western Germany in 1953, earned a degree in illustration at the technical college in Trier, Germany, in 1979 before becoming

SPIEGEL-Titel 29/1983
Gewalt gegen Eltern

*Immer häufiger kommt
es in Familien zu Tätlich-
keiten von Kindern gegen
ihre Eltern. Als Ursache
vermuten Wissenschaftler
aggressive Vorbilder einer
Ellenbogen-Gesellschaft,
aber auch allzu nachgiebige
Erziehungsmodelle der
zurückliegenden Jahre.*

SPIEGEL cover 29/1983
Violence against parents

*More and more teenagers
are physically attacking their
parents. Scientists blame
aggressive role models in our
dog-eat-dog world and
an all too lenient approach
to child rearing.*

SPIEGEL-Titel 10/1987
Der Steuer-Bluff

*Das Jahrhundertwerk
Steuerreform wurde ein
Flop. Kanzler Helmut Kohl
stand kurz vor dem
Rücktritt, Finanzminister
Gerhard Stoltenberg verlor
seine Glaubwürdigkeit.*

SPIEGEL cover 10/1987
The tax bubble

*The tax reform of the
century has flopped.
Chancellor Helmut Kohl
nearly stepped down,
and Finance Minister
Gerhard Stoltenberg has
run out of credibility.*

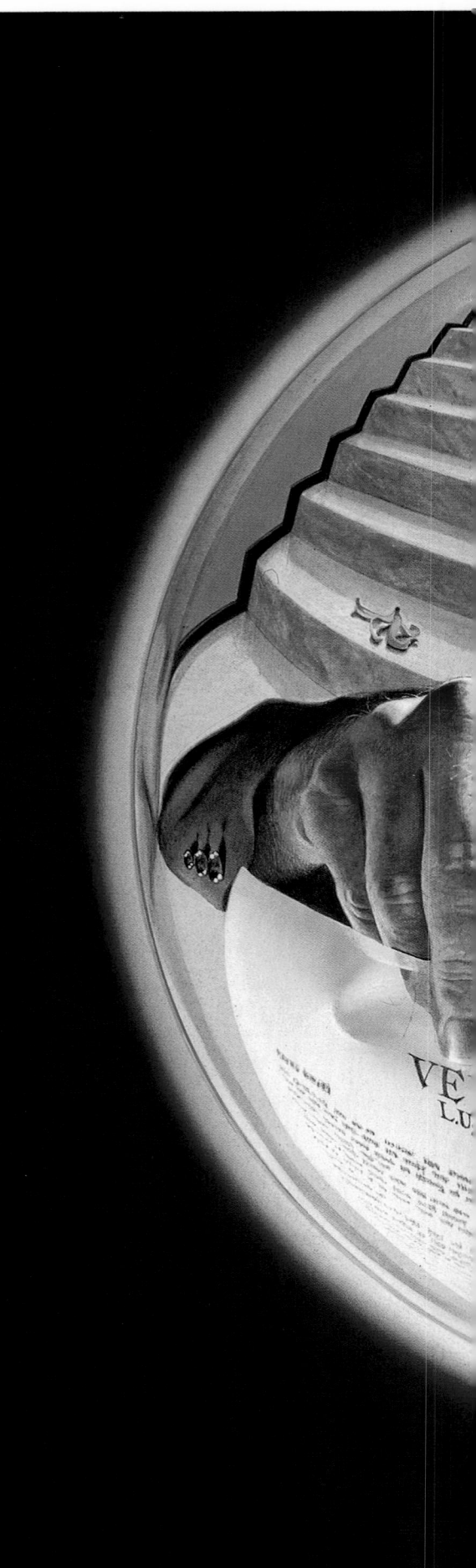

SPIEGEL-Titel 32/1994
Vorsicht! Versicherung

Drückerkolonnen verkaufen aggressiv unsinnige Versicherungen. Experten erwarten eine weitere Zunahme durch die Öffnung des europäischen Markts für Assekuranz-Produkte.

SPIEGEL cover 32/1994
Look out! Insurance

Door-to-door salesmen are using aggressive methods to push entirely unnecessary insurance policies. Experts expect the situation will worsen when the European market for insurance products opens.

SPIEGEL-Titel 31/1999
Wem gehört Mallorca?

*Dreieinhalb Millionen
Deutsche machen jährlich
Urlaub auf Mallorca, viele
besitzen eine eigene
Wohnung auf der Mittel-
meer-Insel. Die Mallor-
quiner haben Angst vor
Überfremdung.*

SPIEGEL cover 31/1999
Who owns Majorca?

*Three and a half million
Germans spend their
vacation on Majorca each
year. Many even own
apartments on the
Mediterranean island.
The Majorcan fear
they are being overrun
by foreigners.*

SPIEGEL-Titel 5/2000
Die Aufklärer: Wer lügt?

*Ex-Kanzler Helmut Kohl
war tief in das System der
schwarzen CDU-Kassen
verstrickt. Die Suche
nach der Wahrheit gestaltet
sich überaus schwierig.*

SPIEGEL cover 5/2000
**The whistle-blowers:
Who's lying?**

*Former Chancellor
Helmut Kohl was deeply
involved in the CDU's
slush-fund system.
Finding the truth is proving
extremely difficult.*

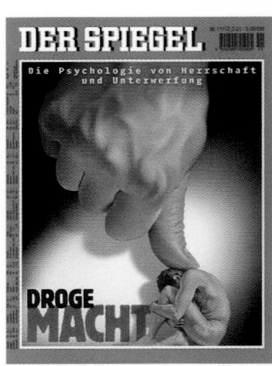

SPIEGEL-Titel 11/2001
Droge Macht

Wie verändert sich der Mensch, wenn er Macht über andere gewinnt? Stachelt ihn ein innerer Dämon zu Erniedrigung und Quälereien an?

SPIEGEL cover 11/2001
The drug of power

How does a person change when he or she gains power over others? Does an evil inner force compel the person to humiliate and torment them?

SPIEGEL-Titel 2/2004
Der letzte Deutsche

*Die Geburtenrate ist in
Deutschland dramatisch
gesunken. Der Kinder-
mangel gefährdet zuneh-
mend das Sozialsystem.*

SPIEGEL cover 2/2004
The last German

*Birth rates in Germany
have declined dramatically.
The lack of children is
also exerting increased
pressure on the country's
social system.*

**Das Duell
(unveröffentlicht 2002)**

*Wer soll die CDU/CSU
im Bundestagswahlkampf
gegen SPD-Kanzler
Gerhard Schröder führen?
Angela Merkel und
Edmund Stoiber streiten
um die Aufgabe.*

**The duel
(unpublished 2002)**

*Who will lead the
CDU/CSU in the election
campaign against Chancel-
lor Gerhard Schröder
of the Social Democratic
Party? Angela Merkel
and Edmund Stoiber are
fighting over the assign-
ment.*

**Der Pate
(unveröffentlicht 2003)**

*Der italienische Regierungs-
chef Silvio Berlusconi
demontiert die Justiz und
lässt Gesetze nach eigenem
Bedarf gestalten. Nun
wird er für ein halbes Jahr
EU-Ratspräsident.*

**The godfather
(unpublished 2003)**

*Italian Prime Minister
Silvio Berlusconi is tearing
apart his country's judicial
system and is drafting
laws tailor-made to suit his
own needs. Now, he will
assume the EU presidency
for six months.*

MATHIAS WASKE

und arbeitet Mathias Waske in München und in der Provence.

A wall painting for the Krupp palace in Marrakech in 1969 marked a first milestone in Mathias Waske's life as a freelance artist. Born in Crailsheim, southern Germany, in 1944, Waske studied at the State College of Fine Arts in Frankfurt/Main between 1962 and 1967. During the 1980s, he designed cover illustrations for Ufa's classic editions of movies from the 1930s to the 1970s. In 1991, his works were exhibited in a one-man show in the Villa Stuck museum in Munich. Mathias Waske, who calls himself an "academic art painter," favors acrylic tempera paints and oil on canvas, but he also makes panel paintings on wood. His paintings are generally bought by private art collectors in the industrial and business communities. Waske's work has been awarded numerous prizes and has been shown in many exhibitions in Europe, Japan and the United States. Mathias Waske lives and works in Munich and in Provence, southern France.

Eine Wandmalerei für den Krupp Palast in Marrakesch war 1969 Mathias Waskes erste wichtige Arbeit als freischaffender Künstler. Geboren 1944 in Crailsheim, Württemberg, studierte Waske von 1962 bis 1967 an der Staatlichen Hochschule für Bildende Künste in Frankfurt am Main. In den achtziger Jahren gestaltete er Cover für die Ufa-Klassik-Edition zu Filmen der dreißiger bis siebziger Jahre. 1991 wurden seine Werke in einer Einzelausstellung der Villa Stuck in München gezeigt. Bevorzugt arbeitet Mathias Waske, der sich „akademischer Kunstmaler" nennt, mit Acryl-Tempera Farben und Öl auf Leinwand, fertigt aber auch Tafelbilder auf Holz. Seine Malereien gehen vor allem an private Kunstsammler aus Industrie und Wirtschaft. Waskes vielfach ausgezeichnete Arbeiten wurden auf zahlreichen Ausstellungen in Europa, Japan und den USA gezeigt. Gegenwärtig lebt

**Michail Gorbatschow
(unveröffentlicht 1991)**

*Rund 70 Jahre nach ihrer
Gründung löst sich die
UdSSR auf. Präsident
Michail Gorbatschow hat
mit seiner Perestroika die
Welt verändert.*

**Mikhail Gorbachev
(unpublished 1991)**

*The USSR is dissolving
about 70 years after
it was founded. President
Mikhail Gorbachev's
perestroika has changed
the face of the world.*

**SPIEGEL-Titel 51/1983
Maria**

*Seit der Wahl von Papst
Johannes Paul II. feiert
der Marienkult in der
katholischen Kirche seine
Auferstehung.*

**SPIEGEL cover 51/1983
Mary**

*Since the election of Pope
John Paul II, the
cult of Mary is celebrating
its resurrection in the
Catholic Church.*

RITA MÜHLBAUER

cally." Today, the artist, who was born in Immenstadt, southern Germany, in 1941, works mostly with watercolors and watercolor pens, but also in mixed technique with slide photo colors, acrylic and oil paint. After her training as a commercial artist at the Rabenbauer School in Munich, Rita Mühlbauer studied for 12 semesters at the Munich Academy of Fine Arts. Her customers include textbook and magazine publishers. As a painter, Rita Mühlbauer has presented her work in numerous individual exhibitions in Germany and abroad.

Schon als Kind zeichnete Rita Mühlbauer „unentwegt und mit Begeisterung" Tiere und Pflanzen sowie Porträts von Verwandten und Freunden. Heute arbeitet die 1941 in Immenstadt im Allgäu geborene Künstlerin hauptsächlich mit Aquarellfarben und -stiften, aber auch in Mischtechnik mit Diafotofarben und Acryl sowie mit Ölfarben. Nach ihrer Ausbildung zur Gebrauchsgrafikerin an der Rabenbauer-Schule in München studierte Rita Mühlbauer zwölf Semester an der Münchner Akademie der Bildenen Künste. Zu ihren Auftraggebern gehören Schulbuch- und Zeitschriftenverlage. Als Malerin präsentierte Rita Mühlbauer ihre Bilder in zahlreichen Einzelausstellungen im In- und Ausland.

Even as a child, Rita Mühlbauer drew animals and plants as well as portraits of relatives and friends "ceaselessly and enthusiasti-

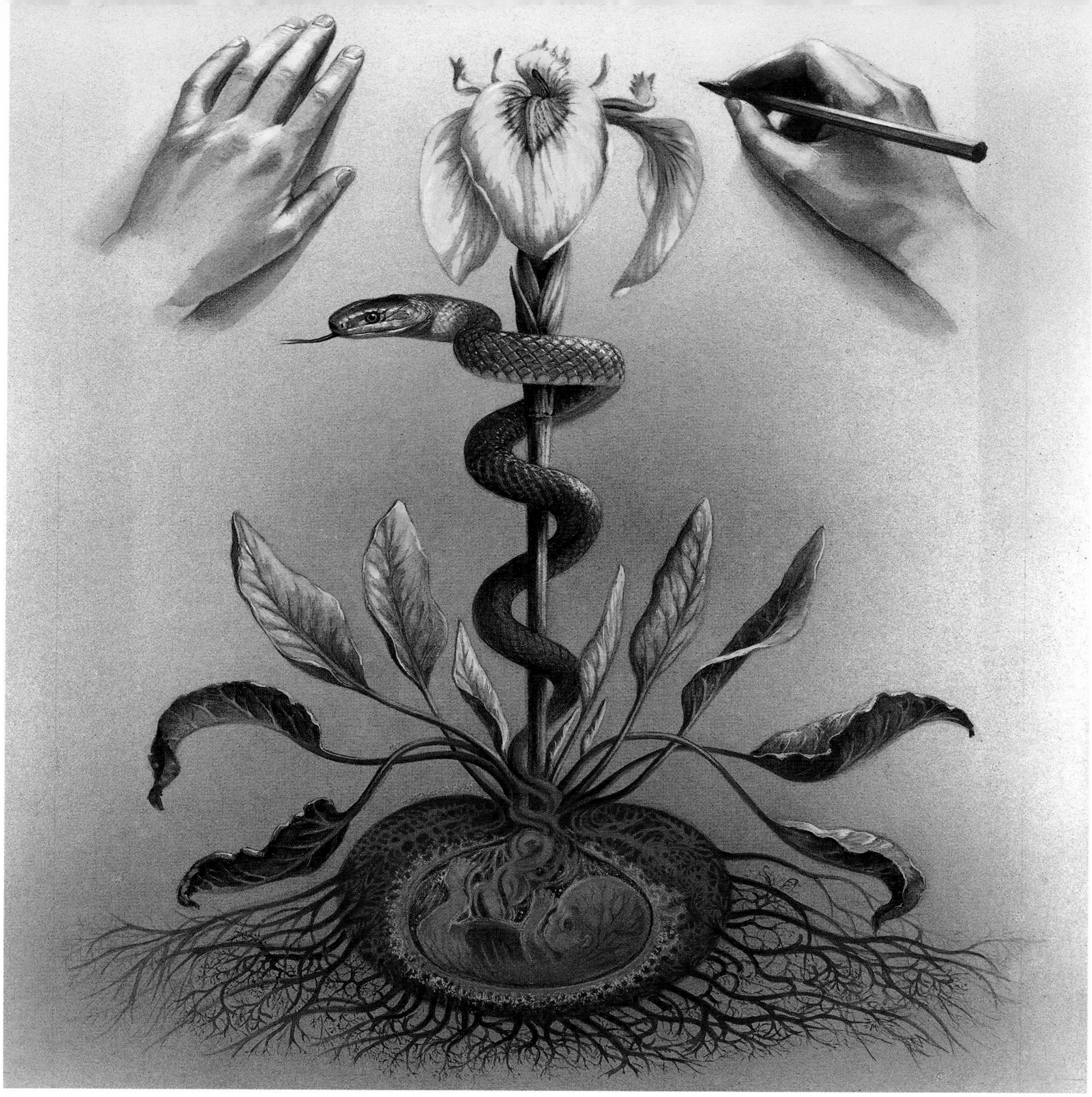

SPIEGEL-Titel 17/1984
Anthroposophen
in Deutschland

Die Anthroposophen haben eigene Schulen, eigene Altersheime und eigene Banken. Viele junge Menschen faszinieren die Ideen Rudolf Steiners, dem vor 60 Jahren gestorbenen Vordenker dieser Bewegung.

SPIEGEL cover 17/1984
Anthroposophers
in Germany

Anthroposophers have their own schools, nursing homes and banks. Many young people are fascinated by the ideas of Rudolf Steiner, the pioneer of this movement, who died 60 years ago.

SPIEGEL-Titel 39/1984
Bauen mit der Natur

Junge Stadtplaner und „Öko-Architekten" suchen die Harmonie von Wohnen und Umwelt neu zu entdecken.

SPIEGEL cover 39/1984
Building with nature

Young urban planners and "eco architects" are trying to rediscover the harmony of housing and the environment.

SPIEGEL-Titel 3/1993
Verlotterte Republik

*Politiker werben für
Firmen, die ihnen Spenden
gewähren – ein dichtes
System von Gefälligkeiten
und Absprachen regiert
die politische Szene. Statt
Führung oder Perspektive
dominiert der Filz.*

SPIEGEL cover 3/1993
The rotten republic

*Politicians do advertising
for companies that have
given them contributions –
a tightly knit network of
favors and deals governs the
political scene. Corruption,
not leadership or vision,
calls the shots.*

PETER SCHÖSSOW

Dass bei seinen Eltern immer Material zum Malen, Zeichnen, Basteln und Modellieren herumlag, prägte den 1953 in Hamburg geborenen Peter Schössow. Nach seiner Ausbildung an der Fachhochschule für Gestaltung in Hamburg von 1971 bis 1975 arbeitete der Illustrator für SPIEGEL, „Stern" und „Transatlantik", für den Carlsen-Verlag, den Rowohlt-Verlag, den WDR und für „Die Sendung mit der Maus". Seine Bilder, Titelseiten und Bücher wurden vom Art Directors Club Deutschland ausgezeichnet (1994 der SPIEGEL-Titel „Gaukler oder Heiler"). Die Stiftung Buchkunst ehrte drei von Schössow illustrierte Bücher jeweils als „eines der schönsten Bücher der Bundesrepublik Deutschland", drei weitere bekamen den Troisdorfer Bilderbuchpreis.

The parents of Peter Schössow, who was born in Hamburg, Germany, in 1953, made their mark on their son because they always had material for painting, drawing, handicrafts and molding lying around their home. After studying at the Hamburg College for Design from 1971–1975, the illustrator worked for DER SPIEGEL, "Stern", "Transatlantik", Carlsen Verlag, Rowohlt Verlag, the WDR broadcasting network and the German "Sendung mit der Maus" (The Program With the Mouse) television program. His pictures, covers and books were honored by the Art Directors Club for Germany (including the 1994 SPIEGEL cover "Impostors or healers"). The Stiftung Buchkunst foundation selected three of Schössow's illustrated books for individual recognition as "one of the most beautiful books in the Federal Republic of Germany." Three others received the Troisdorf illustrated book prize.

SPIEGEL-Titel 30/1994
Gaukler oder Heiler

*Die Kritik an der
Psychotherapie wächst:
Neue Untersuchungen
belegen mangelnde oder
fehlende Wirksamkeit
der meisten Methoden.*

SPIEGEL cover 30/1994
Impostors or healers

*Psychotherapy is the target
of growing criticism:
New studies have found that
most methods are lacking
or ineffective.*

**Banken im Gewinnrausch:
Das große Geld
(unveröffentlicht 1986)**

*Deutschlands Banken
verdienen prächtig wie
nie zuvor.*

**Banks' profit frenzy:
big money
(unpublished 1986)**

*German banks are cashing
in like never before.*

**Brauchen wir Eliten?
(unveröffentlicht 1994)**

*Muss Deutschland mehr
für die Förderung seiner
Eliten tun?*

**Do we need elites?
(unpublished 1994)**

*Does Germany have to do
more to promote its elites?*

SPIEGEL-Titel 49/1985
Die sanfte Heilkunst

Enttäuscht von kaltherziger Apparate-Medizin, sehnen sich mehr und mehr Patienten nach „sanften" und „natürlichen" Formen der Heilkunst. Was können alternative Anwendungen wie Akupunktur und Zelltherapie wirklich leisten?

SPIEGEL cover 49/1985
The gentle art of healing

Disappointed by a cold-hearted medical apparatus, more and more patients are yearning for "gentle" and "natural" forms of medical care. What can such alternative approaches as acupuncture and cell therapy actually achieve?

FRIEDRICH DE BOER

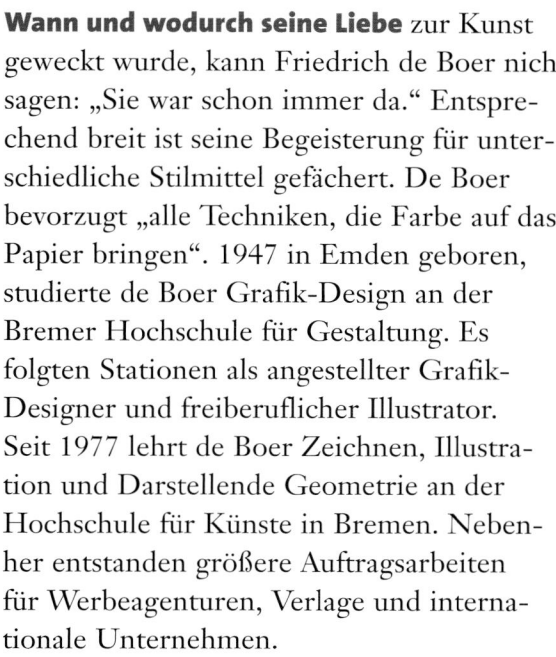

Wann und wodurch seine Liebe zur Kunst geweckt wurde, kann Friedrich de Boer nicht sagen: „Sie war schon immer da." Entsprechend breit ist seine Begeisterung für unterschiedliche Stilmittel gefächert. De Boer bevorzugt „alle Techniken, die Farbe auf das Papier bringen". 1947 in Emden geboren, studierte de Boer Grafik-Design an der Bremer Hochschule für Gestaltung. Es folgten Stationen als angestellter Grafik-Designer und freiberuflicher Illustrator. Seit 1977 lehrt de Boer Zeichnen, Illustration und Darstellende Geometrie an der Hochschule für Künste in Bremen. Nebenher entstanden größere Auftragsarbeiten für Werbeagenturen, Verlage und internationale Unternehmen.

Friedrich de Boer cannot say when and how he developed his love for art. "It was always just there," he says. His interests include an array of stylistic devices, and he prefers "all techniques that put color on paper." De Boer, who was born in 1947 in Emden, studied graphic design at the Bremen Design College. He then worked as a full-time graphic designer and freelance illustrator. He has been teaching drawing, illustration and projective geometry at the University of the Arts in Bremen since 1977. On the side, he has done major projects for advertising agencies, media and international companies.

H. U. OSTERWALDER

Geboren wurde Hans Ulrich Osterwalder 1936 in Zürich, wo er von 1952 an die damalige Kunstgewerbeschule besuchte – „noch ganz in der Bauhaus-Tradition, mit dem viereckigen Blick". Anschließend absolvierte er eine vierjährige Ausbildung zum „Qualitätsfanatiker in Layout und Typografie". Didaktische und dokumentarische Darstellungen für Themen der Medizin und Wissenschaft, die Umsetzung von Sinnzusammenhängen als Information und Gebrauchsanweisung bezeichnet Osterwalder als besondere berufliche Schwerpunkte: „Der Stil entsteht, wenn überhaupt, durch die Anpassung an die spezielle Aufgabe." Bemerkenswert war für ihn die „Twen-Zeit" beim Verlag Insel & Suhrkamp, in der er Buchumschläge in Serie realisiert hat. Seit 1967 führt Osterwalder ein eigenes Studio. Seine international bekannteste und am häufigsten gedruckte Illustration ist die Darstellung des HI-Virus, die 1986 (in leicht abgewandelter Form) als SPIEGEL-Titel entstanden war.

Zurich, Switzerland, is where Hans Ulrich Osterwalder was born in 1936, and it is also where he studied at the college of applied arts from 1952 – "wholly in the Bauhaus tradition, with a square perspective." He subsequently completed a four-year training as a "quality fanatic in layout and typography." Osterwalder focuses on didactic and documentary illustrations for medical and science subjects as well as the illustration of contexts as information and user manuals: "The style emerges, if at all, through the adaptation to the particular task at hand." An important period in his life was the time he spent during his twenties at publishing house Insel & Suhrkamp, where he illustrated book covers. Osterwalder has run his own studio since 1967. His internationally best known illustration is the picture of the HIV (the AIDS virus) that was created (in a slightly adapted form) for a SPIEGEL cover in 1987.

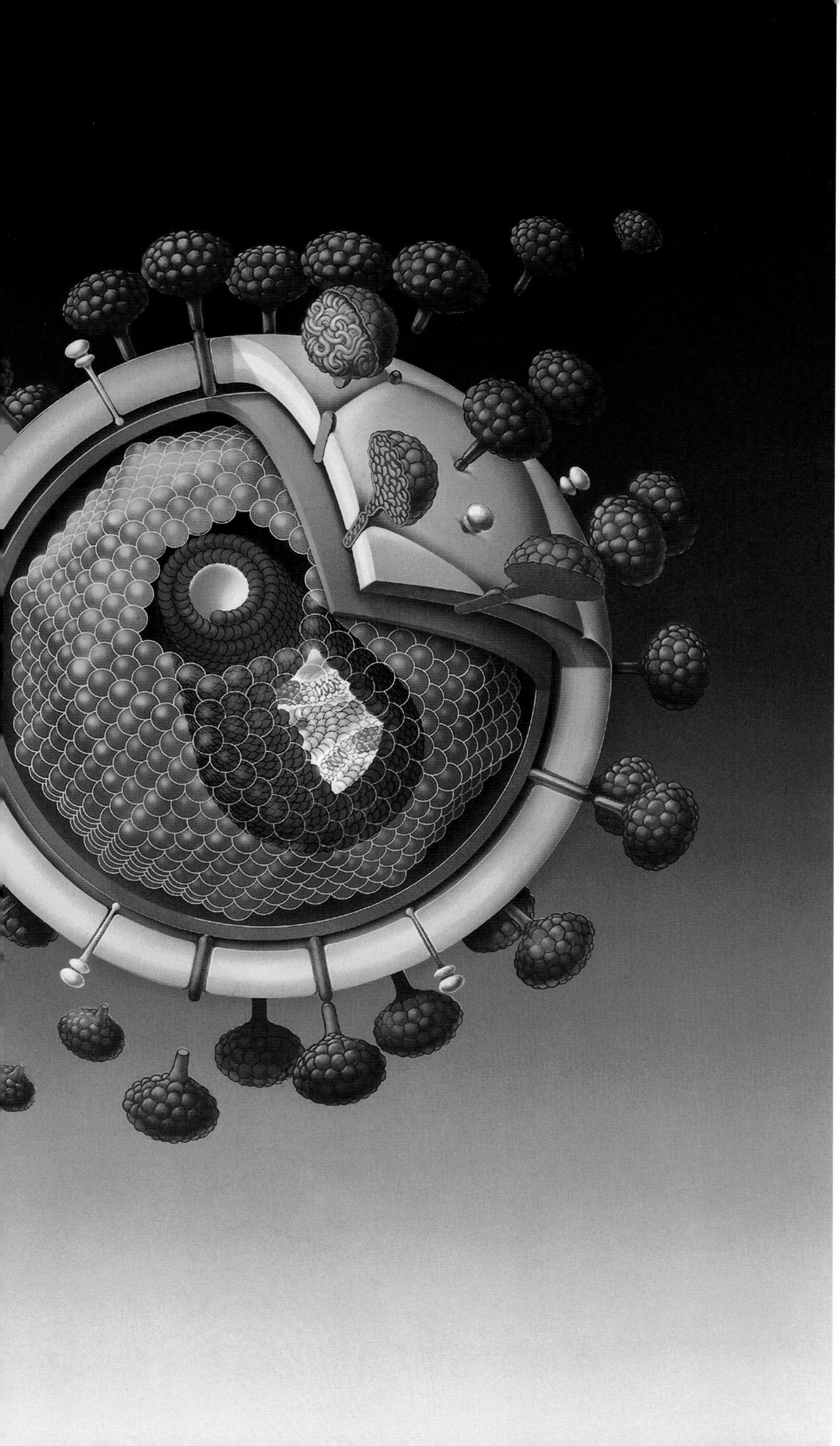

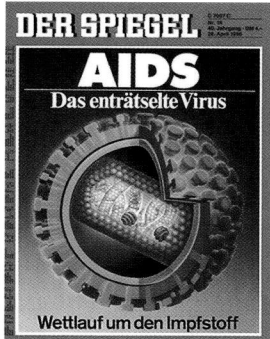

SPIEGEL-Titel 18/1986
Aids

*Die Immunschwächekrank-
heit Aids hat die Welt
umrundet. Überall steigen
die Infektions- und Todes-
zahlen. Doch es gibt
auch erste Erfolge im Kampf
gegen die Seuche.*

SPIEGEL cover 18/1986
AIDS

*The immune deficiency
disease AIDS has toured the
world. Infection and death
rates are on the rise around
the globe. But initial
successes in the fight against
the killer can also be
reported.*

SPIEGEL-Titel 40/1986
Kohls gefährlicher
Gehilfe

*Im Bundestagswahlkampf
will CDU-Generalsekretär
Heiner Geißler gegen
SPD und Grüne „richtig
zuschlagen". Sein Credo:
„Wer Begriffe und Gedan-
ken bestimmt, hat auch
Macht über die Menschen".*

SPIEGEL cover 40/1986
Kohl's menacing helper

*CDU General Secretary
Heiner Geißler wants to
"really stick it to" the
Social Democrats and the
Greens in the federal
election campaign. His credo:
"Those who set the agenda
have power over the people".*

DEWA WAWORKA

Ein Schwan war es, der Dewa Waworka schon als Kind auf die Laufbahn zum Künstler brachte: „Er hat mich so sehr beeindruckt, dass ich ihn immer wieder zeichnete", sagt der 1953 in Augsburg geborene Illustrator, „von da an habe ich nie mehr aufgehört zu zeichnen und zu malen." Die Technik brachte er sich selbst bei – Dewa Waworka ist Autodidakt. Anfangs bevorzugte er Feinmalerei in Lasurtechnik, heute in Acryl. Zunächst arbeitete Waworka als grafischer Zeichner, Bühnenmaler und Theaterplastiker. Seit 1983 ist er freiberuflich als Kunstmaler und Illustrator tätig. Für den Film „Die unendliche Geschichte" entwarf Waworka Plakate, eine SPIEGEL-Titelillustration („Der Verreißer") erhielt vom Art Directors Club Deutschland eine Silbermedaille.

It was a swan that made Dewa Waworka think of an artistic career when he was a child: "I was so impressed by it that I had to draw it again and again," says the illustrator, who was born in Augsburg, Germany, in 1953. "From then on, I never stopped drawing and painting". In an autodidactical manner, Dewa Waworka taught himself the necessary technique. At the beginning, he preferred fine painting in glaze technique. Today, he works mostly with acrylic colors. Waworka initially worked as a graphic designer, scene painter and set maker. He has been working as a freelance painter and illustrator since 1983. Waworka designed posters for the movie "The Never-Ending Story". A SPIEGEL cover ("The carper") was awarded a silver medal from the Art Directors Club Germany.

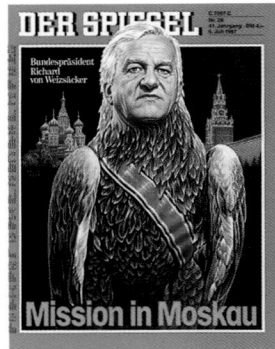

SPIEGEL-Titel 28/1987
Mission in Moskau

*Beim Staatsbesuch
in Moskau will Präsident
Richard von Weizsäcker
politische Fehler von
Kanzler Helmut Kohl
korrigieren und eine
Generalüberholung der
deutsch-sowjetischen
Beziehungen einleiten.*

SPIEGEL cover 28/1987
Mission in Moscow

*German President Richard
von Weizsäcker wants to
use his state visit to Moscow
to correct Helmut Kohl's
political mistakes and renew
German-Soviet relations.*

SPIEGEL-Titel 38/1997
RAF – Herbst des Terrors

*Vor 20 Jahren hatten
Terroristen der Roten
Armee Fraktion Arbeit-
geberpräsident Martin
Schleyer entführt und
ermordet. Jetzt gibt es neue
Erkenntnisse über jene
45 Tage, die Deutschland
in Atem hielten.*

SPIEGEL cover 38/1997
RAF – autumn of terror

*Twenty years ago, terrorists
from West Germany's Red
Army Fraction kidnapped
and killed the country's chief
employer representative,
Martin Schleyer. New reve-
lations about the 45 days
of national crisis have now
come to light.*

SPIEGEL-Titel 30/1998
Der verlogene
Wahlkampf

Die Politiker trauen sich nicht, den Wählern die Wahrheit zu sagen. Denn nötige Reformen sind unbequem und könnten ihre Klientel verschrecken.

SPIEGEL cover 30/1998
The dishonest election campaign

Politicians do not dare to tell voters the truth because necessary reforms are uncomfortable and could scare off their bases of support.

SPIEGEL-Titel 40/1999
Ein Mann sieht rot

Oskar Lafontaine meldet sich in der Politik zurück. Viel Unterstützung hat er nicht: Die meisten Sozialdemokraten scharen sich um den von ihm angefeindeten Kanzler Gerhard Schröder.

SPIEGEL cover 40/1999
A man sees red

Oskar Lafontaine has returned to politics. He does not have a lot of support: Most Social Democrats have rallied around his intra-party enemy, Chancellor Gerhard Schröder.

SPIEGEL-Titel 25/2000
Marlene

*Der Jahrhundertstar
Marlene Dietrich – von
der lasziven Kindfrau zur
weltweit angehimmelten
Göttin der Filmgeschichte.
In ihrer Heimat war sie
oft geschmäht.*

SPIEGEL cover 25/2000
Marlene

*Star of the century
Marlene Dietrich – from
the lustful child-woman
to the worldwide goddess
of the movie history. She
was frequently taunted
in her home country,
Germany.*

SPIEGEL-Titel 38/2000
Der Bruch

*Das Verhältnis der früher
engen Kampfgefährten
Wolfgang Schäuble und
Helmut Kohl ist nicht mehr
zu kitten.*

SPIEGEL cover 38/2000
The break-up

*The relationship of the
former brothers in arms
Wolfgang Schäuble
and Helmut Kohl can
no longer be mended.*

SPIEGEL-Titel 4/2002
Der künstliche
Kindersegen

*Die einst verteufelte
künstliche Fortpflanzung
ist zum globalen Geschäft
geworden. Jedes 80. Kind
in Deutschland kommt
heute aus der Petrischale.*

SPIEGEL cover 4/2002
Artificial birth boom

*Once vilified, artificial
reproduction has become
a global business.
Today, every 80th child
in Germany is created
in the petri dish.*

SPIEGEL-Titel 21/2000
Generation Ich

Die Internet-Generation will hart arbeiten, aber auch viel Spaß haben. Sie hält die ergrauten 68er für spießig und griesgrämig.

SPIEGEL cover 21/2000
The "Me"-generation

The Internet generation wants to work hard and play hard. It considers the graying generation of student protesters of the 1960s narrow-minded and churlish.

Moloch Medizin (unveröffentlicht 1999)

Im deutschen Gesundheitswesen profitieren Industrie und Ärzte von einem für beide Seiten einträglichen Kartell.

The medical moloch (unpublished 1999)

In the German health care system, industry and physicians live well off a mutually beneficial cartel.

PETER KRÄMER

Auf einem flachen Blatt Papier dreidimensionale Illusionen schaffen zu können (die in der wirklichen Welt unmöglich sind) faszinierte den jugendlichen Peter Krämer so sehr, dass er nicht mehr davon loskam. Als Kind fesselten ihn zunächst die Bilder von M. C. Escher. Nachdem ihm später bei den eigenen Arbeiten über viele Jahre Airbrush und Klebefolie gute Dienste leisteten, entstehen seine Bilder heute am Rechner. Seine Ausbildung erfuhr der 1954 in Mühlheim an der Ruhr geborene Krämer an der Folkwang-Schule und der Universität Essen. Erste praktische Erfahrungen sammelte er in Werbeagenturen, dazu kamen noch während des Studiums Illustrationsaufträge für das „FAZ"-Magazin. Weitere Kunden sind Design-Agenturen sowie die Lufthansa. Im Jahr 1997 gab es eine umfangreiche Ausstellung im Hamburger Stilwerk, über die „ein oder andere

Auszeichnung" führe er „nicht Buch", sagt Krämer.

The young Peter Krämer was so fascinated by the idea of creating three-dimensional illusions on a flat piece of paper (which are impossible in the real world) that he became attached to this type of art. As a child, he was enthralled by the works of M. C. Escher. Today, Peter Krämer creates his works with the computer, but for many years, air brushes and adhesive film served him well. He was born in Mülheim an der Ruhr, Germany, in 1954 and attended the Folkwang School and the University of Essen. While studying, he gained his first work experience at advertising agencies and as an illustrator for a magazine supplement to the newspaper "Frankfurter Allgemeine Zeitung". His customers include design agencies and Deutsche Lufthansa. His work was shown in an exhibition at the Stilwerk mall in Hamburg in 1997. Krämer says he does not "keep track of one or the other award."

SPIEGEL-Titel 16/1987
Die Republik wird
schwarz

*Seit Gründung der
Bundesrepublik im Jahr
1949 wurden noch nie
so viele Länder von
konservativen Regierungen
geführt. Die CDU hält
zudem beinahe alle
Schlüsselpositionen im Bund.*

SPIEGEL cover 16/1987
The conservative republic

*Since the Federal Republic
of Germany was founded in
1949, there have never been
so many federal states led
by conservative govern-
ments. Christian Democrats
hold nearly all key positions
at the national level as well.*

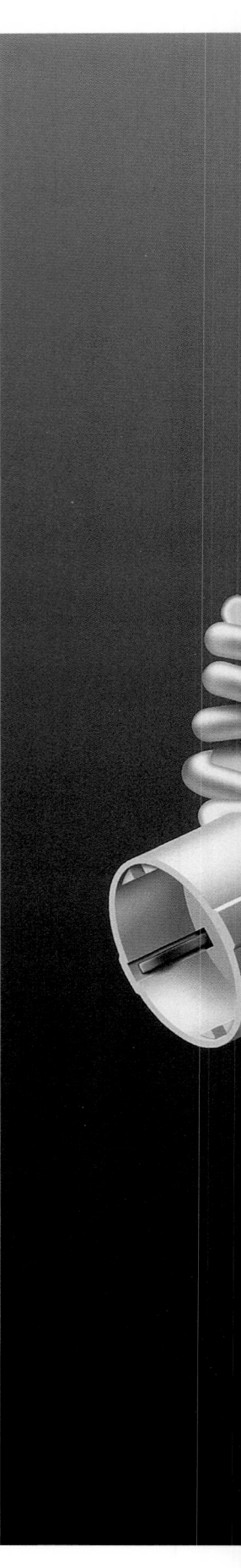

SPIEGEL-Titel 15/1993
Der Gen-Fraß

*Wissenschaftler experimen-
tieren mit gentechnisch
veränderten Lebensmitteln.
Risiken für die Verbraucher
sind kaum erforscht.*

SPIEGEL cover 15/1993
Gene cuisine

*Scientists are experimenting
with genetically modified
foods. But hardly any
research has been done
on the risks consumers
may face.*

**Das Stromkartell
(unveröffentlicht 1995)**

*Deutschland im Griff der
Stromkonzerne: Die
Elektrizitätsgiganten setzen
auf Stromverschwendung
und kassieren überhöhte
Monopolpreise. Wirksame
Kontrolle findet nicht statt:
Viele Politiker sind mit
gut bezahlten Posten ruhig
gestellt.*

**The power cartel
(unpublished 1995)**

*Utility groups control
Germany: The country's
electricity giants count on
wasted power and exorbitant
monopoly prices. No effective
control mechanism is in
place. Many politicians have
been silenced with well-paid
positions.*

SPIEGEL-Titel 28/1984
Deutsch: Ächz, Würg

Ob in Schulen, Betrieben, Büros oder Behörden – Wissenschaftler beobachten eine zunehmende Nachlässigkeit im Umgang mit der deutschen Sprache.

SPIEGEL cover 28/1984
German: in a bad way

Whether it's in schools, factories, offices or government agencies – academics report that people are paying less and less attention to their use of the German language.

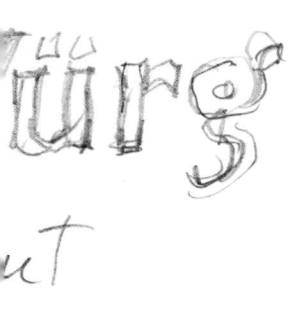

MARIE MARCKS

Mutter Else betrieb eine private Kunst-schule, da lagen immer und überall Papier und Stifte herum. So fand die 1922 in Berlin geborene Marie Marcks als kleines Kind zur Kunst. Und, „da weiter nichts rechtes gelernt", hat sie später „aus dem Gekritzel meinen Beruf gemacht". Nach Ausbildung an der Kunstschule ihrer Mutter studierte Marie Marcks vier Semester Architektur in Berlin und Stuttgart. Sie hat fünf Kinder und lebt als freie Malerin und Grafikerin in Heidelberg.

Marie Marcks fertigt wissenschaftspolitische und tagespolitische Karikaturen, entwirft Cartoons für Jugendsendungen, Plakate und Bucheinbände. Zu ihren Auftraggebern zählen „Die Zeit", „Süddeutsche Zeitung", „Vorwärts", „Titanic" und der SPIEGEL. Zahlreiche Einzelausstellungen im In- und Ausland zeigten ihre Arbeiten. Marie Marcks ist Trägerin des Bundesverdienstkreuzes. 2002 erhielt sie den Satirepreis „Göttinger Elch", und 2004 wurde sie mit dem Karika-turenpreis der Bundesrechtsanwaltskammer ausgezeichnet.

Her mother, Else, ran a private art school, and there were always pens and paper lying about everywhere. That's how Marie Marcks, born in Berlin in 1922, discovered art as a child. And since she "didn't learn anything useful," she later "made scribbling my profession." After attending her mother's art school, Marie Marcks spent four semesters studying architecture in Berlin and Stuttgart. She has five children and works as a freelance painter and illustrator in Heidelberg.

Marie Marcks draws political caricatures and designs cartoons for youth television pro-grams, posters and book covers. Her cus-tomers include such newspapers and maga-zines as "Die Zeit", "Süddeutsche Zeitung", "Vorwärts", "Titanic" and DER SPIEGEL. Her pieces have been shown in numerous individual exhibitions in Germany and abroad. Marie Marcks received the Order of Merit of the German Federal Republic (Bundesverdienstkreuz). In 2002, she was awarded the satire prize "Göttinger Elch" and in 2004 she received the caricature prize of the Federal Chamber of Attorneys.

SPIEGEL-Titel 15/1988
Tollhaus Schule

*Gewalt und Gefühlsarmut
verändern das Klima
an den Schulen. Mit Radau,
Aggressivität und
Clownerien machen Schüler
den Unterricht zur Farce.
Den Kindern des Fernseh-
Zeitalters, klagen Lehrer,
fehle es an „innerer
Disziplin".*

SPIEGEL cover 15/1988
Madhouse school

*Violence and emotional
poverty are changing the
climate at schools. By
squabbling, fighting and
clowning around, students
are turning classes into a
joke. Teachers complain that
the kids of the television
age lack "inner discipline."*

Frauen – Opfer der Einheit (unveröffentlicht 1990)

Welche Chancen haben die Frauen im vereinigten Deutschland?

Women – victims of unification (unpublished 1990)

What opportunities are open to women in unified Germany?

131

KINUKO CRAFT

Als Buch- und Zeitschriftenillustratorin
hat sich die 1940 im japanischen Kanazawa
geborene Kinuko Craft weltweit einen
Namen gemacht. Mehr als hundert ihrer
Arbeiten wurden mit Preisen bedacht –
darunter sind fünf Goldmedaillen der New
Yorker Society of Illustrators. Ihren Weg
zur Künstlerin beschreibt Kinuko Craft so:
„Schon als kleines Kind haben mich Licht
und Farben fasziniert. Auf allen möglichen
Oberflächen habe ich gemalt, und wenn man
deswegen mit mir schimpfte und mir zur
Strafe meine Malstifte wegnahm, habe ich
einfach die Stifte meiner Schwester gestoh-
len. Mein Großvater, ein Meister der Kalli-
grafie, unterstützte mich und erlaubte mir, in
seinen Büchern über Kunst in aller Welt zu
schmökern. Diese Bücher haben mir auf
visuelle Art viele phantastische Geschichten
und Märchen erzählt. Derzeit benutze ich
Wasser- und Ölfarben für meine Bilder.

Zunächst fertige ich eine Skizze an und
übermale sie anschließend mit Wasserfarben.
So entsteht eine Grundierung, die danach
mit Ölfarben übermalt wird. Bilderbücher
wie ‚Dornröschen' oder ‚Cinderella' haben
mir viel kreativen Freiraum gelassen. Seit
ihrer Veröffentlichung habe ich von Privat-
leuten Aufträge erhalten, die mir neue Aus-
drucksmöglichkeiten eröffnen."

Kinuko Y. Craft was born in Kanazawa,
Japan, in 1940 and made a name for herself
internationally as an illustrator of books and
magazines. More than 100 of her works have
won prizes – including five gold medals from
the New York Society of Illustrators.
"From the time I was a little child, light and
color have always fascinated me. I drew on
any available surface, and when I was scolded
for it, I stole my sister's crayons when they
took mine away. My grandfather, who was a
master at calligraphy, encouraged me and
allowed me to look at his books on the arts
of the world. Those books showed me many
fantastic stories and fairy tales in a visual
way. At the moment, I'm using watercolors
and oil paints for my works. I begin with a
tight drawing. I then paint over it with
watercolors. That serves as a base. The work
is then painted over in oils. Picture books
such as 'Sleeping Beauty' and 'Cinderella'
have allowed me a great deal of creative freedom. Since publication, I have been given
jobs by private customers that represent a
new potential avenue of expression."

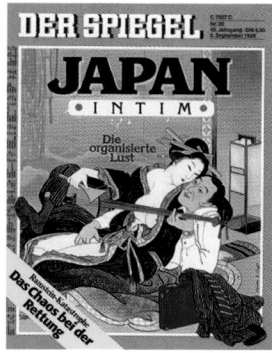

SPIEGEL-Titel 36/1988
Japan Intim

Japaner gelten als äußerst fleißig und hochdiszipliniert. Doch was tun sie nach Feierabend? Sie vergnügen sich in Bars, Spielsalons und „Love Hotels". Und sie trinken reichlich Alkohol.

SPIEGEL cover 36/1988
Intimacy in Japan

The Japanese are known as industrious, highly disciplined workers. But what happens after they've clocked out for the day? They entertain themselves in bars, casinos and "Love Hotels". And they down loads of alcohol.

SPIEGEL-Titel 4/1990
Gefahr für
den Wohlstand?

*Hunderttausende DDR-
Bürger siedeln nach
Westdeutschland um.
Der Kampf um Jobs und
Wohnungen wird immer
härter. Die sozialen
Sicherungssysteme stehen
vor erheblichen Zusatz-
belastungen.*

SPIEGEL cover 4/1990
Affluence imperiled?

*Hundreds of thousands
of East German citizens are
moving to West Germany.
The battle for jobs and
apartments is becoming
tougher and tougher. The
social service systems are
facing immense additional
burdens.*

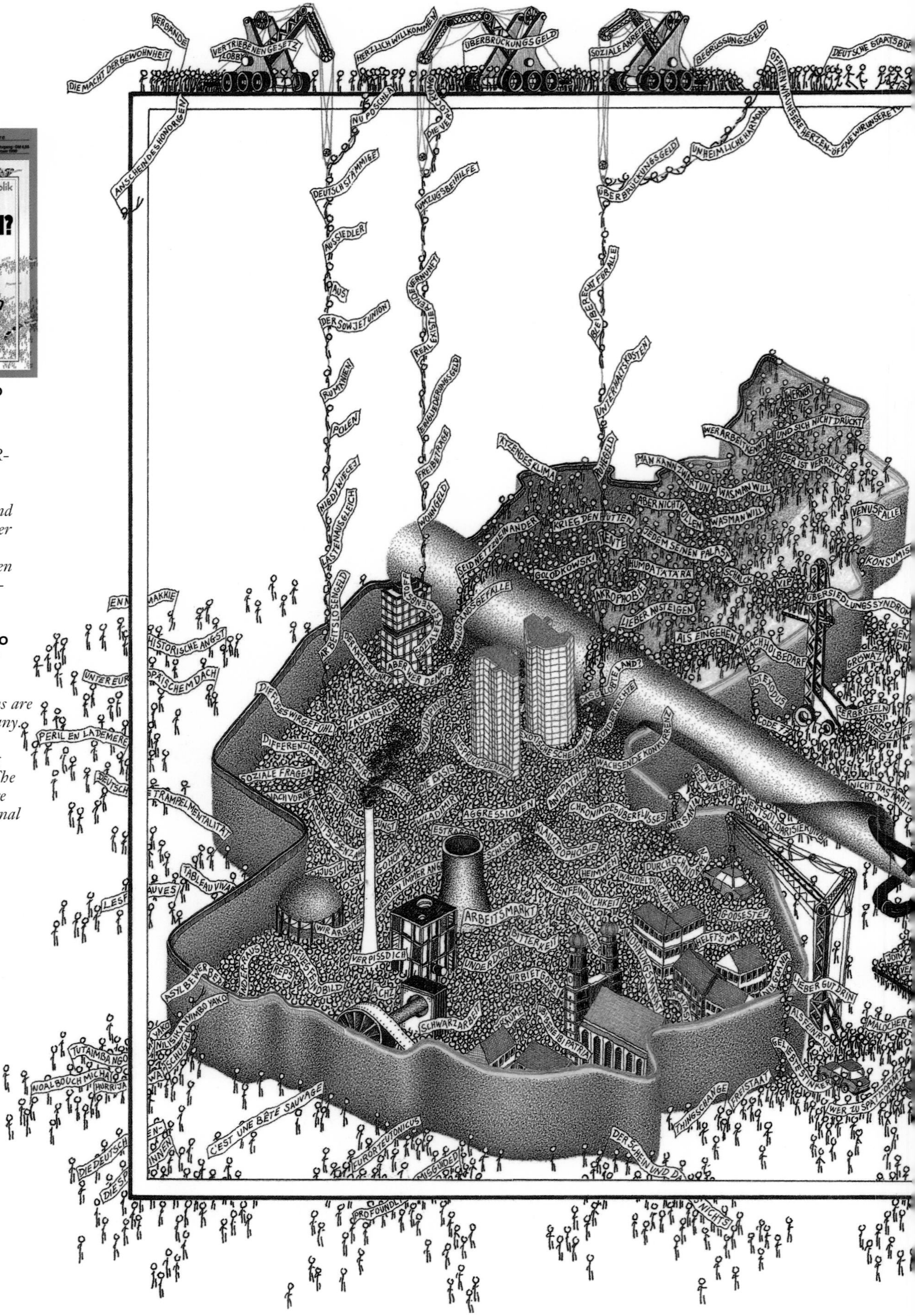

UWE BRANDI

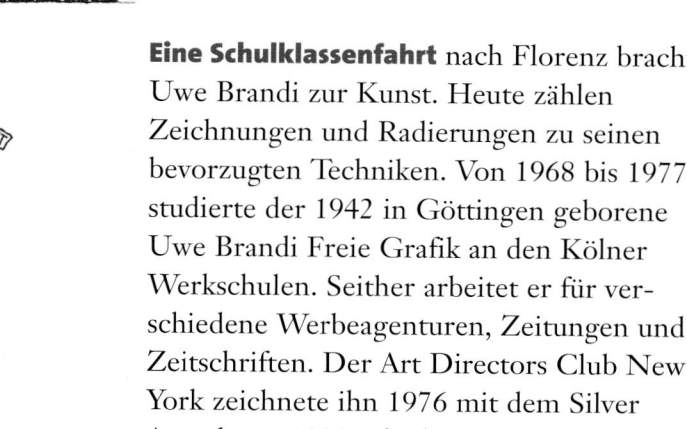

Eine Schulklassenfahrt nach Florenz brachte Uwe Brandi zur Kunst. Heute zählen Zeichnungen und Radierungen zu seinen bevorzugten Techniken. Von 1968 bis 1977 studierte der 1942 in Göttingen geborene Uwe Brandi Freie Grafik an den Kölner Werkschulen. Seither arbeitet er für verschiedene Werbeagenturen, Zeitungen und Zeitschriften. Der Art Directors Club New York zeichnete ihn 1976 mit dem Silver Award aus, 1989 erhielt er zusammen mit Christiane Maether den Albert-Haueisen-Preis.

Uwe Brandi's artistic journey began with a school trip to Florence. Etching and drawing still remain the artist's favorite techniques. Uwe Brandi, who was born in Göttingen in 1942, studied graphic arts from 1968-1977 at the Cologne Werkschulen. Since then, he has worked for advertising agencies, newspapers and magazines. The Art Directors Club New York gave him the Silver Award in 1976, and he received the Albert Haueisen Prize with Christiane Maether in 1989.

**Die erstarrte Republik
(unveröffentlicht 1996)**

*Nichts geht, nichts bewegt
sich mehr – Deutschland
wird zum Auslaufmodell.*

**The rigid republic
(unpublished 1996)**

*No movement, no
progress – Germany is
becoming obsolete.*

SPIEGEL-Titel 42/1993
Dr. Arbeitslos

*Ein akademischer Abschluss
ist keine Garantie mehr
für einen Job. Die Rezession
trifft nun auch Hochschul-
absolventen.*

SPIEGEL cover 42/1993
Dr. Jobless

*A university degree is no
longer a guarantee for a job.
University graduates are
now feeling the full impact
of the recession.*

DIETRICH EBERT

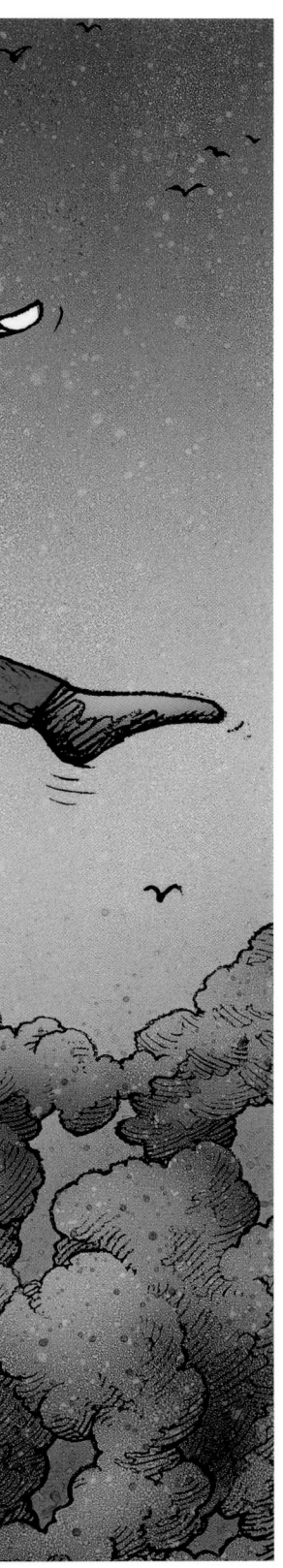

Erst kam eine Lithografenlehre, dann eine Ausbildung als grafischer Zeichner in einem Werbeatelier und schließlich ein Studium an der Akademie der bildenden Künste in Stuttgart – der 1948 in St. Peter geborene Dietrich Ebert lernte seinen Beruf von der Pike auf. Nach dem Studium machte er sich als Illustrator selbständig und ist es bis heute (nur unterbrochen von einer zweijährigen Professur für Grafik-Design an der Hochschule für bildende Künste in Braunschweig). Ebert arbeitet für Werbeagenturen, Industriekonzerne und Verlage. „Der kompositionelle Aufbau seiner Illustrationen ist frisch und unverkrampft", lobt sein ehemaliger Stuttgarter Professor Albrecht Ade.

Dietrich Ebert was born in St. Peter in 1948 and learned his profession from the bottom. He first earned a degree in lithography and then worked as a graphic designer at an advertising agency. Dietrich Ebert later completed studies at the Academy of Fine Arts in Stuttgart, Germany. After his studies, he worked as a freelance illustrator. A two-year professorship in Graphic Design at the Academy for Fine Arts in Braunschweig aside, he has worked as a freelance illustrator ever since. Dietrich Ebert works for advertising agencies, indstrial companies and publishing houses. "The compositional construction of his illustrations is fresh and relaxed," said his former Stuttgart Professor Albrecht Ade.

Nils Fliegner

"Mad" and an array of advertising agencies ("I've received an ADC award"). Fliegner now lives in Hamburg or, to be more exact, in the St. Pauli amusement district.

Westerland auf Sylt war am 5. Mai 1966 der Geburtsort von Nils Fliegner. Richtig Lust auf Kunst bekam der Nordsee-Insulaner bei der intensiven Betrachtung von Donald-Duck-Heften. Das Zeichnen brachte er sich selbst bei, allerdings: „Ich war mir ein lausiger Lehrer." Für SPIEGEL, „Stern", „Mad" und diverse Werbeagenturen reichte es gleichwohl („hab mal eine ADC-Auszeichnung bekommen"). Inzwischen lebt Fliegner in Hamburg. Genauer: „Grüsse aus St. Pauli!"

Nils Fliegner was born in Westerland on the northern German island of Sylt on May 5, 1966. The North Sea islander developed his profound interest in art through intense reading of Donald Duck magazines. He taught himself to draw, and although he says "I was a lousy teacher," his talent is more than enough for DER SPIEGEL, "Stern",

SPIEGEL-Titel 33/1994
Der Osten is' stark

Der Dramatiker Klaus Pohl ist 4000 Kilometer quer durch Deutschland gereist, vor allem durch die neuen Bundesländer.

SPIEGEL cover 33/1994
The East flexes its muscles

The dramatist Klaus Pohl traveled 4,000 kilometers through Germany, in particular the eastern states.

SPIEGEL-Titel 50/2001
**Sind deutsche Schüler
doof?**

*Im internationalen Ver-
gleich versagen die deutschen
Schulen – das zeigt
die OECD-Studie Pisa.*

SPIEGEL cover 50/2001
**Are German
pupils dumb?**

*In international comparison,
German schools aren't
making the grade – at least
according to the OECD's
PISA study.*

**Die roten Mörder
(unveröffentlicht 1998)**

*Die weltweite Opfer-
bilanz kommunistischer
Diktaturen.*

**The Red murderers
(unpublished 1998)**

*Communist dictators and
their worldwide victims.*

**SPIEGEL-Titel 39/1995
Feldzug der Moralisten**

*Die Deutschen sind auf
der Suche nach der
einfachen, guten Moral.
Tugendwächter genießen
hohes Ansehen.
Die angeblich egozentrische
Jugend hungert nach
neuen Werten.*

**SPIEGEL cover 39/1995
Moralists on the attack**

*Germans are searching
for a morality that is both
simple and good. The
sentinels of virtue are highly
respected. Young people,
supposedly so egocentric,
actually hunger for new
values.*

140

SILKE BACHMANN

Zeichnungen von Wilhelm M. Busch begeisterten Silke Bachmann für die Kunst. Ihre Ausbildung erfuhr sie an der Hamburger Fachhochschule für Kunst und Gestaltung. Seit 1986 ist sie als Malerin, Zeichnerin und Illustratorin tätig. Einen Namen machte sich die 1955 in Hamburg geborene Silke Bachmann auch mit Porträts und Gemäldekopien. Außerdem beschäftigt sie sich mit Zeichentrick. Ihre Arbeiten zeigte die Künstlerin auf mehreren Ausstellungen in Deutschland, Spanien und den USA.

Silke Bachmann's enthusiasm for art goes back to the drawings of Wilhelm M. Busch. She received her formal training at the Hamburg College for Art and Design. She has been working as a painter, drawer and illustrator since 1986. Silke Bachmann, who was born in Hamburg, Germany, in 1955, has also made a name for herself with portraits and copied paintings. She takes an active interest in animation as well. The artist has shown her works at exhibitions held in Germany, Spain and the United States.

LUDVIK GLAZER-NAUDÉ

"I think I was seven years old when my mother whipped off a fantastic, surreal snow landscape on a piece of writing paper for me," recalls Ludvik Glazer-Naudé. From that day on, he has looked at the world of pictures with "more open eyes." He was born in 1961 in Maribor, Slovenia, and attended the Technical College for Visual Communication in Hildesheim, Germany, from 1982 to 1984, before transferring to the Berlin University of the Arts. Since then, he has worked as a freelance painter, graphic designer and illustrator for theaters, publishers, magazines, newspapers and advertising agencies. Glazer-Naudé prefers drawing with pens and India ink or acrylics. He has received numerous awards – his most recent prize came from the Art Directors Club Germany in 1997 for his SPIEGEL cover "The divine devil."

„Ich war vielleicht sieben Jahre alt, als meine Mutter mir mit wenigen Strichen eine phantastische und surreale Schneelandschaft auf ein Briefpapier zeichnete", erinnert sich Ludvik Glazer-Naudé. Seither betrachte er die Welt der Bilder mit „bewussteren Augen". 1961 in Maribor, Slowenien, geboren, studierte Ludvik Glazer-Naudé von 1982 bis 1984 an der Fachhochschule für Visuelle Kommunikation in Hildesheim, anschließend an der Universität der Künste in Berlin. Seitdem ist er selbständig für Theater, Buchverlage, Magazine, Zeitungen und Werbeagenturen tätig. Bevorzugt arbeitet Glazer-Naudé mit Zeichenfeder und Tusche sowie Künstleracryl. Für seine Arbeiten wurde er mit zahlreichen Auszeichnungen bedacht – zuletzt 1997 vom Art Directors Club Deutschland für die SPIEGEL-Titelbildillustration „Der göttliche Teufel".

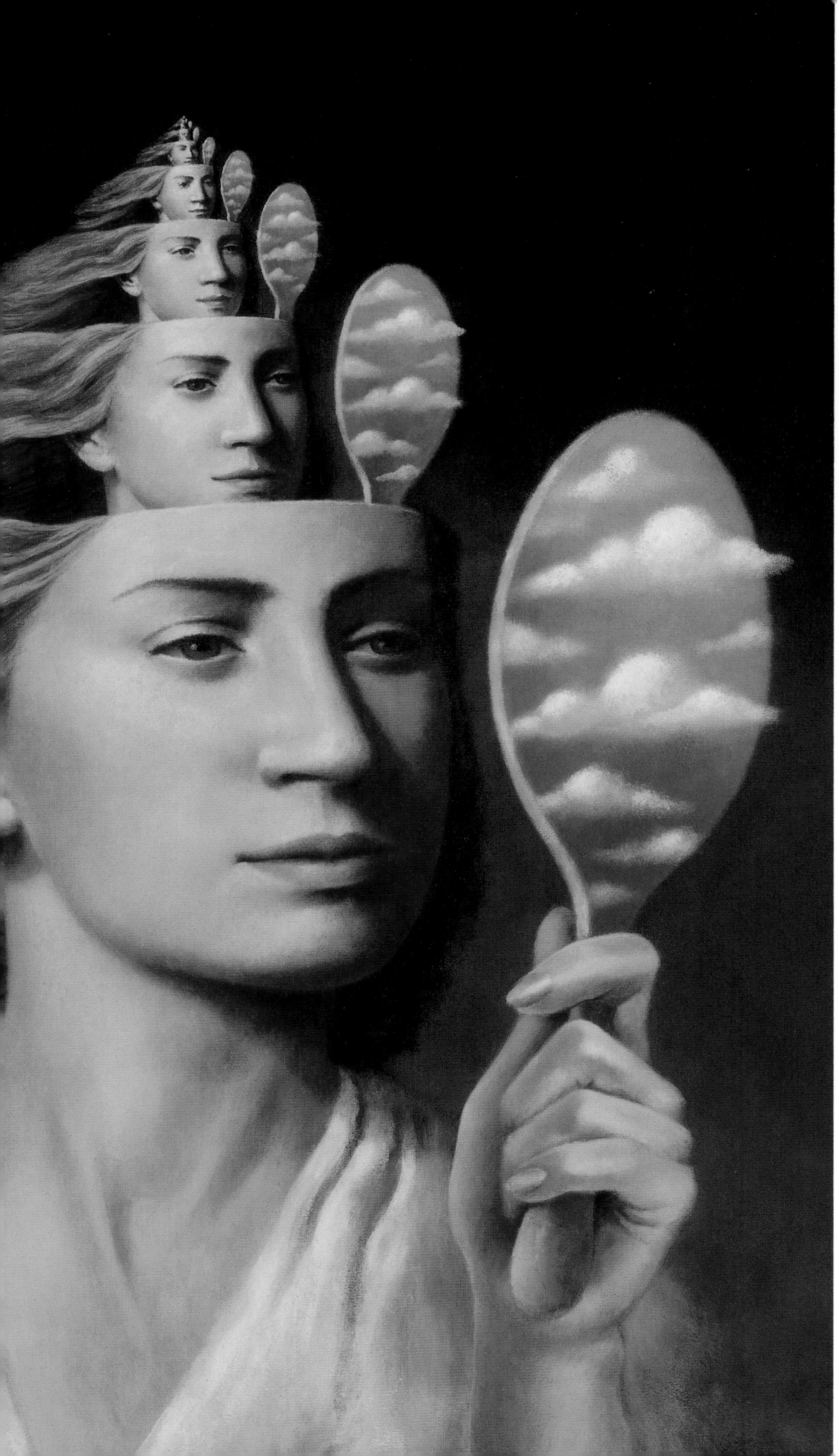

SPIEGEL-Titel 16/1996
Wer ist Ich?

*Neurologen, Informatiker
und Psychologen wollen
gemeinsam ein Urrätsel
der Philosophie lösen:
Was ist Bewusstsein?
Größtes Problem dabei ist,
die Rolle von Gefühlen
und Empfindungen wissen-
schaftlich zu erfassen.*

SPIEGEL cover 16/1996
Who is I?

*Neurologists, computer
experts and psychologists
have joined forces to answer
one of mankind's oldest
philosophical questions:
What is consciousness?
The key challenge is to
scientifically grasp emotions
and sensations.*

SPIEGEL-Titel 52/1996
Der göttliche Teufel

*Er kommt aus der Tiefe
der Geschichte und
den Abgründen der Seele,
und der Mensch kann
offenbar ohne ihn nicht sein:
der Teufel, alias Satan,
die Verkörperung des Bösen.*

SPIEGEL cover 52/1996
The divine devil

*His roots run far back
into history and the darkest
depths of the human soul.
It seems that humans cannot
live without him: the devil,
alias Satan, the incarnation
of evil.*

SPIEGEL-Titel 1/1998
Zeit: Die große Illusion

Forscher haben genetisch programmierte „Uhren" entdeckt, die dem Leben den Takt vorgeben. Sie zerstören eine Illusion: Eine absolute Zeit gibt es nicht, die Zeit entsteht im Kopf.

SPIEGEL cover 1/1998
Time: the great illusion

Scientists have discovered genetically programmed clocks that make life tick. They have destroyed an illusion: There is no such thing as absolute time. Time exists only in our minds.

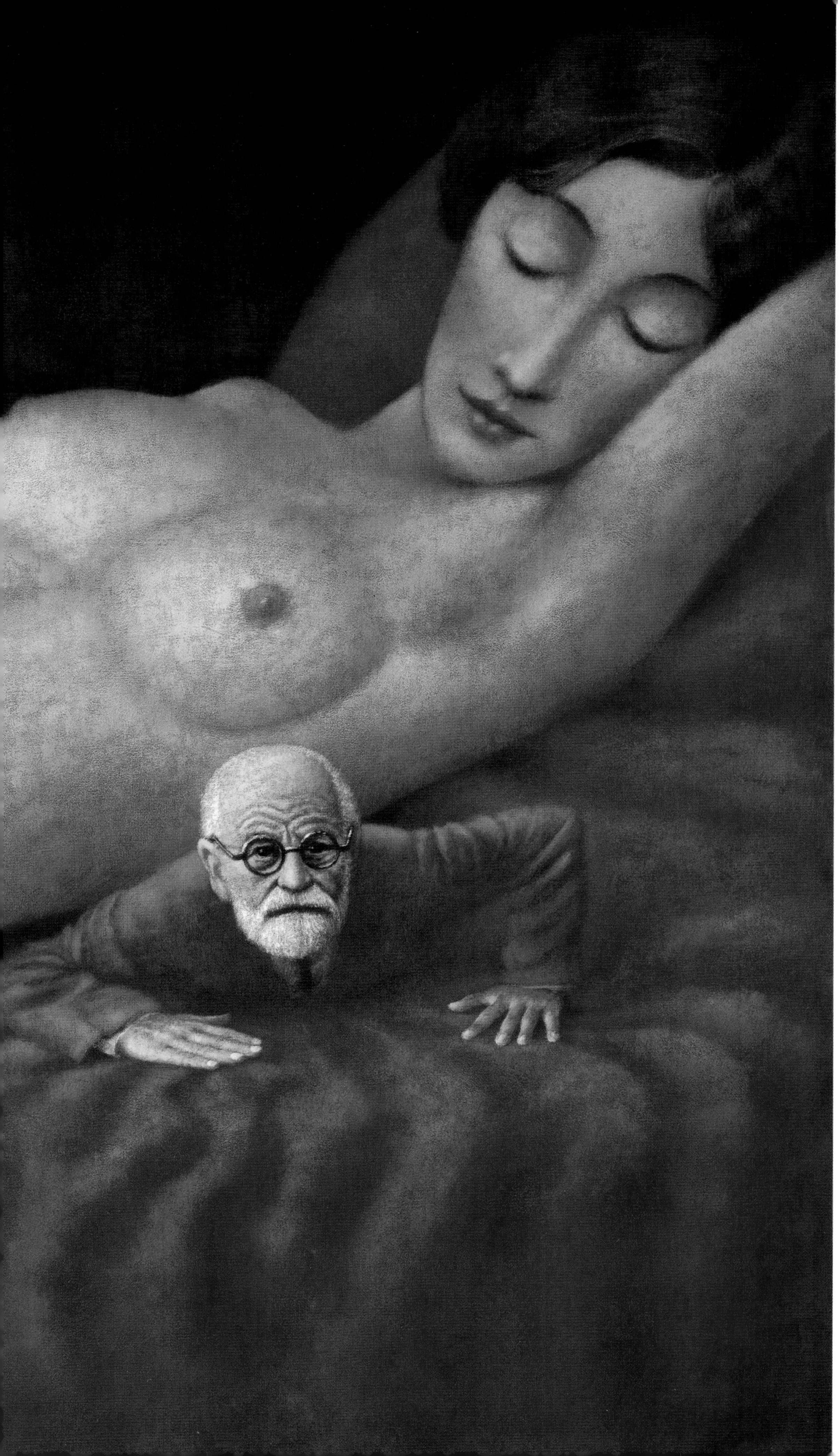

SPIEGEL-Titel 25/1998
Die Psycho-Falle

*Als Schöpfer der Psycho-
analyse hat Sigmund Freud
das 20. Jahrhundert wie
kaum ein anderer geprägt.
Nun stellen radikale
Kritiker seine Lehre in
Frage und sind dabei, das
überlebensgroße Denkmal
des Tiefenpsychologen
zu stürzen.*

SPIEGEL cover 25/1998
The psyche trap

*As the creator of psychoan-
alysis, Sigmund Freud
shaped the 20th century like
no other. Radical critics are
now challenging his doctrine
and toppling the larger-
than-life Freud monument
that still looms over depth
psychology.*

SPIEGEL-Titel 52/1998
Gottes Urknall

Viele Himmelsforscher können sich die immer wundersamer erscheinende Entstehung des Universums nur durch einen Weltenlenker erklären – Astronomen entdecken Gott.

SPIEGEL cover 52/1998
God's big bang

Many astronomers have only one explanation for the ever more wondrous creation of the universe. There must be some sort of controlling force. They are discovering God.

**Casanova
(unveröffentlicht 1998)**

*Der 1725 geborene
italienische Abenteurer
Giacomo Girolamo
Casanova gilt als sagen-
haftester Frauenflüsterer
aller Zeiten.*

**Casanova
(unpublished 1998)**

*The Italian adventurer
Giacomo Girolamo
Casanova, born in 1725,
is considered to be the most
legendary woman chaser
of all times.*

TOM JÜTZ

Geboren wurde Tom Jütz 1965 in Braunschweig. Dort lernte er zunächst an der Hochschule für Bildende Künste, danach an der Fachhochschule für Gestaltung in Hamburg. Seit 1995 arbeitet Tom Jütz als freier Illustrator und Maler. Er gewann mehrere Preise bei der künstlerischen Gestaltung von Wänden.

Tom Jütz was born in Braunschweig, Germany, in 1965. He attended the city's University of Fine Arts before transferring to the Technical College of Design in Hamburg. Since 1995, he has worked as a freelance illustrator and painter. Jütz has won several awards for his artistic wall designs.

SPIEGEL-Titel 25/1996
Absturz Ost

*Die ostdeutsche Wirtschaft
steht vor dem Kollaps.
Zunächst erfolgreiche neue
Betriebe gehen Pleite, die
Industrie schrumpft weiter.*

SPIEGEL cover 25/1996
The collapse of the East

*The eastern German
economy is facing collapse.
Companies that initially
enjoyed success are going
bankrupt. The industrial
base continues to shrink.*

SPIEGEL-Titel 35/1997
Nichts geht mehr

*Auflösungstendenzen in
der konservativ-liberalen
Koalition: Kanzler
Helmut Kohl scheint
die Kontrolle über sein
Kabinett zu verlieren.*

SPIEGEL cover 35/1997
No go

*The erosion of Germany's
coalition: Chancellor
Helmut Kohl seems to
be losing his grip on the
cabinet.*

BRALDT BRALDS

Braldt Bralds likes to work with oil on wood, canvas or copper most of all. "It enables you to make countless variations in technique, and its gloss is beautiful beyond compare," he says. Bralds' interest in art began to grow after he visited a museum for the first time when he was 12. The artist, who was born in Hoogkerk, the Netherlands, in 1951, largely tought himself to draw – he never attended an art college. He was driven by the desire to earn his living like the American illustrators he admired so much. With this goal in mind, he headed off to the United States to live: "Measuring up to your heroes keeps you in shape." Bralds works for "Rolling Stone" magazine, "Celestial Seasons" and "National Geographic", and designs covers for "Newsweek", "Time" and DER SPIEGEL. He also has been honored by the Society of Illustrators (New York and Los Angeles), among others.

Mit Öl auf Holz, Leinwand oder Kupfer arbeitet Braldt Bralds am liebsten: „Es erlaubt endlose Variationen in der Technik, und sein Glanz hat eine unvergleichliche Schönheit." Bralds' Interesse für die Kunst wuchs nach einem ersten Museumsbesuch als Zwölfjähriger. 1951 im niederländischen Hoogkerk geboren, brachte er sich das Zeichnen weitgehend selbst bei – eine Kunsthochschule hat er nie besucht. Doch ihn trieb der Wunsch, einmal so sein Geld zu verdienen, wie die von ihm bewunderten amerikanischen Illustratoren. Deshalb lebt er auch in den Vereinigten Staaten: „Dich mit deinen Helden zu messen hält dich auf dem Laufenden." Bralds arbeitet für das „Rolling Stone Magazine", „Celestial Seasons" und „National Geographic", und er zeichnet Titel für „Newsweek", „Time" sowie den SPIEGEL. Seine Werke wurden mehrfach ausgezeichnet, unter anderem

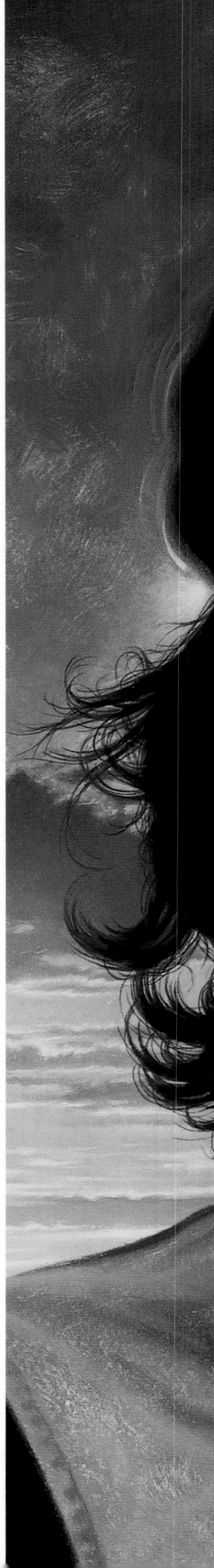

SPIEGEL-Titel 38/1996
Mythos Ché Guevara

*Die genauen Umstände
seines gewaltsamen Todes
vor 37 Jahren sind bis heute
ungeklärt – doch längst ist
Ché Guevara eine Kultfigur
geworden: vom Revolutionär
zum Poster-Helden.*

SPIEGEL cover 38/1996
The myth of Ché Guevara

*The exact circumstances
surrounding his violent
death 37 years ago remain
unclear – but Ché Guevara
lives on as a cult figure:
the revolutionary fighter
turned poster boy.*

SPIEGEL-Titel 33/1999
Mephisto Goethe

Vor 250 Jahren wurde Johann Wolfgang von Goethe geboren. Er gilt als Dichter der Deutschen, aber auch als Mann der Widersprüche: „Zwei Seelen wohnen, ach! in meiner Brust."

SPIEGEL cover 33/1999
Mephisto Goethe

Johann Wolfgang von Goethe was born 250 years ago. He is considered to be the Germans' poet. But he is also a man of contradictions: "Two souls are living, ah!, in my breast."

SPIEGEL-Titel 50/1999
Das Gehirn des
Jahrhunderts

*Mit der Kraft seiner Gedan-
ken schuf Albert Einstein
ein Universum. Im privaten
Leben scheiterte das Genie.*

SPIEGEL cover 50/1999
The brain of the century

*With the power of his
thoughts, Albert Einstein
created a universe.
But the genius failed in
his private life.*

SPIEGEL-Titel 35/2000
Bruder Affe

*Die Menschenaffen stehen
dem Homo sapiens näher
als alle anderen Lebewesen.
Jetzt sind sie vom Ausster-
ben bedroht.*

SPIEGEL cover 35/2000
Brother ape

*Apes are closer to Homo
sapiens than any other
form of life. Today, they are
facing extinction.*

SPIEGEL-Titel 51/2003
Die Manns

*Als Romancier und
Gegner Hitlers wurde
Thomas Mann der
berühmteste deutsche
Schriftsteller im 20. Jahr-
hundert. Nun ist seine
Familie Gegenstand eines
dreiteiligen TV-Films.*

SPIEGEL cover 51/2003
The Manns

*As a novelist and an
opponent of Hitler,
Thomas Mann became the
most famous German
writer of the 20th century.
Now, his family has become
the focus of a three-part
television movie.*

**Mordfall Jesus Christus
(unveröffentlicht 2004)**

*Wer war Jesus Christus, wie
lebte er, und wie starb er?
Bücher, Fernsehsendungen
und Filme dokumentieren
ein ungebrochenes Interesse
am Schicksal des jungen
Mannes aus Galiläa.*

**The murder case of
Jesus Christ
(unpublished 2004)**

*Who was Jesus Christ?
How did he live and how
did he die? Books, television
programs and films show
that interest in the fate
of the young man from the
former Galilee is unbroken.*

MARK ENTWISLE

Schon als Kind malte er gern – und dabei
ist es auch geblieben. 1961 in Bristol geboren, studierte Mark Entwisle Anfang der
achtziger Jahre am Brighton Art College.
Bevorzugt nutzt er Wasser- und Ölfarben.
Besonders wichtige Arbeiten Entwisles sind
mehrere Plakate für das National Theatre,
London, und Buchumschläge für Werke von
Gabriel García Márquez.

Mark Entwisle has enjoyed drawing since he
was a child. Born in Bristol, Britain, in 1961,
Entwisle studied at the Brighton Art College
in the early 1980s. He prefers watercolors
and oils. Among his most important commissions he includes several posters for the
National Theatre, London, and covers for
books by Gabriel García Márquez.

SPIEGEL-Titel 1/1997
Im Keller

*Viereinhalb Wochen
lang vegetierte der
Hamburger Sozialforscher
und Multimillionär
Jan Philipp Reemtsma
angekettet in einem dunklen
Keller. Entführer hatten
ihn verschleppt und
30 Millionen Mark erpresst.*

SPIEGEL cover 1/1997
In the basement

*The Hamburg social resear-
cher and multimillionaire
Jan Philipp Reemtsma
was held in chains in a dark
basement for four and a half
weeks. His kidnappers got
DM 30 million in ransom.*

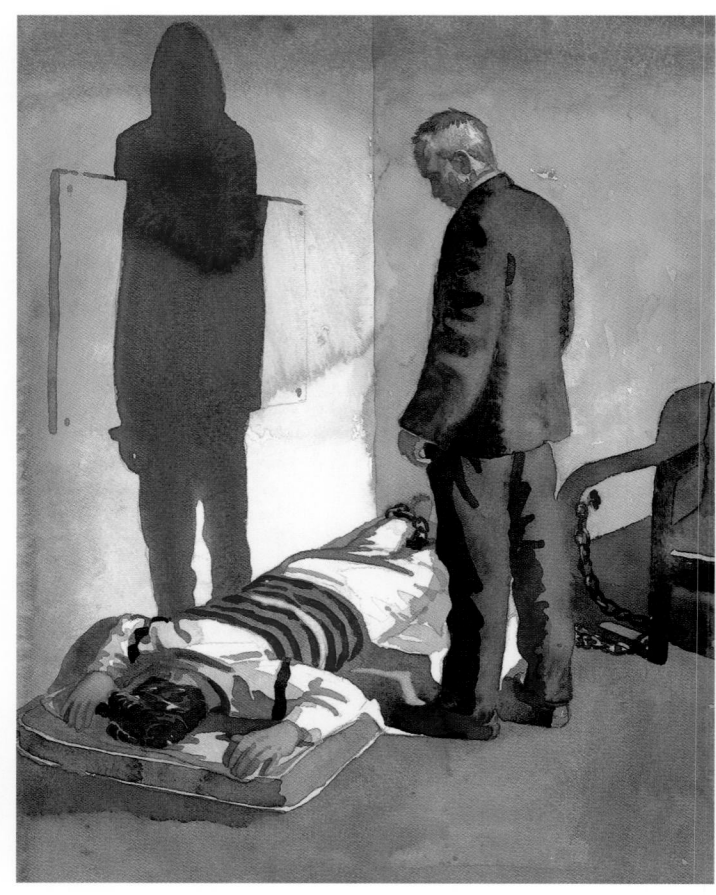

**Im Keller
(Illustrationen im
SPIEGEL 1997)**

*Wie Jan Philipp Reemtsma
die Umstände seiner
Entführung und die Zeit
im Kellerverlies nach
eigener Darstellung
erlebt hat.*

**In the basement
(Illustrations in
DER SPIEGEL 1997)**

*How Jan Philipp
Reemtsma experienced his
kidnapping and his time
in the basement where
he was held captive.*

TIM O'BRIEN

Master's of Fine Art from Paier College of Art in 1987. In the mid-1990s, O'Brien's work became well-known through a series of covers he did for "Time" magazine. Today, he works for "Time", "Business Week", "Fortune", "Rolling Stone", "National Geographic" and other publications. His pieces have been exhibited by the Society of Illustrators, the Norman Rockwell Museum and the Rock and Roll Hall of Fame, among others. He has received numerous awards, including silver medals from the Society of Illustrators in New York and Los Angeles.

Sein Interesse für die Kunst sei „instinktiv", so der 1964 in New Haven, Connecticut, geborene Tim O'Brien. Mit dem Master of Fine Art hatte er 1987 seine Ausbildung am Paier College of Art abgeschlossen. Mitte der neunziger Jahre wurde O'Briens Werk durch eine Reihe von Titelbildern des „Time Magazine" bekannt. Heute arbeitet er für „Time", „Business Week", „Fortune", „Rolling Stone", „National Geographic" und andere Publikationen. Seine Werke wurden unter anderem von der Society of Illustrators, dem Norman Rockwell Museum und der Rock and Roll Hall of Fame gezeigt und oft prämiert – etwa mit Silbermedaillen der Society of Illustrators in New York und in Los Angeles.

His interest in art is "instinctive," says Tim O'Brien, who was born in New Haven, Connecticut, in 1964. He graduated with a

SPIEGEL-Titel 8/1997
Abenteuer Euro

*Das Experiment Euro droht
zu scheitern, noch ehe es
begonnen hat: Ausgerechnet
die Deutschen verfehlen
offenkundig die Stabilitätskriterien.*

SPIEGEL cover 8/1997
The euro adventure

*The euro experiment is
threatened with failure even
before it begins: It seems
the Germans, of all people,
are not meeting the stability
criteria.*

**SPIEGEL-Titel 28/1997
Aufräumen wie in
New York?**

*Deutsche Polizeichefs
pilgern nach New York,
um von der amerikanischen
Metropole zu lernen,
wie sie das Verbrechen
zurückgedrängt hat.*

**SPIEGEL cover 28/1997
Clean up, New York-style?**

*German police chiefs are
going on pilgrimage to
New York to learn how the
U.S. metropolis fought
off crime.*

SPIEGEL-Titel 18/1998
Abschied von der Mark

*Die Europäische Einheits-
währung kommt gewiss –
aber noch streiten sich
die Euro-Mitglieder um
Stabilitätskriterien
und einflussreiche Posten
in Kontrollgremien.*

SPIEGEL cover 18/1998
Bidding farewell to
the deutschmark

*The common European
currency is bound to come –
but the euro members are
still haggling over stability
criteria and influential posts
on supervisory bodies.*

Die Kirche und der Holocaust (unveröffentlicht 1997)

Hätte Papst Pius XII. durch sein Eingreifen viele Juden vor der Ermordung retten können?

The church and the Holocaust (unpublished 1997)

Could Pope Pius XII have saved the lives of many Jews?

Nazi-Geld in der Schweiz (unveröffentlicht 1997)

Die Schweiz ist stolz auf ihr Bankgeheimnis – wie viel von den Nazis geraubtes und erpresstes Geld liegt immer noch auf Alpenkonten?

Nazi money in Switzerland (unpublished 1997)

Switzerland is proud of its bank secrecy – how much of the money that was stolen and extorted by the Nazis is still lying in Swiss accounts?

**Die Party ist aus
(unveröffentlicht 2001)**

Die Internet-Aktien stürzen ab, die Börsen-Blase ist geplatzt. Jetzt herrscht allenthalben Katzenjammer.

**The party's over
(unpublished 2001)**

Internet stocks are crashing, and the stock market bubble has burst. Now everybody is suffering from a hangover.

**Weicher Euro
(unveröffentlicht 2002)**

Nach seiner Einführung schwächelt der Euro – die Deutschen trauern um ihre D-Mark und haben Angst vor einer weichen europäischen Währung.

**Weak euro
(unpublished 2002)**

After its introduction, the euro is languishing – the Germans mourn for their beloved deutsche mark and are afraid that the new European currency will be weak.

KAZUHIKO SANO

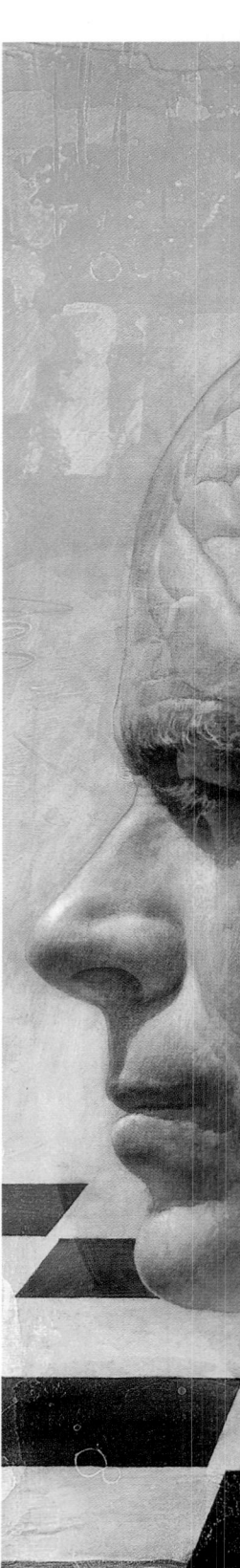

and then in San Francisco. He says his note-worthy pieces include drawings for the movie "Return of the Jedi" and illustrations for stamps issued by the U.S. Postal Service. Sano's works have been shown in numerous exhibitions in Japan and the United States. The San Francisco Society of Illustrators awarded him a gold medal. Kazuhiko Sano lives and works in the United States.

Comic-Zeichner, Maler, Schlagzeuger in einer Rockband und Designer wollte Kazu-hiko Sano als Kind werden. Beim Künstleri-schen ist der 1952 in Tokio geborene Kazu-hiko Sano geblieben: Er studierte in Japan, danach in San Francisco. Als besonders bemerkenswerte Arbeiten nennt er Zeich-nungen für den Star-Wars-Film „Rückkehr der Jedi-Ritter" sowie Illustrationen für Briefmarken der US-Post. Sanos Werke wurden auf etlichen Ausstellungen in Japan und den USA gezeigt. Die San Francisco Society of Illustrators verlieh ihm eine Goldmedaille. Kazuhiko Sano lebt und arbeitet in den USA.

As a child, Kazuhiko Sano wanted to become a comic-strip artist, then a painter, a drum-mer in a rock band and a designer. Sano, who was born in Tokyo in 1952, stayed true to the arts in the end: He studied in Japan

**Homo erectus
(unveröffentlicht 2003)**

*Vom Raubtier zum
Menschen – wie aus dem
Jäger das Kulturwesen
wurde.*

**Homo erectus
(unpublished 2003)**

*From the wild beast to the
human being – how hunters
became cultured creatures.*

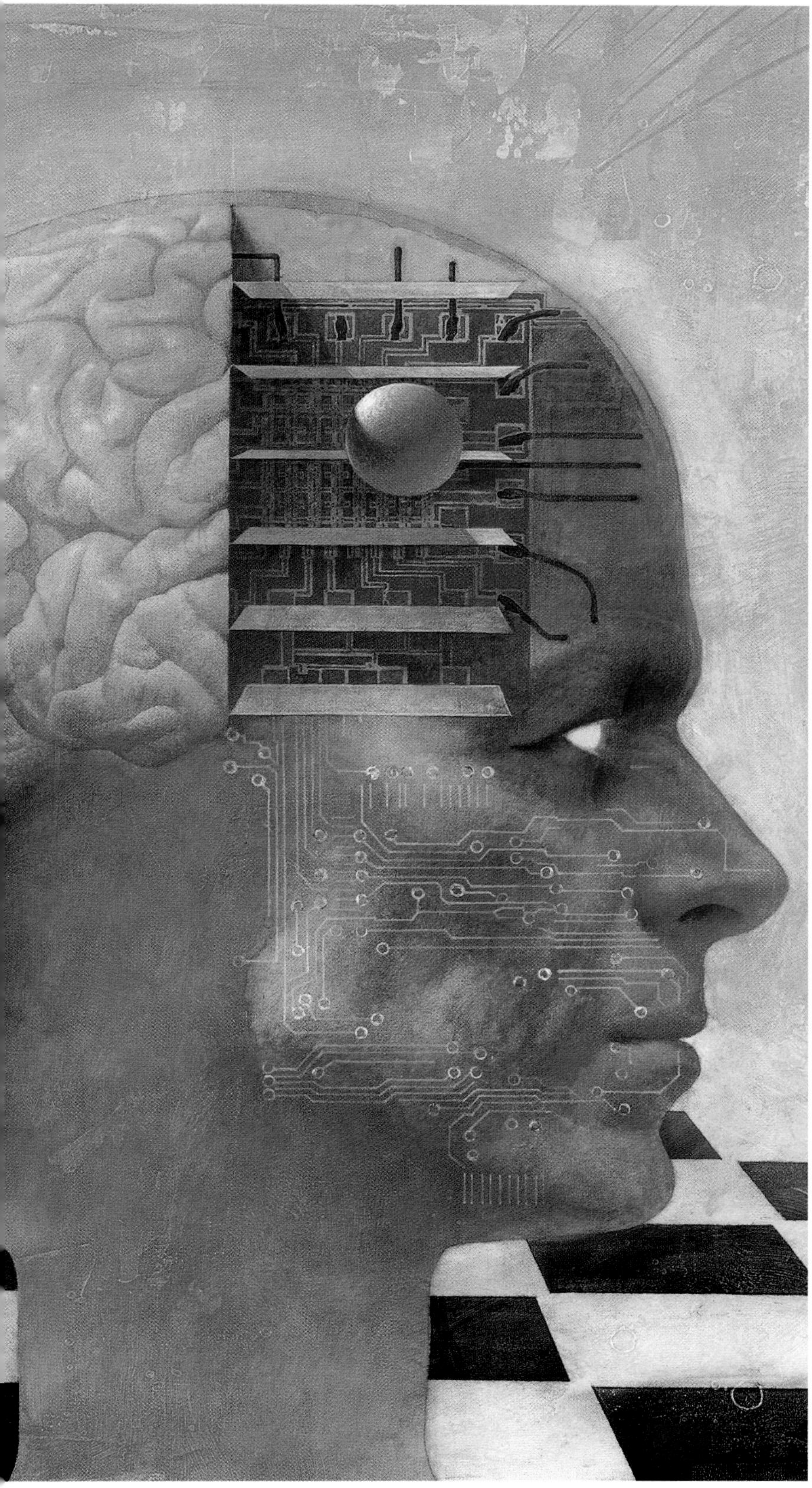

SPIEGEL-Titel 18/1997
Mensch gegen Maschine

*Schachweltmeister
Garri Kasparow tritt zum
Match gegen den Super-
Rechner „Deep Blue" an.*

SPIEGEL cover 18/1997
Man vs. machine

*Chess world champion
Garry Kasparov is taking
on the super-computer
"Deep Blue".*

SPIEGEL-Titel 52/1997
Jesus, allein zu Haus

*Den Kirchen droht in
Deutschland der Absturz
in die Bedeutungslosigkeit.
Das entstehende geistliche
Vakuum füllen Sektierer
und obskure Vereine.*

SPIEGEL cover 52/1997
Jesus, home alone

*The churches in Germany
are on the verge of becoming
meaningless. Sects and
obscure groups are taking
their place.*

MARVIN MATTELSON

Bisweilen führen eher ungünstige Umstände zu einer erfreulichen Entwicklung: Marvin Mattelson, geboren 1947 in Philadelphia, sagt, seine „langweilige Kindheit" habe ihm den Weg zur Kunst gewiesen. Seine Ausbildung erhielt er am Philadelphia College of Art sowie durch Privatstunden. Mattelson verließ das College wieder, um Geld zu verdienen, und konzentrierte sich ganz auf das Porträtmalen, am liebsten mit Öl auf Leinwand. Sein wichtigster Auftraggeber? „Der nächste." Mattelsons oft prämierte Arbeiten wurden in der National Portrait Gallery und von der Society of Illustrations gezeigt.

Occasionally, rather unfavorable circumstances result in a favorable development: Marvin Mattelson, born in Philadelphia in 1947, says it was his "boring childhood" that led him to the art world. He was educated at the Philadelphia College of Art and through private lessons. Mattelson left the college to earn money and concentrated fully on portraits, with oil on canvas his preferred technique. His key client? "The next one." Mattelson has received numerous awards for his work, which has been shown in the National Portrait Gallery and by the Society of Illustrators.

SPIEGEL-Titel 16/1998
Buddhismus

*Noch nie war der
Buddhismus so im Gespräch,
noch nie war Tibet im
Westen so populär.
Gleichzeitig wird die Lage
in dem von China besetzten
Land immer verzweifelter.*

SPIEGEL cover 16/1998
Buddhism

*Buddhism has never before
been the topic of so much
conversation and Tibet has
never before been so popular
in the West. All the while,
the situation in the country
under Chinese occupation
is becoming more and more
desolate.*

SPIEGEL-Titel 7/2000
Im Land der Lügen

Parteien-Finanzskandale erschüttern die Republik – und die Politiker geben sich unwissend. Auf der Flucht vor der Wahrheit jonglieren sie mit Fakten, verbreiten Halbwahrheiten und üben sich in Tricksereien.

SPIEGEL cover 7/2000
In the land of lies

Party financing scandals are rocking Germany – and politicians feign ignorance. On their flight from the truth, they are juggling facts, spreading half-truths and playing dirty tricks.

GUY BILLOUT

„Eine offensichtliche Fähigkeit zu zeichnen" gab den Ausschlag für seine künstlerische Karriere, so Guy Billout. 1941 in Decize, Frankreich, geboren, studierte er von 1956 bis 1960 an der École des Arts Appliqués de Beaune in Burgund, um zunächst als Grafik-Designer für Werbeagenturen zu arbeiten. Billouts bevorzugte Techniken sind Aquarell, Airbrush und Buntstift. Seit seiner Auswanderung nach New York arbeitet Billout für „The Atlantic Monthly", „The New Yorker", „The New York Times" und verschiedene internationale Werbeagenturen und Unternehmen. Einen besonderen Impuls habe ihm die Anfrage von Harlin Quist gegeben, ein eigenes Kinderbuch zu schreiben und zu illustrieren – bei dieser Arbeit habe er, so Billout, „totale Freiheit" genossen. Inzwischen wurden vier seiner Kinderbücher von der „New York Times" auf ihre Liste der besten illustrierten Kinderbücher gesetzt.

Guy Billout erhielt drei Gold- und zwei Silbermedaillen von der Society of Illustrators in New York sowie den Hamilton King Award für beste Illustration.

As Guy Billout tells the story, it was his "apparent ability to draw" that led him to pursue a career in art. Guy Billout, who was born in Decize, France, in 1941, studied at the École des Arts Appliqués de Beaune in Burgundy from 1956 to 1960 in preparation for becoming a graphic designer at advertising agencies. Billout prefers to use watercolors, airbrushes and colored pencils. Since emigrating to New York, he has worked for "The Atlantic Monthly", "The New Yorker", "The New York Times" and various international advertising agencies and multinational companies. His work gained new impetus when Harlin Quist suggested that he should write and illustrate his own children's book. Billout says he had "total freedom" to perform the project. Since then, "The New York Times" has placed four of his works on the list of best illustrated children's books. He has also received three gold and two silver medals from the Society of Illustrators in New York and the Hamilton King Award for best illustrations.

**Die Weltformel
(unveröffentlicht 1999)**

*Die internationale Elite
der Physiker versucht auf
einer Konferenz im Sommer
1999, die ganze Welt
mit einer einzigen Formel
zu erklären.*

**The theory of everything
(unpublished 1999)**

*At a conference in the
summer of 1999, members
of the physics elite
community try to boil the
entire world down into
one formula.*

SPIEGEL-Titel 2/1998
2 vor 2000

*Bis zum Jahr 2000 stehen
den Deutschen einschneiden-
de Ereignisse ins Haus:
Der Euro kommt, Berlin
wird Hauptstadt, und
ein Regierungswechsel ist
absehbar.*

SPIEGEL cover 2/1998
2 before 2000

*In the time remaining
before 2000, Germans will
experience some sweeping
changes: The euro is
arriving, Berlin is becoming
the capital, and a change
of government appears to be
in the cards.*

SPIEGEL-Titel 10/1998
Der göttliche Funke

*Ist die Evolution eine
Geschichte des Fortschritts,
oder schuf allein der Zufall
die heutige Welt? Auch
Molekularbiologen suchen
jetzt nach Antworten –
im Erbgut der Lebewesen.*

SPIEGEL cover 10/1998
The divine spark

*Is evolution a story of
progress or is today's world
merely a product of chance?
Molecular biologists are
searching for answers –
in the genetic material of
the world's living creatures.*

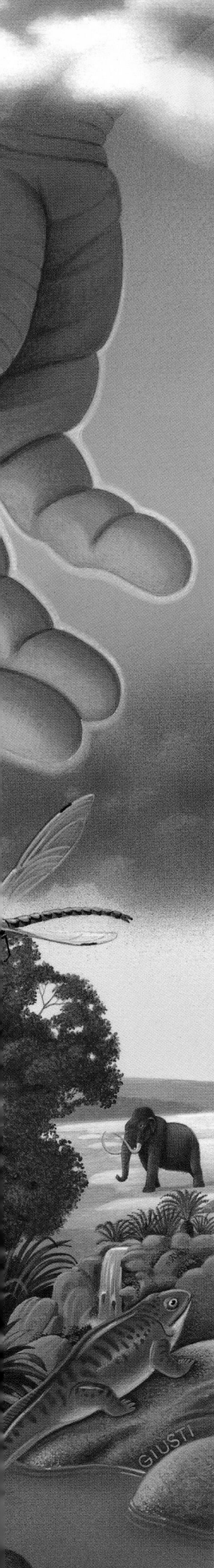

ROBERT GIUSTI

Als Sohn eines Grafikers und einer Mode-Illustratorin wuchs der 1937 in Zürich geborene Robert Giusti in New York auf. Seine Kindheit verbrachte er in einem von Kunst und Kreativität geprägten Umfeld. Giusti studierte an der Tyler School of Fine Arts in Philadelphia und erwarb später einen Bachelor of Fine Arts an der Cranbrook Academy of Art in Michigan. Nach Ende seines Studiums arbeitete er zunächst im Anzeigengeschäft, bevor er als Art Director und Designer zum Verlagshaus Random House ging. Einige Jahre später machte sich Robert Giusti als Grafiker und Illustrator selbständig. Er entwarf unter anderem mehrere Briefmarken für den U. S. Postal Service, ein Superbowl-Poster für die N.F.L. und Buchtitel für Stephen King.
Seine Werke wurden in vielen internationalen Ausstellungen gezeigt und oft ausgezeichnet, etwa mit Medaillen des Art Directors Club of New York.
Robert Giusti hat ein Studio in seinem Haus in Bridgewater, Connecticut, das er mit seiner Frau Grace und zwei Hunden, Lupo und Baci, teilt.

Born in Zurich, Switzerland, in 1937 and raised in New York City, Robert Giusti is the son of a graphic artist and a fashion illustrator who enabled him to grow up in an artistic and creative environment. He attended the Tyler School of Fine Arts in Philadelphia and earned a Bachelor of Fine Arts from the Cranbrook Academy of Art in Michigan. After graduation, he worked in advertising before joining the Random House publishing company as art director and designer.
A few years later, Robert Giusti began freelancing as a graphic designer and illustrator. He designed several stamps for the U. S. Postal Service, a Super Bowl poster for the NFL and book covers for Stephen King. His works have been displayed in many international exhibitions and received numerous awards, including medals from the Art Directors Club of New York.
Giusti has a studio in his house in Bridgewater, Connecticut, where he lives with his wife, Grace, and their two dogs, Lupo and Baci.

SPIEGEL-Titel 12/2000
Der Krieg
der ersten Menschen

*Vor rund 40 000 Jahren
entdeckte der Mensch die
Kultur. Vermutlich als
Resultat eines Kampfes,
nachdem der Homo sapiens
auf einen ebenbürtigen
Rivalen gestoßen war – den
Neandertaler.*

SPIEGEL cover 12/2000
The war between
the first men

*About 40,000 years ago,
mankind discovered culture
– most likely in the wake of
a struggle that pitted Homo
sapiens against an equal
rival, the Neanderthal.*

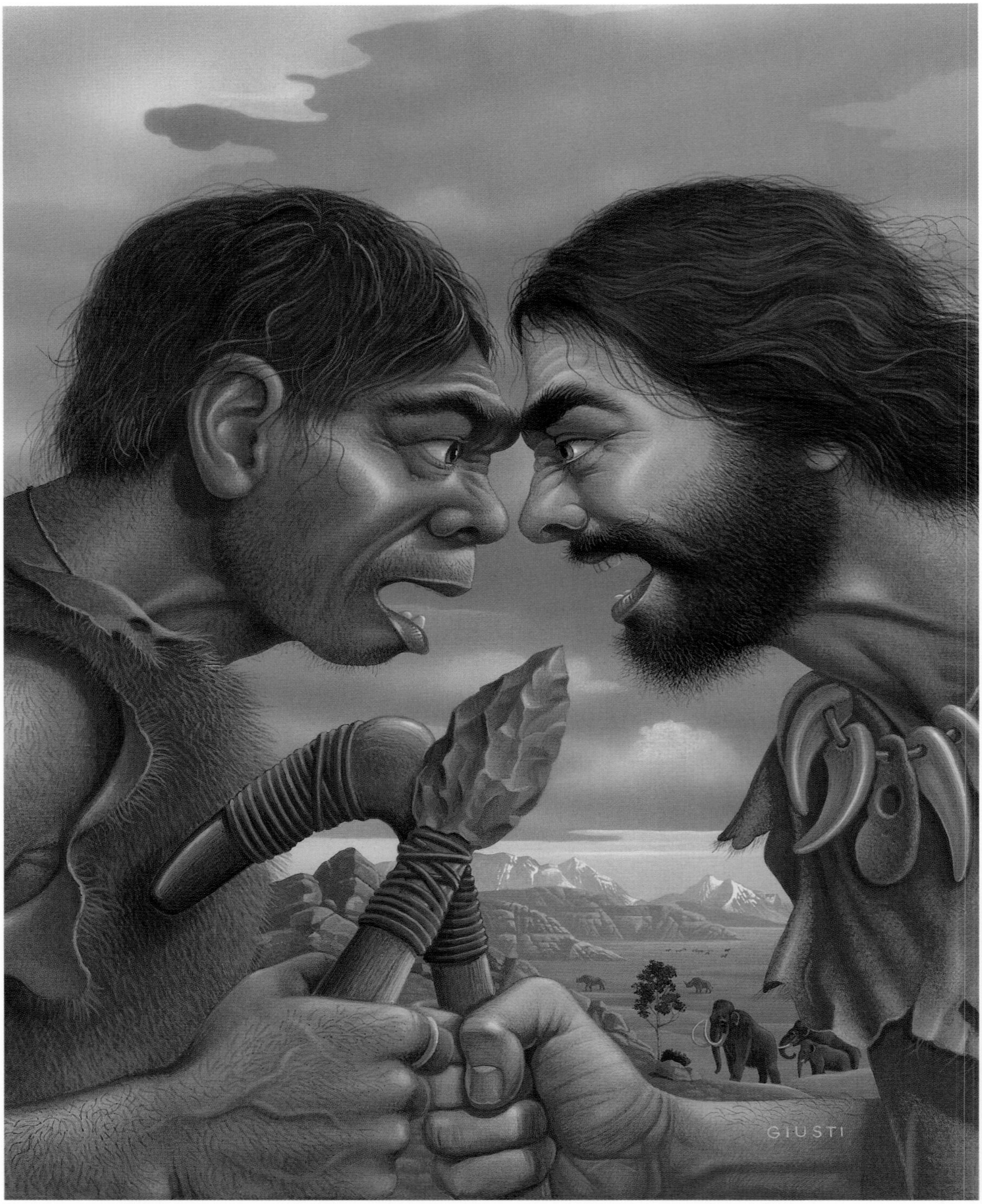

Amazonas
(unveröffentlicht 2001)

Die Bemühungen von Umweltschützern zeigen Erfolge: Am Amazonas wird weniger Wald vernichtet als je zuvor, ein Netzwerk gut gemeinter Projekte hat sich etabliert. Aber der Dschungel ist immer noch voller Mythen.

Amazon
(unpublished 2001)

The efforts of environmentalists are paying off: Less rainforest is being destroyed in the Amazon region than before, and a network of well-meaning projects has been established. But the jungle remains filled with myths.

at the Berlin Hilgemann gallery in 1995. Their most successful work, "Happy Day", is an allegory of German reunification in a wedding party with Helmut Kohl. It was this work that led DER SPIEGEL to commission Alexander Vinogradov and Vladimir Dubosarsky to do a portrait of the former chancellor for the cover. The original cover can be seen at the Haus der Geschichte (House of History) museum in Bonn.

Das kreative Duo Alexander Vinogradov (geboren 1963 in Moskau) und Vladimir Dubosarskij (geboren 1964 in Moskau) arbeitet seit 1994 zusammen. 1995 zeigten die russischen Künstler in der Berliner Hilgemann Galerie ihre Ausstellung „Painting for Reichstag". Ihr erfolgreichstes Werk („Happy Day") ist eine Allegorie des wiedervereinten Deutschland auf einer Hochzeitsversammlung mit Helmut Kohl. DER SPIEGEL beauftragte daraufhin Alexander Vinogradov und Vladimir Dubosarskij mit einem Porträt des Altkanzlers für ein Titelblatt. Das Original hat das Bonner Haus der Geschichte angekauft.

The creative duo Alexander Vinogradov and Vladimir Dubosarsky has worked together since 1994. The two artists, who were born in Moscow in 1963 and 1964 respectively, held an exhibition "Painting for Reichstag"

SPIEGEL-Titel 11/1998
Abschied vom Gestern

*Kanzler Helmut Kohl
erleidet beim Lauschangriff
eine Niederlage, Gerhard
Schröder gewinnt unverhofft
hoch die Landtagswahlen
in Niedersachsen – kommt
jetzt die Nachkriegs-
generation an die Macht?*

SPIEGEL cover 11/1998
Farewell to yesteryear

*Chancellor Helmut Kohl
suffers political defeat in the
"great bugging operation,"
Gerhard Schröder wins an
unexpectedly clear victory in
the state election in Lower
Saxony. Is the postwar
generation now coming into
power?*

181

Dynamic Duo

„Comic-Kunsthistoriker". Dynamic Duo wurde mit Auszeichnungen wie dem Gold Medal Award for Illustration von „Creativity 28" geehrt.

Arlen Schumer, born in Detroit in 1958, started to draw when he was only three years old, painting characters from television and comics, among other things. Schumer prefers to work with pencil and ink and scans his sketches electronically. That is when his partner, Sherri Wolfgang, takes over. Wolfgang, who was born in New York in 1961, colors the sketches digitally. Both Arlen Schumer and Sherri Wolfgang worked in an advertising agency before they came together in 1986 to form The Dynamic Duo Studio. Their clients are well-known advertising agencies in New York and across the United States. The two artists have created illustrations for such publications as "Time", "Newsweek", the "New York Times Magazine", "Forbes" and the "Washington Post". Schumer continues to enjoy comics and prefers to refer to himself as a "comic art historian". Dynamic Duo has been honored with such awards as the Gold Medal Award for illustration from "Creativity 28".

Mit drei Jahren schon begann der 1958 in Detroit geborene Arlen Schumer zu zeichnen – er malte unter anderem Figuren aus dem Fernsehen und aus Comics ab. Schumer arbeitet bevorzugt mit Bleistift und Tinte und scannt die Zeichnungen dann in den Computer. Hier übernimmt seine Partnerin Sherri Wolfgang. Die 1961 in New York geborene Künstlerin koloriert die Arbeiten digital. Arlen Schumer und Sherri Wolfgang arbeiteten beide in einer Werbeagentur, bevor sie sich 1986 als The Dynamic Duo Studio zusammenfanden.
Ihre Auftraggeber sind namhafte Werbeagenturen in New York und dem Rest der Vereinigten Staaten. Schumer und Wolfgang fertigen Illustrationen unter anderem für „Time", „Newsweek", „The New York Times Magazine", „Forbes" und „Washington Post". Schumer hat nach wie vor Spaß an Comics: Er bezeichnet sich gern als

SPIEGEL-Titel 15/1998
Die kleinen Monster

Was tun, wenn Kinder zu Schlägern, Dieben und Mördern werden? Pädagogen, Polizisten und Sozialarbeiter suchen nach Wegen aus der Jugendkriminalität.

SPIEGEL cover 15/1998
Pint-sized monsters

What's to be done when children become thugs, thieves and murderers? Educators, police officers and social workers are searching for ways out of youth crime.

SPIEGEL-Titel 29/2002
Das Zappelphilipp-Syndrom

Zu viele Kinder, die leicht erregbar, hyperaktiv oder unkonzentriert sind, werden mit Medikamenten behandelt. Oft überdeckt dies nur Erziehungsmängel.

SPIEGEL cover 29/2002
Fidgeting child syndrome

Too many easily excitable, hyperactive or inattentive children are treated with drugs. Often this just covers deficits in child rearing.

SPIEGEL-Titel 26/1998
Japan

Noch vor wenigen Jahren galt Japan als die kommende Nummer eins auf der Welt und wurde als Erfolgsmodell gepriesen. Jetzt steckt die Wirtschaft in einer Rezession, und die Politiker sind ratlos.

SPIEGEL cover 26/1998
Japan

Until a few years ago, Japan was considered the prospective No. 1 in the world and praised as a success model. Now, its economy is stuck in a recession, and politicians are at a loss.

NANCY STAHL

In einem Vorort von New York wurde Nancy Stahl 1949 geboren. „Als jüngstes Mitglied einer von Ehrgeiz und Konkurrenzdenken geprägten Familie entwickelte ich eine eigene Identität, als ich mein Talent für das Zeichnen entdeckte", sagt sie. Zwei Jahre lang studierte Nancy Stahl an der Universität von Arizona Kunstwissenschaft, danach absolvierte sie ein Studium am Art Center in Los Angeles. Die Künstlerin gestaltet Firmenlogos sowie CD-Hüllen und arbeitet für Zeitschriften wie „Business Week" und „Atlantic Monthly". Der U.S. Postal Service hat fünf Briefmarken mit ihren Motiven herausgegeben. 1990 hatte sie eine eigene Ausstellung in der Lustrare Galerie in SoHo (New York). Außerdem sind ihre Werke Teil der Wanderausstellung „Women Illustrators Past and Present" („Weibliche Illustratoren gestern und heute") der amerikanischen Society of Illustrators.

Nancy Stahl was born in a suburb of New York City in 1949. "Being the youngest in a competitive household, my identity was formed when I discovered that I could excel at drawing," she says. Nancy Stahl was a fine arts major at the University of Arizona for two years, and then earned a degree at the Art Center in Los Angeles. Nancy Stahl designs corporate logos and CD covers, and works for magazines like "Business Week" and "Atlantic Monthly". The U.S. Postal Service has produced five stamps with her images. In 1990, she had a one-woman show at Lustrare gallery in SoHo, New York. Her work has also been included in the touring exhibit "Women Illustrators Past and Present" of the American Society of Illustrators.

SPIEGEL-Titel 37/1999
Was ist soziale
Gerechtigkeit?

*Die Sozialausgaben steigen
stetig, das System staatlicher
Fürsorge ist außer Kontrolle
geraten. Dennoch wird
die Forderung nach „mehr
sozialer Gerechtigkeit"
lauter.*

SPIEGEL cover 37/1999
What is social justice?

*Social expenditures are
rising, and the system
of state welfare has gotten
out of control. Nonetheless,
demands for "more social
justice" are growing louder.*

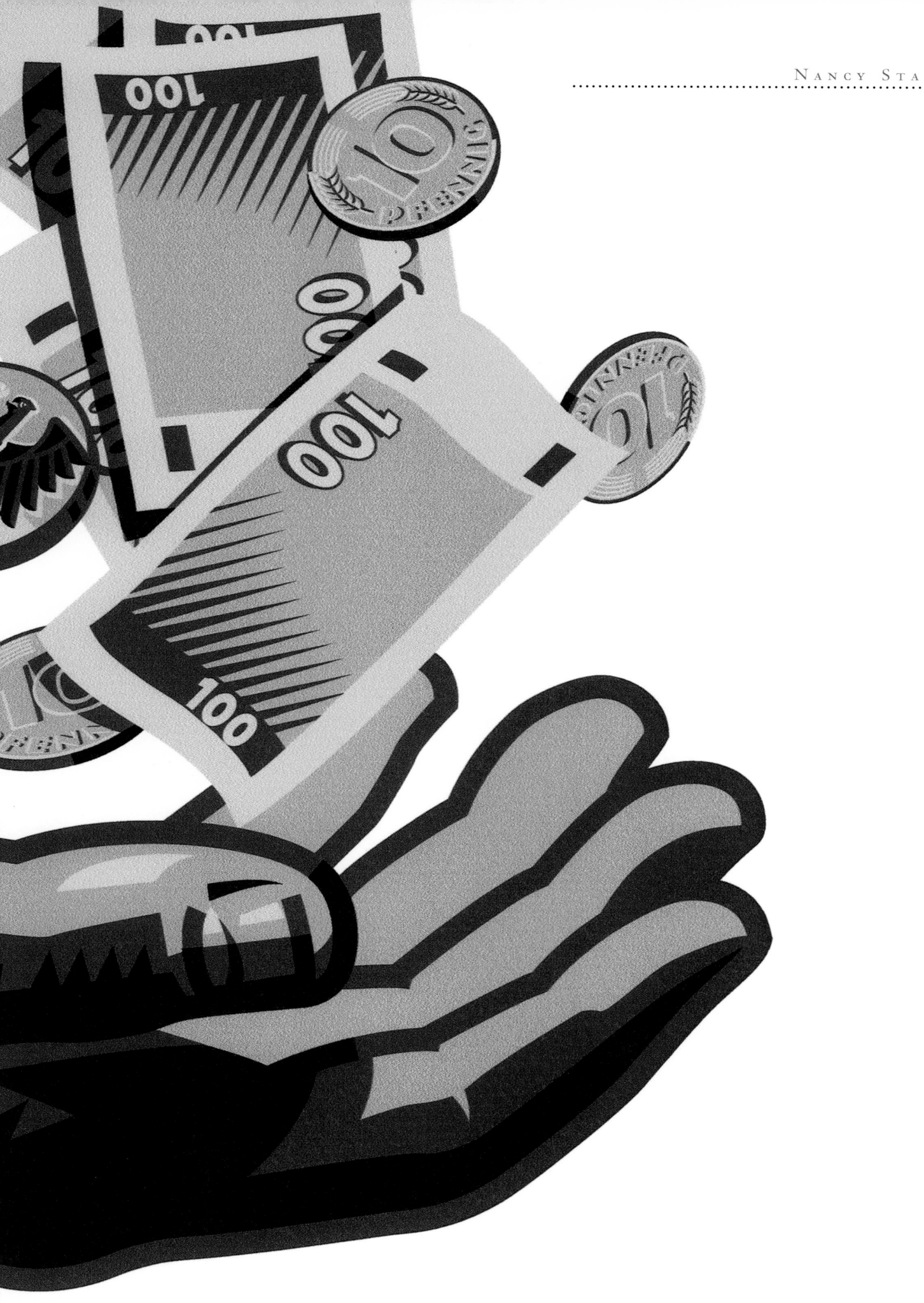

SPIEGEL-Titel 1/1999
Aufbruch ins Euro-Land

Der alte Kontinent erscheint mit der Euro-Einführung in neuer Größe. Wird Europa die neue friedliche Weltmacht?

SPIEGEL cover 1/1999
The dawning of Euroland

The introduction of the euro gives the old continent new grandeur. Will Europe become the new peaceful world power?

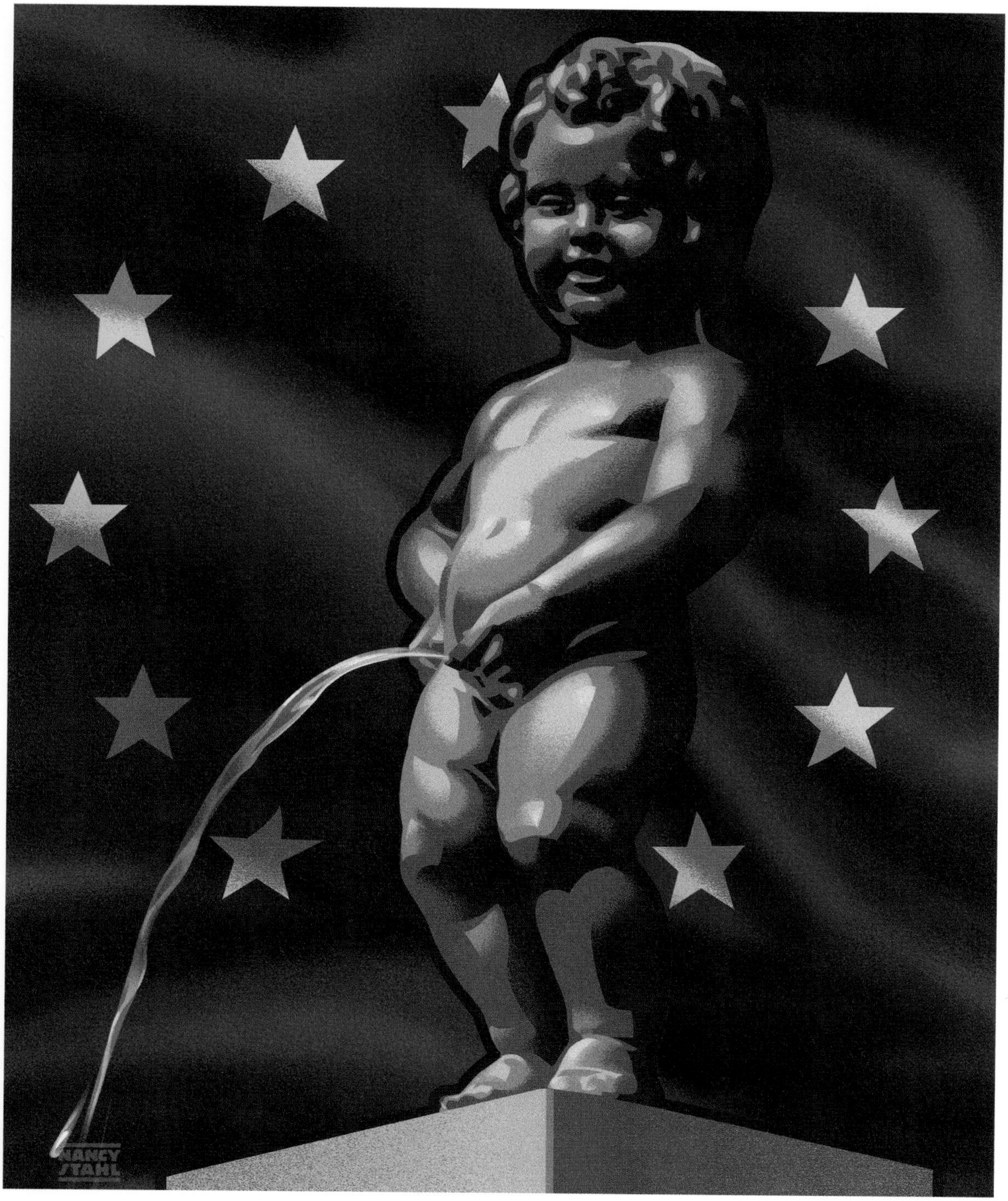

SPIEGEL-Titel 12/1999
Ist Europa
noch zu retten?

*Ein Bericht über Miss-
management und Betrug
in der EU-Kommission
löst die größte Krise aus,
die europäische Gremien
je erlebt haben.*

SPIEGEL cover 12/1999
Can Europe
still be saved?

*A report about mismanage-
ment and fraud in the
EU Commission sparks
the biggest crisis ever seen
in a European institution.*

SPIEGEL-Titel 29/1998
Rasender Stillstand

*Überfüllte Flughäfen,
verspätete Bahnen und
Rekordstaus auf den
Straßen: Die Leistungs-
gesellschaft bekommt ihre
Verkehrsprobleme nicht
in den Griff. Das Tempo
der Fortbewegung sinkt.*

SPIEGEL cover 29/1998
Frenzied standstill

*Overcrowded airports,
late trains and record con-
gestion on the roads: Our
performance-geared society
cannot get a grip on its
traffic problems. Movement
slows down.*

JEAN-PIERRE KUNKEL

Airbrush, Mischtechnik, Öl auf Leinwand, Aquarell, Fotografie, Bildbearbeitung und Illustration – eigentlich ist jede Technik die von Jean-Pierre Kunkel bevorzugte. Kunkel wurde 1950 in Lievin, Frankreich, geboren und interessierte sich schon als Jugendlicher für das künstlerische Handwerk. Er besuchte die Kunstakademie in München und die Kunsthochschule Lerchenfeld in Hamburg ohne Examina. Malerei und Illustration lernte er als Autodidakt. Hinzu kamen längere Studienaufenthalte in Paris und New York. Kunkel ist als Fotorealist einer der meistbeschäftigten Illustratoren Deutschlands.

Airbrush, mixed techniques, oil on canvas, watercolors, photography, photo processing and illustration – Jean-Pierre Kunkel seems to like all techniques. Kunkel, who was born in Lievin, France, in 1950, discovered art as a teenager. He attended the Academy of Arts in Munich, Germany, and the University of Fine Arts in Hamburg, but never earned a degree. He learned the art of painting and illustration as an autodidact and spent some time studying in Paris and New York. Today, Kunkel, a fotorealist, is one of Germany's busiest illustrators.

SPIEGEL-Titel 6/1999
Der Prinz, der Schatz
und die Nazis

*Zwei politische Affären
um die legendären
Welfenschätze rücken
den hannoverschen Prin-
zen Ernst August, Chef
eines der ältesten Adels-
geschlechter Europas, ins
Zwielicht.*

SPIEGEL cover 6/1999
The prince, the treasure
and the Nazis

*Two political affairs
surrounding the legendary
treasures of the Welf
dynasty are casting a
shadow on the reputation
of Prince Ernst August
of Hanover, head of
one of Europe's oldest
aristocratic dynasties.*

SPIEGEL-Titel 16/1999
Krieg ohne Sieg

Der Nato-Luftkrieg gegen den jugoslawischen Despoten Slobodan Milošević blieb bislang erfolglos. Und immer mehr zivile Opfer sind zu beklagen.

SPIEGEL cover 16/1999
War without victory

NATO's air warfare against Yugoslav despot Slobodan Milošević has not been successful so far. And the number of civil casualties is rising.

SPIEGEL-Titel 52/1999
Abschied mit Schimpf
und Schande

*Durch sein System der
schwarzen Kassen und seine
halsstarrige Verweigerung
von Auskünften demontiert
sich Helmut Kohl,
der Kanzler der deutschen
Einheit, selbst.*

SPIEGEL cover 52/1999
Fall into disgrace

*With his slush-fund system
and his stubborn refusal
to provide information,
"unification chancellor"
Helmut Kohl is tearing
down his own image.*

SPIEGEL-Titel 22/2001
Die Entmachtung
der Eltern

*In der Pubertät begehren
Heranwachsende gegen ihre
Eltern auf. Was können
Vater und Mutter tun,
um in dieser Lebensphase
den Kontakt zu ihren
Kindern nicht zu verlieren?*

SPIEGEL cover 22/2001
The divestment
of parents

*When they hit puberty,
adolescents rebel against
their parents. What can
mothers and fathers do
to stay in touch with their
children during this phase?*

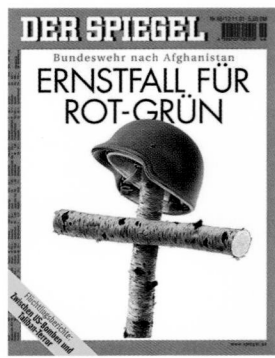

SPIEGEL-Titel 46/2001
Ernstfall für Rot-Grün

Erstmals nach dem Zweiten Weltkrieg soll die Bundeswehr in den Kampf ziehen. Der Einsatz in Afghanistan könnte die rot-grüne Koalition sprengen.

SPIEGEL cover 46/2001
Alarm for coalition

For the first time since World War II, the German army is supposed to go to war. The Afghanistan mission could blow up in the face of the coalition of Social Democrats and Greens.

SPIEGEL-Titel 8/2002
Die Bush-Krieger

*Im Kampf gegen den
Terror hat US-Präsident
George W. Bush den
Irak im Visier. In Europa
ist die Bereitschaft zu
einem Schlag gegen Saddam
Hussein jedoch gering.*

SPIEGEL cover 8/2002
Bush's warriors

*U.S. President George W.
Bush is targeting Iraq in
his war against terrorism.
In Europe, however, there
is little support for an attack
on Saddam Hussein.*

SPIEGEL-Titel 25/2001
Was man lesen muss

*Der Literaturkritiker
Marcel Reich-Ranicki stellt
seinen persönlichen Kanon
deutscher Dichtung
vor – Orientierungshilfe
für Schüler und erwachsene
Leser.*

SPIEGEL cover 25/2001
Must-read books

*Literary critic Marcel
Reich-Ranicki presents his
personal canon of German
literature - a guide for
students and adults alike.*

Putin und die Milliardäre
(unveröffentlicht 2003)

*Präsident Wladimir Putin
wird in Washington ebenso
umworben wie in Berlin –
die russische Wirtschaft
boomt. Jetzt legt sich
der Kreml-Herrscher mit
den Oligarchen im Land an.*

Putin and the billionaires
(unpublished 2003)

*Russian President Vladimir
Putin is being wooed by
both Washington and Berlin
- the Russian economy is
booming. Now, the head
of the Kremlin is going after
the country's oligarchs.*

Lafontaine und Gysi
(unveröffentlicht 2002)

*Die SPD streitet über
ihren Umgang mit der
SED-Nachfolgepartei PDS
und deren Galionsfigur
Gregor Gysi. Der Saar-
länder Oskar Lafontaine
will eine politische
Zusammenarbeit nicht
ausschließen.*

Lafontaine and Gysi
(unpublished 2002)

*The Social Democrats are
wrestling with the issue
of how they should deal with
the PDS, the successor to
East Germany's state party,
and its front man, Gregor
Gysi. Social Democratic
leader Oskar Lafontaine
does not want to rule
out political cooperation.*

SPIEGEL-Titel 10/1999
Das Ost-West-Gefühl

*Vor knapp zehn Jahren
fiel die Mauer, und mit ihr
erlosch die DDR.
Eine Bestandsaufnahme.*

SPIEGEL cover 10/1999
The east-west feeling

*Nearly 10 years ago, the
wall that divided Berlin fell,
and East Germany
soon collapsed. It's time
to take stock.*

RAFAL OLBINSKI

Geboren in Polen und ausgebildet am Warschauer Polytechnikum, emigrierte Rafal Olbinski 1981 in die Vereinigten Staaten. Dort etablierte er sich rasch als angesehener Maler, Illustrator und Designer. Seitdem sind seine Arbeiten häufig auf den Titelseiten internationaler Zeitschriften wie „Time", „Newsweek" oder DER SPIEGEL zu sehen. Für sein künstlerisches Schaffen erhielt Olbinski bereits über 150 Auszeichnungen, darunter auch Gold- und Silbermedaillen des Art Directors Club, New York, und der Society of Illustrators in New York und Los Angeles. 1994 bekam er in Paris den Prix Savignac verliehen, einen Preis für das bemerkenswerteste Poster der Welt. Ein Jahr später wurde ein von Olbinski entworfenes Motiv in einem Wettbewerb als „New York City Capital of the World"-Poster ausgewählt. Einige seiner Werke waren Teil der Installation „Grand Space" in der New Yorker Grand Central Station anlässlich der Aktionen zum Earth Day. Auch Keith Haring, Roy Lichtenstein, Robert Raushenberg und Andy Warhol waren hier vertreten. Rafal Olbinskis Arbeiten finden sich im National Arts Club in New York, in der Library of Congress in Washington, im Suntory Museum in Osaka und an vielen Orten Europas.

Born in Poland and educated at the polytechnic college in Warsaw, Rafal Olbinski emigrated to the United States in 1981. There, he soon established himself as a prominent painter, illustrator and designer. His work frequently appears on the covers of international magazines such as "Time", "Newsweek" and DER SPIEGEL. For his artistic achievement, he has already received more than 150 awards, including gold and silver medals from the Art Directors Club of New

York and the Society of Illustrators in New York and Los Angeles. In 1994, he was awarded the Prix Savignac, an international prize for the world's most memorable poster. In 1995, his poster was chosen as the official New York City Capital of the World poster in an invitational competition. A selection of his paintings was included in the "Grand Space" projection in Grand Central Station on the occasion of the Earth Day celebration in New York. The other artists featured in the show were Keith Haring, Roy Lichtenstein, Robert Raushenberg and Andy Warhol. Rafal Olbinski's paintings are included in the collections of the National Arts Club in New York, the Library of Congress in Washington, Suntory Museum in Osaka and throughout Europe.

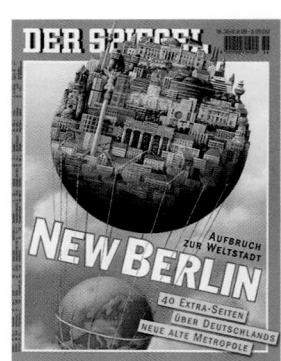

SPIEGEL-Titel 36/1999
New Berlin

Zwischen Vergangenheit und Zukunft sucht Berlin, die Baustelle der Nation, eine neue Identität.

SPIEGEL cover 36/1999
New Berlin

Caught between the past and the future, Berlin, Germany's biggest construction site, is searching for a new identity.

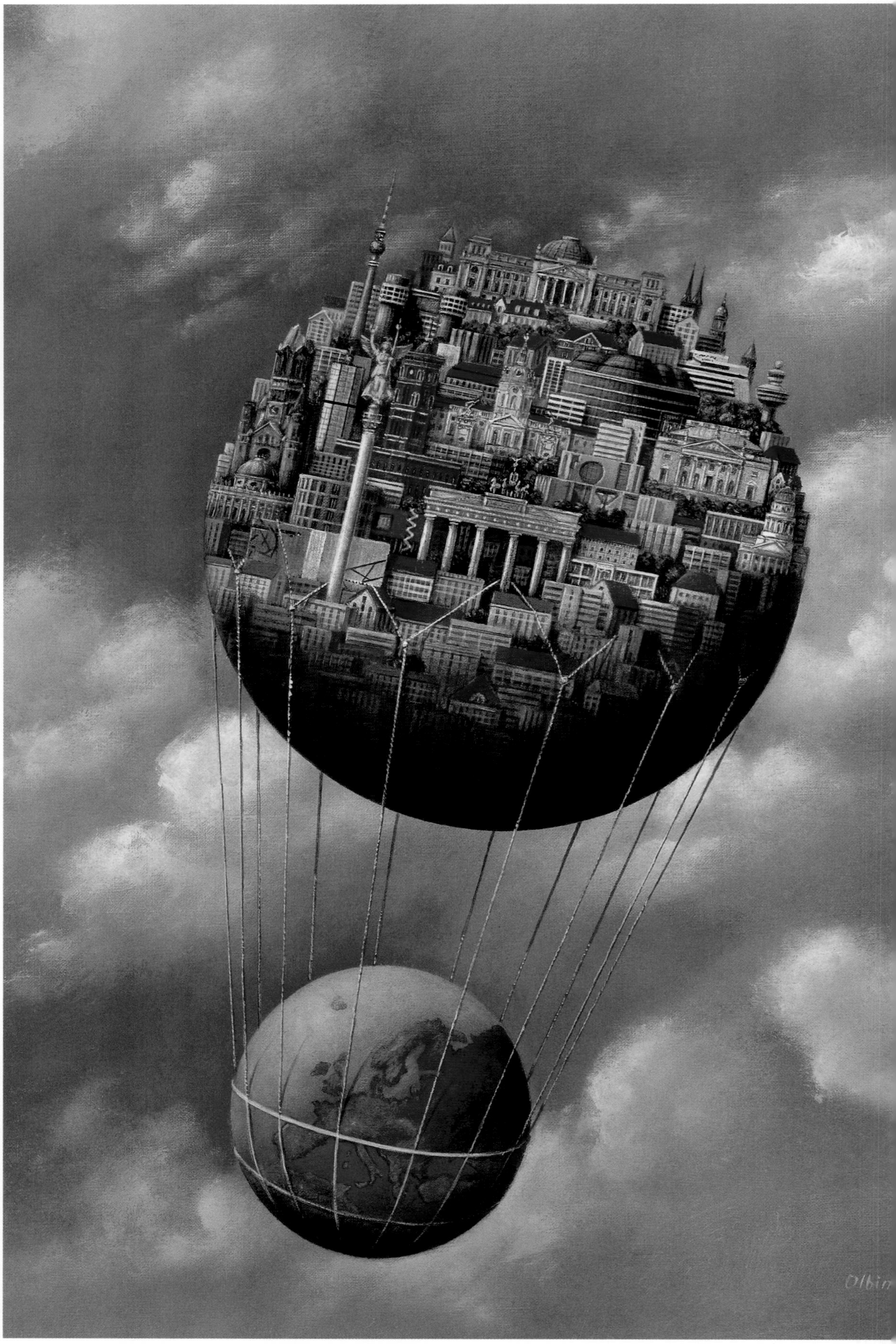

COURTESY OF GERALD D. WAGNER, NEW YORK CITY

SPIEGEL-Titel 36/2000
Was kann
Psycho-Therapie?

*Das neue Psychotherapeu-
tengesetz verhilft der
Branche zu staatlicher
Anerkennung. Doch der
Streit um die Wirksamkeit
von Therapieformen
geht weiter.*

SPIEGEL cover 36/2000
What can
psychotherapy do?

*The new psychotherapy
law accords the sector state
recognition. But the fight
over the effectiveness of
different therapies continues.*

SPIEGEL-Titel 2/2002
Das Ende des Universums

*Wann erlöschen die letzten
Sterne? Astrophysiker haben
herausgefunden, wie sich Son-
nen und Galaxien in ferner
Zukunft entwickeln werden.*

SPIEGEL cover 2/2002
The end of the universe

*When will the last stars be
extinguished? Astrophysicists
have discovered what will
happen to the suns and gal-
axies in the distant future.*

SPIEGEL-Titel 39/2002
Die blockierte Republik

*Ob Arbeitsmarkt,
Staatsbürokratie, Bildungs-
oder Gesundheitswesen –
der Reformbedarf ist riesig.
Die Rezepte sind bekannt,
doch Parteien und Verbände
verteidigen verbissen
den Status quo.*

SPIEGEL cover 39/2002
The republic in fetters

*From the job market to the
state bureaucracy and
education and health care
systems – the need for
reform is immense. The
recipes are well-known, but
parties and associations
are fiercely clinging to the
status quo.*

SPIEGEL-Titel 31/2003
Musik

*Forscher entschlüsseln,
wie sich physikalische
Schwingungen in Gefühle
verwandeln. Macht erst
die Musik den Menschen
zum sozialen Wesen?*

SPIEGEL cover 31/2003
Music

*Researchers decipher
how physical vibrations
translate into emotions.
Does man become a social
being through music?*

SPIEGEL-Titel 39/2003
**Wer arbeitet,
ist der Dumme**

*Die Kosten für die über-
forderten Wohlfahrtssysteme
tragen einseitig die Beschäf-
tigten. Längst hat sich die
Belastung des Faktors
Arbeit durch Steuern und
Abgaben zum Konjunktur-
killer entwickelt.*

SPIEGEL cover 39/2003
**Paying for the
privilege of work**

*The costs of overtaxed
welfare systems are borne
solely by employees.
The burden on labor caused
by taxes and payroll
withholdings has long
become a growth killer.*

SPIEGEL-Titel 18/2004
Das neue Europa

Am 1. Mai 2004 treten zehn neue Mitglieder in die EU ein. Die Osterweiterung wird die Gemeinschaft grundlegend verändern.

SPIEGEL cover 18/2004
The new Europe

Ten new members will join the EU on May 1, 2004. The eastward enlargement will fundamentally alter the union.

**Dem Frieden (k)eine Chance?
(unveröffentlicht 1999)**

Nach dem Bombenkrieg laufen jetzt Vorbereitungen für eine Invasion von Nato-Bodentruppen in Jugoslawien.

(No) chance for peace? (unpublished 1999)

After the bombing war, preparations for an invasion of Yugoslavia by NATO ground troops are now under way.

Putin und die Milliardäre (unveröffentlicht 2003)

Der russische Staats-präsident Wladimir Putin legt sich mit den Oligarchen im Land an.

Putin and the billionaires (unpublished 2003)

Russian President Vladimir Putin attacks the country's oligarchs.

WERNER BANDEL

the 1990s, he was a member of the team put together by the Canadian illusionist Doug Henning. Nearly all of the works produced by the independent artist become parts of private collections assembled by international art lovers.

Die Leitz-Kamera-Werke lagen in der Nähe, und so kam der 1951 in Wetzlar geborene Werner Bandel in Kontakt zur Fotografie. Von 1969 bis 1973 studierte er an der Kunsthochschule Kassel mit dem Schwerpunkt Experimentelle Fotografie. Malerei und Illustration lernte Werner Bandel als Autodidakt. Anfang der neunziger Jahre war er im Team des kanadischen Illusionisten Doug Henning. Nahezu sämtliche Arbeiten des freischaffenden Künstlers gehen inzwischen an private Sammlungen internationaler Kunstliebhaber.

Thanks to a nearby Leitz camera factory, photography caught the eye of Werner Bandel, who was born in Wetzlar, Germany, in 1951. From 1969 to 1973, he majored in experimental photography at the Kassel Art College. Werner Bandel taught himself painting and drawing. At the beginning of

Wie Glaube entsteht (unveröffentlicht 2002)

Warum Menschen Götter anbeten, lässt sich wissenschaftlich bislang nicht erklären. Hirnforscher suchen den Ursprung der Religion nun in einer bestimmten Hirnregion.

The genesis of belief (unpublished 2002)

Scientists have been unable to determine why humans pray to gods. Researchers are hunting for the fountain of religion in a particular region of the brain.

SPIEGEL-Titel 53/1998
Mythos Atlantis

Die Debatte um einen „historischen Kern" der angeblich im Meer versunkenen sagenhaften Insel Atlantis wurde durch Grabungsfunde neu entfacht.

SPIEGEL cover 53/1998
The myth of Atlantis

New archaeological discoveries have rekindled the debate about the "historical core" of Atlantis, the city that legend says sank into the sea.

ROBERT RODRIGUEZ

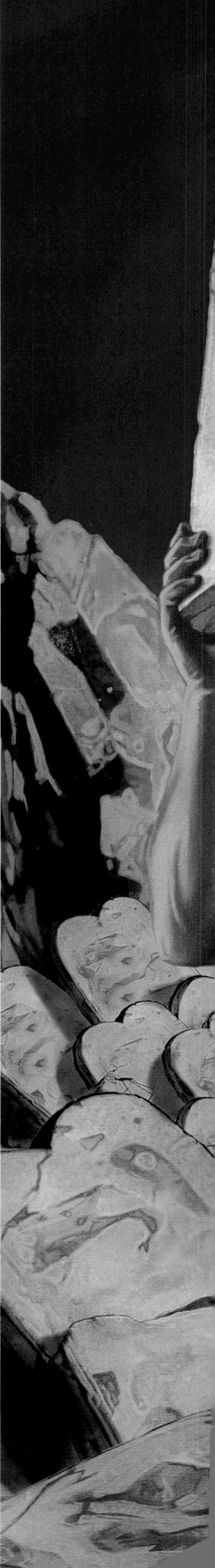

Geboren 1947 in New Orleans, lebt Robert Rodriguez seit 1965 in Kalifornien. Nach Abschluss seines Studiums am Chouinard Art Institute im Jahr 1969 arbeitete er als freischaffender Illustrator. In seiner Kindheit träumte Rodriguez davon, Trickfilmzeichner zu werden. Während eines Besuchs der Walt-Disney-Studios an seinem 14. Geburtstag kam die Ernüchterung: „Ich beobachtete, wie ein Trickfilmzeichner das gleiche Bild mit minimalen Abweichungen immer und immer wieder zeichnete. Es war faszinierend, aber ich wusste, dass das nichts für mich war." Seit jener „abschreckenden Erfahrung" wollte Rodriguez immer Illustrator werden.

Zunächst arbeitete er mit Acrylfarbe und Farbstiften. Dann wechselte er zu Ölfarben und begann auch, digital zu arbeiten. Der Computer ist gegenwärtig sein Hauptarbeitsmittel: „In den letzten vier Jahren sind sogar die wenigen Arbeiten, die ich noch in Öl gemalt hatte, gescannt und elektronisch abgegeben worden."

Der vielfach ausgezeichnete Künstler gestaltete mehrere Briefmarken, darunter die „Cinco de Mayo" – die erste Briefmarke, die von den USA gemeinsam mit einem anderen Staat (Mexiko) in Auftrag gegeben wurde.

Robert Rodriguez was born on May 3, 1947, in New Orleans and has lived in California since 1965. After completing his degree at the Chouinard Art Institute in 1969, he began working as a freelance illustrator. As a child, he dreamed of drawing animated cartoons. But that changed when he visited the Walt Disney Studios on his 14th birthday. "I watched an animator draw the same picture, with minor variations, over and over again. It was magical, but I knew that was not for me." After this "scary experience," Rodriguez set his sights on becoming an illustrator. At first, he worked with acrylic paint and color pencils. Then, he moved to oil paints and also began to work digitally. Today, the computer is his primary artistic tool. "Over the last four years or so, even the few pieces that were done in oils have been scanned and delivered electronically."

The winner of many awards has designed several stamps, including the "Cinco de Mayo" – that was the first stamp that the United States commissioned with another country (Mexico).

SPIEGEL-Titel 51/1999
Wo ist die Moral?

*Am Ende des Jahrtausends
steckt die Gesellschaft in
einer tiefen ethischen Krise.
Der Konsens darüber, was
gut und böse ist, schwindet.
Sind die Deutschen
ein Volk ohne Moral?*

SPIEGEL cover 51/1999
Where are the morals?

*At the end of the century,
society is mired in a deep
ethical crisis. The consensus
about good and evil is
vanishing. Are the Germans
a people without a moral
compass?*

215

SPIEGEL-Titel 21/2002
Der gedachte Gott

*Warum beten Menschen
Götter an? Wissenschaftler
suchen im Hirn nach dem
Ursprung der Religion.*

SPIEGEL cover 21/2002
The god in mind

*Why do people pray to gods?
Scientists look in the brain
for the fountain of religion.*

SPIEGEL-Titel 45/2000
Wohin steuert Amerika?

*Beim Kampf um die
US-Präsidentschaft liegen
George W. Bush und
Al Gore Kopf an Kopf –
aber die meisten
Amerikaner geben
sich desinteressiert und
selbstzufrieden.*

SPIEGEL cover 45/2000
Where is America
headed?

*George W. Bush and
Al Gore are locked in a
neck-and-neck presidential
race – but most Americans
show little interest in
the campaign and remain
complacent.*

JOHN MACDONALD

cover of "U. S. News" and "World Report" at the height of the Lewinsky scandal: "Talk about pressure!" MacDonald, who was born in Lafayette, Indiana, in 1957, studied painting and illustration at the Washington University in St. Louis. Before earning a living as a freelance illustrator, MacDonald painted oil landscapes that sold well in galleries. He also worked as a political cartoonist. John MacDonald lives with his wife and two sons in Williamstown, Massachusetts.

Die ihm wichtigste Arbeit ist John MacDonald ein Porträt des ehemaligen US-Präsidenten Bill Clinton für die Titelseite des „U. S. News and World Report" zum Höhepunkt der Lewinsky-Affäre: „Da stand ich unter echtem Druck!" Studiert hat der 1957 in Lafayette, Indiana, geborene MacDonald Malerei und Illustration an der Washington University in St. Louis. Bevor er als freischaffender Illustrator sein Geld verdiente, hatte MacDonald zunächst vor allem Landschaftsbilder in Öl gemalt, die sich in Galerien gut verkaufen ließen. Außerdem arbeitete er als politischer Karikaturist. John MacDonald lebt mit seiner Frau und zwei Söhnen in Williamstown, Massachusetts.

His most important project, John Mac-Donald says, was a portrait of the former U. S. President Bill Clinton he did for the

SPIEGEL-Titel 8/2000
Die www.Welt

*Das Online-Leben wird
zum Alltag, der Computer
gerät zum Lifestyle-Attri-
but. Das Internet beflügelt
die Wirtschaft.*

SPIEGEL cover 8/2000
The www.world

*Online life is becoming
our everyday reality, and
computers are becoming
lifestyle products. The
Internet is the force behind
the economy.*

SPIEGEL-Titel 3/2004
Die teure Billig-Uni

Überforderte Lehrer,
frustrierte Studenten,
marode Gebäude und
mittelmäßige Forschung –
die deutschen Universitäten
stehen vor dem Kollaps.
Studiengebühren könnten
ein Ausweg sein.

SPIEGEL cover 3/2004
The costly free university

Stressed-out lecturers,
frustrated students, ram-
shackle buildings and
mediocre research – German
universities are reaching
the breaking point. Tuition
could offer one way out.

**Die Party ist aus
(unveröffentlicht 2001)**

*Der Internet-Boom
ist zu Ende, die Aktienkurse
fallen ins Bodenlose. Viele
junge, noch vor kurzem
euphorisch gefeierte
Start-up-Unternehmen
gehen Pleite.*

**The party is over
(unpublished 2001)**

*The Internet boom is over;
stock prices are plummeting.
The euphoria of many
start-up businesses is turning into bankruptcy.*

GREGORY BRIDGES

sports, Gregory Bridges, who was born in Melbourne in 1951, exploited his creative potential early on. His mother, who was also an artist and lecturer of photography in Swinbourne, did all she could to support his talent. Gregory Bridges soon showed an interest in drawings on futuristic subjects and developed a fascination for surrealism when he discovered the work of Salvador Dalí in 1965. Bridges was particularly enthralled by Dalí's famous piece "The Burning Giraffe." Surreal art and science fiction continue to characterize Bridges' work, which has received numerous international awards. His clients are publishers and companies from around the world.

Weil er als Kind an einer seltenen Knochenkrankheit litt und keinerlei Sport treiben durfte, konzentrierte sich der 1951 in Melbourne geborene Gregory Bridges schon früh auf seine kreativen Möglichkeiten. Seine Mutter, Künstlerin und Dozentin für Fotografie in Swinbourne, förderte ihn dabei nach Kräften. Bald interessierte sich Gregory Bridges auch für Zeichnungen zu futuristischen Themen, und nachdem er 1965 die Arbeiten Salvador Dalís entdeckt hatte, faszinierte ihn der Surrealismus. Besonders angetan war Bridges von Dalís berühmtem Werk „Die brennende Giraffe". Surreale Kunst und Science Fiction prägen die international vielfach ausgezeichneten Arbeiten Bridges' bis heute. Seine Auftraggeber sind Verlage und Unternehmen aus aller Welt.

Because he suffered from a rare bone disease as a child and was not allowed to play any

SPIEGEL-Titel 11/2000
Unternehmen Größenwahn

Deutschland im Börsenrausch: Getrieben durch die Internet-Euphorie und eine gigantische Welle von Fusionen, erreichen Aktienwerte immer neue Rekorde. Doch wie lange noch? Viele Profiterwartungen gelten als unrealistisch.

SPIEGEL cover 11/2000
Market megalomania

Germany under the spell of the stock market: Driven by Internet euphoria and a huge merger wave, stock prices are climbing to ever new heights. But for how much longer? Many profit forecasts are considered to be totally unrealistic.

SPIEGEL-Titel 1/2001
Das Universum im Kopf

*Mit der Erforschung
des Bewusstseins stößt die
Wissenschaft an ihre
Grenzen: Ist das Gehirn
des Menschen mit seinem
Gewirr von Milliarden
Nervenzellen fähig,
sich selbst zu erkennen?*

SPIEGEL cover 1/2001
The universe in the mind

*Science is reaching its limits
in research of the human
conscience: Is the human
brain, with its web of
billions of neurons, capable
of recognizing itself?*

SPIEGEL-Titel 12/2001
Hightech-Welt 2001

Handys spielen Musik und verwalten Termine, Fotokameras zeichnen Videos auf. Bald soll jedes Gerät alles können. Allerdings – die Bedienung der Geräte überfordert schon heute viele.

SPIEGEL cover 12/2001
High-tech world 2001

Cell phones play music and manage appointments, photo cameras are recording videos. Soon every device is supposed to be able to do everything. But there's just one catch – many people are still befuddled by the equipment they already own.

CHRIS F. PAYNE

he studied art at Miami University in Ohio and completed training at the Illustrators Workshop in Terrytown, New York. From 1980, Payne worked as a freelance artist, above all for "Reader's Digest", "Time" magazine and "Rolling Stone" magazine. "DER SPIEGEL has now taken my work to the European continent and a new international audience." Payne has received several awards for his work, including gold and silver medals from the Society of Illustrators in New York and Los Angeles.

Seit seiner Kindheit habe er immer gewusst, was er später beruflich machen wolle, sagt Chris F. Payne: „Zeichnen". Geboren 1954 in Cincinnati, Ohio, studierte er Kunst an der Miami University in Ohio und absolvierte eine Ausbildung am Illustrators Workshop in Terrytown, New York. Seit 1980 arbeitet Payne als freischaffender Künstler vor allem für „Reader's Digest", „Time" und „Rolling Stone". Payne: „Nun hat DER SPIEGEL meine Arbeit nach Europa gebracht und damit einem neuen internationalen Publikum zugänglich gemacht."
Paynes Illustrationen wurden mehrfach ausgezeichnet, etwa mit Gold- und Silbermedaillen der Society of Illustrators in New York und Los Angeles.

Since his childhood, Chris F. Payne has always known what he wanted to do: "draw pictures." Born in 1954 in Cincinnati, Ohio,

SPIEGEL-Titel 33/2000
Die verwöhnten Kleinen

*Luxuskleidung, Reiz-
überflutung, innere
Verwahrlosung – Eltern
und Pädagogen suchen
nach Auswegen aus der
Verwöhnungsfalle.*

SPIEGEL cover 33/2000
The spoiled brats

*Luxury clothing, stimulus
overload, emotional neglect –
parents and educators
are looking for ways out of
the indulgence trap.*

SPIEGEL-Titel 46/2003
Klassenkrampf

*Der Berufsstand der Lehrer
steckt in der Krise.
Bildungsreformer wollen
Unterricht, Schule und
Ausbildung jetzt neu
organisieren. Machen die
Lehrer mit?*

SPIEGEL cover 46/2003
Class conflict

*The teaching profession
is in crisis. Education
policy makers want
to fundamentally reform
teaching, schools and
training. Will the teachers
go along?*

**Abgehauen
(unveröffentlicht 2001)**

*Wenn die Hormone
verrückt spielen, wächst
der Wunsch nach Distanz
und Abgrenzung von
Heranwachsenden zu
ihren Eltern.*

**Runaways
(unpublished 2001)**

*When the hormones start
to go crazy, adolescents
develop a growing desire to
get away from their parents.*

**Beute Kind
(unveröffentlicht 2002)**

Wenn Eltern sich trennen, werden Kinder im Scheidungskampf oft zu Opfern. In neuen Studien belegen Psychologen die fatalen Folgen.

**Children as loot
(unpublished 2002)**

When parents split up, children often become the victims of the divorce war. In new studies, psychologists highlight the fatal consequences.

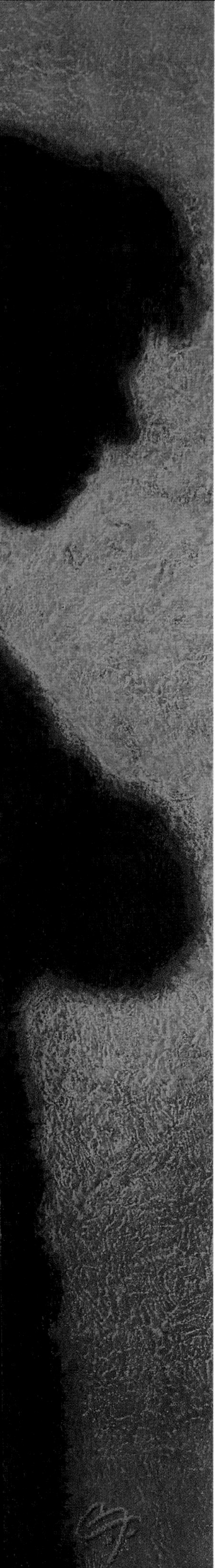

**Mobilmania
(unveröffentlicht 2004)**

*Für viele Jugendliche ist
das Handy zum Status-
symbol und zum beherr-
schenden Kommunikations-
mittel geworden.*

**Mobile mania
(unpublished 2004)**

*For many young people,
the cell phone has become
a status symbol and
the dominant means of
communication.*

HANNES BINDER

work on the scratch board most of all. The Swiss artist gets most of his jobs from magazines. Hannes Binder has received a number of awards and prizes, including the Prix TinTin for comics and the Troisdorfer Bilderbuchpreis (picture book prize).

Dass sein Vater Kunsterzieher war, sei für die eigene Karriere wegweisend gewesen, sagt Hannes Binder. Seine Ausbildung erhielt er in den Jahren 1964 bis 1967 an der Kunstgewerbeschule in Zürich. Der 1947 in der Schweiz geborene Grafiker, Layouter, Maler, Illustrator und Büchermacher arbeitet am liebsten am Scratch Board – vor allem für Zeitschriften und Illustrierte. Hannes Binder erhielt verschiedene Preise und Auszeichnungen wie den Prix TinTin für Comics sowie den Troisdorfer Bilderbuchpreis.

Hannes Binder points to his father's occupation as an art teacher as the key reason for his own artistic career. He received his training from 1964 to 1967 at the Zurich School of Applied Arts. The graphic artist, layout designer, painter, illustrator and book producer, who was born in 1947, likes to

SPIEGEL-Titel 20/2002
Dumm gelaufen

*Das schlechte Abschneiden
deutscher Schüler im
internationalen Vergleich
(Pisa-Studie) hat die
Politiker aufgerüttelt. Der
Umbau des Bildungssystems,
vom Kindergarten bis zur
Universität, ist überfällig.*

SPIEGEL cover 20/2002
Stairway to failure

*The poor performance
by German students on an
international test (Pisa)
has shaken political leaders.
An overhaul of the
education system, from
kindergarten to university,
is overdue.*

Falsches Spiel mit echten Mördern
(unveröffentlicht 2003)

Vor dem Irak-Krieg haben die USA die Welt belogen. Nach dem Feldzug bringen Attentate in Bagdad und Kritik an der Heimatfront George W. Bush in Bedrängnis.

Foul play with real killers
(unpublished 2003)

Before the Iraq war, the United States lied to the world. After the war, attacks in Baghdad and criticism at home are causing major trouble for George W. Bush.

SPIEGEL-Titel 24/2002
Die Droge Wichtigkeit

Politiker inszenieren sich wie Popstars. Die öffentliche Aufmerksamkeit ist der Kick, der sie antreibt, und Macht ist die Droge, die sie nicht loslässt.

SPIEGEL cover 24/2002
The drug: importance

Politicians act like pop stars. Public attention is what propels them, and power is the drug they're hooked on.

PARADA

ROBERTO PARADA

Ein Tag im Metropolitan Museum of Art in New York City veränderte sein Leben: Der Gang des achtjährigen Roberto Parada mit seiner Mutter durch die Ausstellung weckte eine anhaltende Leidenschaft für die Kunst. Von 1987 bis 1991 studierte der 1969 in New Jersey geborene Parada am Pratt Institute in Brooklyn, New York. Seit 1997 arbeitet er regelmäßig für das „Esquire Magazine". Roberto Parada malt bevorzugt mit Ölfarben auf Leinwand. Zu seinen bemerkenswertesten Illustrationen zählt er einen „Time"-Titel mit Saddam Hussein und einen Titel für das „Rolling Stone Magazine" mit dem Rapper Eminem. Seine Arbeiten sind in den Jahresausstellungen der Society of Illustrators zu sehen sowie bei Ausstellungen der American Illustration and Communication Arts.

A day in the Metropolitan Museum of Art in New York changed his life: A walk through the exhibition as an 8-year-old with his mother sparked a lasting passion for art. Between 1987 and 1991, Roberto Parada, who was born in New Jersey in 1969, studied at the Pratt Institute in Brooklyn, New York. He has been working regularly for "Esquire" magazine since 1997. Roberto Parada prefers oil on canvas. He includes among his most noteworthy illustrations a cover for "Time" magazine featuring Saddam Hussein and a cover for "Rolling Stone" magazine showing the rapper Eminem. His work is shown in the annual exhibitions of the Society of Illustrators as well as in exhibitions of the American Illustration and Communication Arts.

ROB BROOKS

Brooks is convinced that he has achieved his goal in life – particularly since he found the courage in the 1990s to earn his living solely by selling his work to galleries. Brooks prefers to work with oil on canvas. He says his greatest honor is to have his work appreciated by art lovers around the world. A happy artist: "Every day, I do something I love more than anything else: PAINT!"

Mit der Liebe zur Kunst sei er bereits auf die Welt gekommen, sagt der 1962 in Massachusetts geborene Rob Brooks: Die Kunst sei seine größte Leidenschaft, solange er denken könne. Mit 42 Jahren ist Brooks nun überzeugt davon, sein Lebensziel erreicht zu haben – vor allem, seit er in den neunziger Jahren den Mut fand, sein Einkommen ausschließlich durch den Verkauf seiner Bilder an Galerien zu finanzieren. Brooks arbeitet am liebsten mit Öl auf Leinwand. Größte Auszeichnung für ihn sei, dass weltweit Kunstliebhaber seine Arbeit schätzten, versichert er. Ein glücklicher Künstler: „Jeden Tag mache ich, was ich mehr als alles andere liebe: MALEN!"

Rob Brooks was born with a love of art, says the man whose life began in 1962 in Massachusetts. Art has been his biggest passion for as long as he can remember, he says. At 42,

SPIEGEL-Titel 26/2002
Radikal-Kur
gegen Arbeitslosigkeit

*Mit Hilfe eines
ungewöhnlichen Konzepts
will Bundeskanzler
Gerhard Schröder
die Arbeitslosigkeit
in Deutschland binnen
drei Jahren halbieren.*

SPIEGEL cover 26/2002
Radical cure
for unemployment

*Employing an unusual
concept, Chancellor
Gerhard Schröder wants
to cut German unemploy-
ment by half within three
years.*

237

MICHAEL PLEESZ

trator. Pleesz, who was born in Vienna in 1964, learned airbrush and other illustration techniques in a graphics studio. He has been working as a freelance illustrator since 1987 and has since replaced the airbrush with digital tools. He has also started working with oil and acrylic paints. In 2000, Michael Pleesz received an award from the German Art Directors Club for the "Playboy" illustration "The street sweep and death".

Während seiner Ausbildung von 1978 bis 1983 auf der Höheren Grafischen Bundes-, Lehr- und Versuchsanstalt in Wien erkannte Michael Pleesz, dass er als Illustrator arbeiten wollte. 1964 in Wien geboren, lernte Pleesz Airbrush- und andere Illustrationstechniken in einem Grafikstudio. Seit 1987 ist er als selbständiger Illustrator tätig. Airbrush ersetzte Pleesz inzwischen durch digitales Werkzeug. Gleichzeitig begann er, mit Ölfarben und Acryl zu arbeiten. Im Jahr 2000 erhielt Pleesz eine Auszeichnung vom deutschen Art Directors Club für die „Playboy"-Illustration „Der Straßenkehrer und der Tod".

It was during his education at the college of applied arts in Vienna, the Höhere Grafische Bundes-, Lehr- und Versuchsanstalt, between 1978 and 1983 that Michael Pleesz realized that he wanted to work as an illus-

Schlaue Mädchen, dumme Jungen (unveröffentlicht 2004)

Lange galten sie als die Stärkeren, doch nun geraten Jungen an den Schulen ins Hintertreffen: Mädchen lernen besser und haben eine größere soziale Kompetenz.

Clever girls, dumb boys (unpublished 2004)

They were long considered stronger, but now boys are falling behind in the schools: Girls learn more easily and are more socially competent.

SPIEGEL-Titel 47/2002
Genosse Schröder

Zu dringend nötigen Reformen kann sich Kanzler Gerhard Schröder nicht durchringen. Das Konzept der neuen Mitte ist passé, Schröder wendet sich den Gewerkschaften zu.

SPIEGEL cover 47/2002
Comrade Schröder

Chancellor Gerhard Schröder cannot bring himself to implement urgently needed reform. The concept of the new middle has been discarded. Now Schröder is turning to the unions.

JOHN HARWOOD

was 13. At the age of 17, the British artist, who was born in 1954, sold his pictures as artwork for posters and received commissions from race drivers who wanted to have pictures of their cars painted. Harwood studied technical design and became a freelance illustrator in 1975. He subsequently worked for a publishing house for several years before switching to advertising. John Harwood currently works mostly on the computer. His clients are major international corporations, such as Apple Computers.

Weil er bereits mehr Auszeichnungen erhalten hatte und häufiger auf Ausstellungen gezeigt wurde als sein Kunstlehrer, nahm John Harwood mit 13 Jahren nicht mehr am Kunstunterricht seiner Schule teil. 17-jährig verkaufte der 1954 geborene Brite seine Bilder als Poster-Vorlagen und erhielt Aufträge von Rennfahrern, die ihre Autos gemalt haben wollten. Harwood studierte Technikdesign und machte sich 1975 als Illustrator selbständig. Danach war er einige Jahre in einem Verlag beschäftigt und wechselte dann zur Werbung. Gegenwärtig arbeitet John Harwood vor allem am Computer. Seine Auftraggeber sind große internationale Konzerne, wie etwa Apple Computers.

Because his work had already received more awards and been shown at more exhibitions than that of his art teacher, John Harwood stopped taking art lessons at school when he

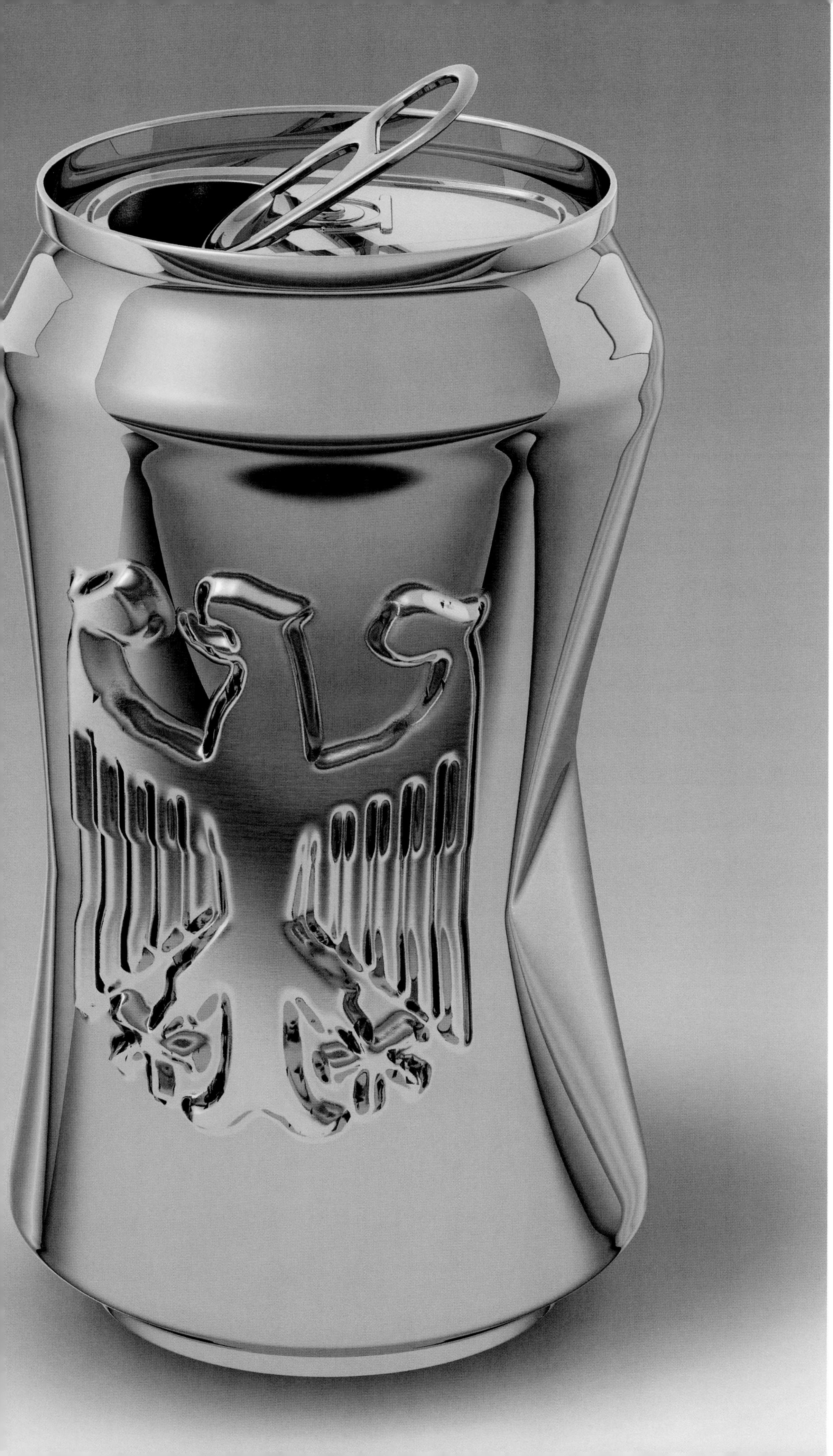

SPIEGEL-Titel 32/2003
Operation Dosenpfand

Eine gute Idee mündet im Chaos: Der seit Jahren andauernde Streit um ein Mehrwegsystem steht für die Reformunfähigkeit der gesamten Republik.

SPIEGEL cover 32/2003
Operation can deposit

A good idea has led to chaos: The years-long dispute over a recycling system for drink containers has come to represent Germany's general inability to reform.

SPIEGEL-Titel 33/2003
Erfundene Krankheiten

*Systematisch erfinden
Pharma-Firmen und Ärzte
neue Krankheiten. Die
Behandlung von Gesunden
sichert das Wachstum
der Medizinindustrie.*

SPIEGEL cover 33/2003
Invented illnesses

*Pharmaceutical companies
and doctors are systemati-
cally creating new sicknesses.
By treating healthy people,
they are taking good care
of the medical industry's
expansion.*

SANDRA SHAP

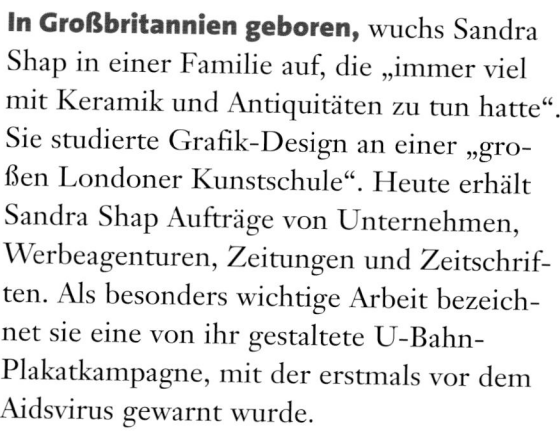

In Großbritannien geboren, wuchs Sandra Shap in einer Familie auf, die „immer viel mit Keramik und Antiquitäten zu tun hatte". Sie studierte Grafik-Design an einer „großen Londoner Kunstschule". Heute erhält Sandra Shap Aufträge von Unternehmen, Werbeagenturen, Zeitungen und Zeitschriften. Als besonders wichtige Arbeit bezeichnet sie eine von ihr gestaltete U-Bahn-Plakatkampagne, mit der erstmals vor dem Aidsvirus gewarnt wurde.

Sandra Shap, a British native, grew up in a family that "always had a lot to do with ceramics and antiques." From there, she went on to study graphic design at a "huge London art school." Today, Sandra Shap does projects for companies, advertising agencies, newspapers and magazines. She considers one of her most important works to be the tube posters she designed for the first campaign conducted against AIDS.

SPIEGEL-Titel 1/2004
Das Projekt Aufklärung

Der vor rund 200 Jahren gestorbene Philosoph Immanuel Kant hat das Nachdenken über Gott, das Weltall und den Menschen revolutioniert. Seine Ideen und kritischen Anstöße sind immer noch aktuell.

SPIEGEL cover 1/2004
The Enlightenment project

The philosopher Immanuel Kant, who died about 200 years ago, revolutionized concepts of god, space and humankind. His ideas and critical thoughts are as timely as ever.

MICHAEL DEAS

Weitgehend Autodidakt ist Michael J. Deas – inzwischen gilt er jedoch als einer der wichtigsten Illustratoren in den USA für altmeisterliche Öltechnik. Während der siebziger Jahre besuchte der 1956 in Norfolk, Virginia, geborene Deas zwar die New Yorker Art School; dort lernte er nach eigener Aussage allerdings „kaum etwas". Zu seinen bedeutendsten Aufträgen zählt Deas das von ihm entworfene Logo für Columbia Pictures sowie zwölf amerikanische Briefmarken. Seine Werke wurden im Norman Rockwell Museum und von der Society of Illustrators gezeigt, von der er vier Gold- und zwei Silbermedaillen für seine Arbeiten erhielt.

Michael J. Deas, who was born in Norfolk, Virginia, in 1956, mostly taught art to himself. Today, he is one of the most important illustrators in the United States who uses the oil techniques of the old masters. During the 1970s, he attended the New York Art School, but "learned hardly anything" there. Among his most important commissions are the logo for Columbia Pictures and 12 U. S. postage stamps. Deas' work has been shown by the Society of Illustrators and in the Norman Rockwell Museum. His illustrations have been honored with four gold and two silver medals from the Society of Illustrators.

DANIEL ADEL

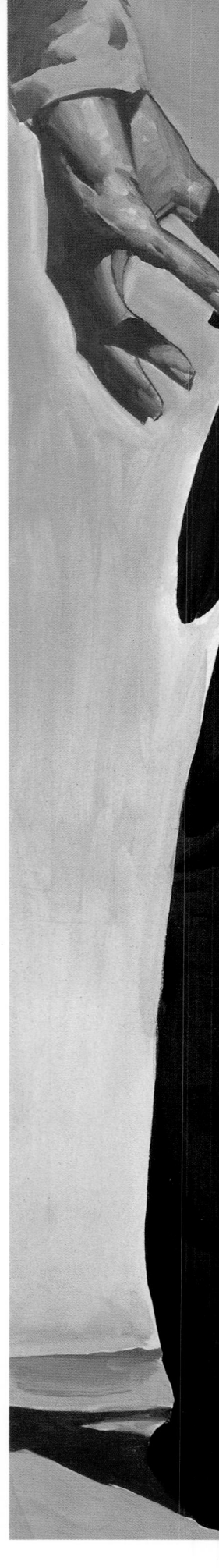

Design in New York. Daniel Adel prefers to work with oil. But, lately, he also has been using watercolors/dry brush. His career took a completely new turn in 1992 when Daniel Adel was asked for the first time to paint something funny and illustrate a children's book by Jon Scieszka ("Book That Jack Wrote"). Today, he does work for such publications as "Esquire" and "The New York Times" and illustrates book covers for Arianna Huffington, among others. Daniel Adel's work has been honored with one gold and one silver medal from the Society of Illustrators.

In New York City wurde Daniel Adel 1962 geboren. Er studierte Kunstgeschichte in Dartmouth und Figürliche Malerei an der National Academy of Design in New York. Bevorzugt arbeitet Daniel Adel mit Öl, in jügster Zeit aber auch gern mit Aquarell/ Drybrush. Dass er 1992 erstmals gebeten wurde, etwas Lustiges zu malen, und das Kinderbuch von Jon Scieszka („Book that Jack wrote") illustrierte, „hauchte meiner Karriere neues Leben ein". Heute arbeitet Adel unter anderem für „Esquire" und die „New York Times" und illustriert Buch- umschläge, etwa für Arianna Huffington. Seine Werke wurden bereits mit einer Gold- und einer Silbermedaille von der Society of Illustrators ausgezeichnet.

Daniel Adel was born in New York City in 1962. He studied art history at Dartmouth and drawing at the National Academy of

SPIEGEL-Titel 10/2004
Wird Amerika
wieder demokratisch?

*Kandidat der Demokraten
für die US-Präsidentschafts-
wahl ist John F. Kerry.
Bislang galt die Wieder-
wahl des Republikaners
George W. Bush als sicher.
Nun ist das Rennen wieder
offen.*

SPIEGEL cover 10/2004
Will America become
democratic again?

*John F. Kerry is the
Democratic presidential
candidate. Up to now, the
re-election of President
George W. Bush had been
considered a sure thing.
But now the race is on.*

Der kleine Sheriff (unveröffentlicht 2001)

Nach der Wahl von George W. Bush machte sich die ganze Welt lustig über den Neuen im Weißen Haus.

Little sheriff (unpublished 2001)

After George W. Bush was elected, the whole world made fun of the new man in the White House.

SPIEGEL-Titel 21/2004
Schlaue Mädchen, dumme Jungen

Die Leistungen von Mädchen an den Schulen werden immer bessser, während den Jungen häufig die Lernlust fehlt. Pädagogen sorgen sich um die Männer von morgen.

SPIEGEL cover 21/2004
Clever girls, dumb boys

Girls are performing better and better in schools. Boys, on the other hand, all too often lack the desire to learn. Educators are worried about the men of tomorrow.

THOMAS FLUHARTY

Das Malen sei ihm schon immer sehr leicht gefallen, sagt der 1962 im kalifornischen Santa Ana geborene Thomas Lively Fluharty: „Als ich meinen Eltern meine erste richtige Zeichnung zeigte, dachten sie, ich hätte sie durchgepaust." Nach dem Studium am Art Institute von Pittsburgh lernte er in New York von Ken Bald, der in den fünfziger Jahren Dr. Kildare-Cartoons und andere Marvel-Comics zeichnete. Außerdem besuchte Fluharty Kurse in Malerei und Zeichnen an der National Academy of Fine Arts sowie an der School of Visual Arts in New York.

1996 hatte er einen ersten großen Erfolg als Illustrator mit der Gestaltung eines Titels der Zeitschrift „Mad". Darauf folgten fünf Karikaturen von Jerry Lewis für die „New York Times": „Das setzte alles in Gang." Fluhartys Arbeiten wurden unter anderem in der Society of Illustrators Gallery gezeigt. Kunstpreise habe er bisher leider noch nicht gewonnen, sagt Fluharty, aber: „Meine wunderbare Familie, meine Frau Krissy und meine fünf Töchter, hat mich mit dem Preis ‚Bester Ehemann und Vater des Jahres' ausgezeichnet."

Thomas Lively Fluharty was born in Santa Ana, California, in 1962. Painting was something that always came easy to him. "When I showed my mom and dad my first real drawing, they thought that I'd traced it," Fluharty said. Following studies at the Art Institute of Pittsburgh, he trained in New York under Ken Bald, who drew Dr. Kildare cartoons and other Marvel Comics during the 1950s. In addition, he attended courses in painting and drawing at the National Academy of Fine Arts as well as at the School of Visual Arts in New York. In 1996, Thomas Lively Fluharty had his first major success as illustrator with the design of a cover for "Mad" magazine. After that, the "New York Times" commissioned Fluharty to do five caricatures of Jerry Lewis: "That really started it all." Fluharty's work has been shown in many places, including in the Society of Illustrators Gallery. Fluharty has yet to win any art awards. But "I've won the Best Husband and Father of the Year Award handed out by my wonderful family of my wife, Krissy, and five girls."

**Der Anfang war das Wort
(unveröffentlicht 2002)**

*Wann hat der Urmensch
das Sprechen gelernt?
Bei der Suche nach dem
Ursprung der Sprache
haben Wissenschaftler
erstaunliche Entdeckungen
gemacht.*

**In the beginning,
there was the word
(unpublished 2002)**

*When did prehistoric man
learn to speak? Scientists
have made astonishing
discoveries in their search
for the origins of language.*

**Die eingebildete
Weltmacht
(unveröffentlicht 2003)**

*Die USA sind unange-
fochten die Nummer eins
in der Welt. Aber die
Supermacht leidet an
Selbstüberschätzung und
Selbstüberforderung.*

**The big-headed
superpower
(unpublished 2003)**

*The United States is the
undisputed No. 1 power
in the world. But the
superpower overestimates
itself and has taken on more
than it can handle.*

ROBERT HUNT

Ein besonderes Ereignis löste bei Robert Hunt den Wunsch aus, Künstler zu werden – es war eine High-School-Exkursion zum San Francisco Museum of Modern Art und zur dortigen Pop-Art Wanderausstellung: „Ich war fasziniert von den Werken Warhols, von Rosenquists ‚F-111‘ und dem ‚Portable War Memorial‘ von Edward Kienholz. Damals erkannte ich, dass es in dieser Welt Menschen gibt, die Kunstwerke schaffen, und ich wollte einer von ihnen sein."

Robert Hunt studierte an der Universität von Berkeley Studio Art und Film und machte einen Abschluss in Kunstgeschichte. Danach besuchte er die Kunstakademie in San Francisco. Die Arbeiten von Robert Hunt sind vielfach prämiert (unter anderem zehn Gold- und vier Silbermedaillen von der San Francisco Society of Illustrators, darunter zwei „Best-in-show awards"): „Am stolzesten bin ich über die Aufnahme meiner Werke in die neueste Ausgabe des Buches „The Illustrator in America".

Asked whether he can pinpoint a particular event that triggered his desire to become an artist, Robert Hunt recalls a high school trip to the San Francisco Museum of Modern Art and the temporary pop art exhibition on display there. "I was fascinated by Warhol's works, Rosenquist's 'F-111' and the 'Portable War Memorial' by Edward Kienholz. At that point, I realized that there are people in this world who create art. And I wanted to be one of them," Hunt says now.

Robert Hunt studied studio art and film at the University of Berkeley, California, and earned a degree in art history before attending the Academy of Arts in San Francisco. His works have received numerous awards, among them ten gold and four silver medals from the San Francisco Society of Illustrators, including two best-in-show awards. "The inclusion of my work into the new edition of the Book 'The Illustrator in America' is what I am most proud of."

Herr der Gene
(unveröffentlicht 2002)

Die Entschlüsselung des menschlichen Genoms hat den umstrittenen US-Wissenschaftler Craig Venter reich und berühmt gemacht.

Lord of the genes
(unpublished 2002)

The controversial U.S. scientist Craig Venter has won riches and fame by decoding the human genome.

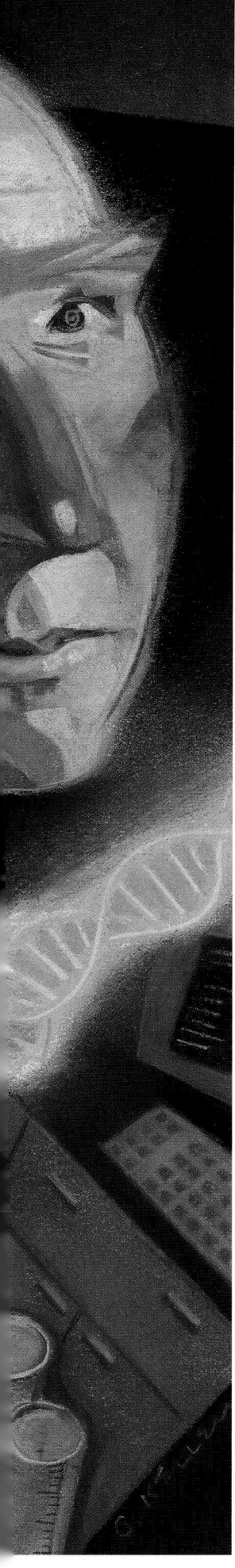

GARY KELLEY

Pastellfarben bevorzugt Gary Kelley, aber
er arbeitet auch gern in Öl. Geboren 1945
in Algona, Iowa, studierte Kelley an der
University of Northern Iowa. Noch während
seiner Schulzeit jobbte er bei einem Schil-
dermaler, danach als Grafik-Designer. Während dieser Zeit wurde sein Interesse an
Malerei und Illustrationen geweckt. Heute
arbeitet Gary Kelley für verschiedene Verlage wie Bantam und Kensington sowie für
Magazine und private Auftraggeber.

Gary Kelley prefers pastels, but he also
likes to work with oil paints. Born in Algona,
Iowa, in 1945, he attended the University
of Northern Iowa. While he was still at high
school, he worked for a sign painter and later
as a graphic designer. During this time, he
developed an interest in painting and illustration. Today, Gary Kelley works for such
publishers as Bantam and Kensington as well
as for magazines and private customers.

LIZ LOMAX

wire armature. They are then baked in an oven and painted with oils. For the CowParade in New York, she created a life-size sculpture of a cow ("Angelicow"). The original was subsequently acquired in a charity auction by former Beatle Ringo Starr for his private collection. Miniature "Angelicows" have been sold all over the world. Liz Lomax has received a multitude of awards and worked for such magazines as "Rolling Stone", "Time", "Newsweek" and DER SPIEGEL.

Die 1975 in New York geborene Künstlerin Liz Lomax ist eine führende Vertreterin der dreidimensionalen Illustration. Mit Fimo-Masse und Drahtgerüsten stellt sie Figuren und deren Umwelt her, härtet sie im Ofen und bemalt sie mit Ölfarbe. Für die CowPa-rade in New York schuf Liz Lomax die lebensgroße Skulptur einer Kuh („Angeli-cow"). Ex-Beatle Ringo Starr ersteigerte das Werk anschließend auf einer Benefiz-Veran-staltung für seine eigene Sammlung. Minia-tur-Angelicows wurden in alle Welt verkauft. Die vielfach ausgezeichnete Künstlerin arbeitet unter anderem für Magazine wie „Rolling Stone", „Time", „Newsweek" und DER SPIEGEL.

Born in New York City in 1975, Liz Lomax is a leading representative of her field, three-dimensional illustration. She creates figures and their environment using Sculpey on a

**Mobilmania
(unveröffentlicht 2004)**

*Das Mobiltelefon hat
sich rasant in der
Gesellschaft verbreitet.
Für viele Jugendliche ist
es zum unentbehrlichen
Lebensmedium geworden.*

**Mobile mania
(unpublished 2004)**

*Cell phones have conquered
our society in no time. For
many adolescents, they have
become an indispensable
medium of life.*

JOHN MARTIN

Initially, John Martin's preferred medium was oil paint, but a severe allergy forced him to switch to a new technique. Now, acrylic paint has become his main medium, although he has also returned to drawing with pen and ink as well as photography. John Martin was born in Toronto, Canada, in 1939. He studied at the Ontario College of Art in Toronto. Between 1967 and 1971, he dedicated himself almost exclusively to his musical interests and traveled extensively throughout Europe, North Africa and Asia. When he returned in 1972, he and four partners formed a design company that worked mostly for the music industry. Since 1980, John Martin has concentrated on illustration. He has won many acclaimed awards, including from the Chicago Art Directors Club and the American Institute of Graphic Arts.

Zunächst arbeitete John Martin am liebsten mit Ölfarben, eine heftige Allergie zwang ihn jedoch zum Wechsel: Nun bevorzugt er Acryl, aber auch Feder und Tinte sowie Fotografie. John Martin wurde 1939 im kanadischen Toronto geboren, wo er später am Ontario College of Art studierte. Zwischen 1967 und 1971 widmete er sich fast ausschließlich seinen musikalischen Interessen und unternahm ausgedehnte Reisen nach Europa, Nordafrika und Asien. Zurückgekehrt gründete er mit Partnern 1972 eine Design-Firma, die vor allem für die Musikindustrie tätig war. Seit 1980 konzentriert sich John Martin im Wesentlichen auf Illustrationen. Viele seiner Arbeiten wurden mit renommierten Preisen ausgezeichnet, etwa vom Chicago Art Directors Club oder dem American Institute of Graphic Arts.

**Was man lesen muss
(unveröffentlicht 2001)**

*Der Literaturkritiker
Marcel Reich-Ranicki stellt
seine persönliche Liste der
ihm wichtigsten Bücher vor.*

**Must-read books
(unpublished 2001)**

*Literary critic Marcel
Reich-Ranicki presents
his personal list of the books
that are most important
to him.*

WILSON MCLEAN

Although he attended an art college, Wilson McLean considers himself an autodidact. McLean, who was born in Glasgow, Scotland, in 1937 and grew up in London, developed his interest in painting early on: "As a young boy I realized that I enjoyed drawing more than anything else, and the streets of Glasgow were a great place for chalk drawings!" One of his favorite techniques is oil on canvas. Looking back, he now considers his decision at the age of 28 to move to New York and "make a fresh start" as a turning point in his career. Today, Wilson McLean works for film studios like Paramount, publishing houses, theaters and magazines. He has received various awards, including gold and silver medals from the New York Society of Illustrators.

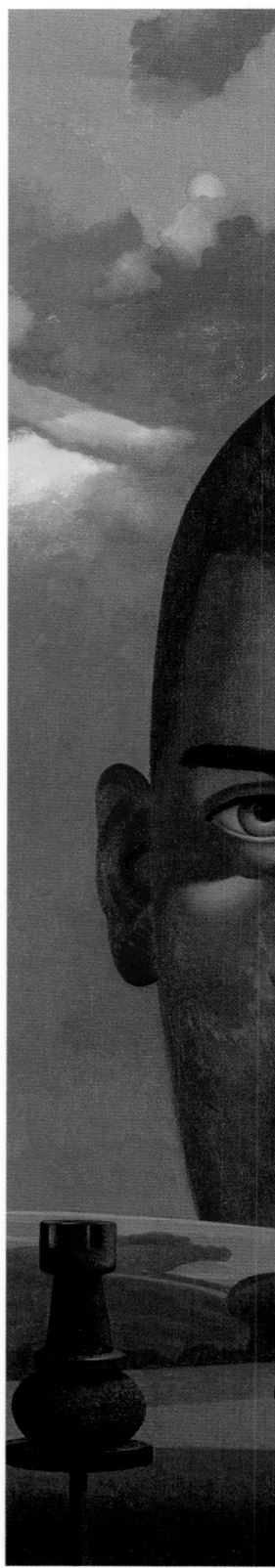

Obwohl er eine Kunsthochschule besuchte, betrachtet sich Wilson McLean als Autodidakt. Sein Interesse an Malerei wuchs früh: „Als kleiner Junge merkte ich, dass mir Zeichnen mehr Spaß als andere Dinge machte, und die Straßen von Glasgow waren ein gutes Pflaster für Kreidezeichnungen!" Zu den bevorzugten Techniken zählt der 1937 in Glasgow geborene und in London aufgewachsenen Wilson McLean Öl auf Leinwand. Seine Entscheidung, mit 28 Jahren nach New York zu ziehen und „neu anzufangen", sieht er als beruflichen Wendepunkt. Heute arbeitet McLean für Filmstudios wie Paramount, für Verlage, Theater und Zeitschriften. Seine Arbeiten wurden mehrfach ausgezeichnet, etwa mit Gold- und Silbermedaillen der New Yorker Society of Illustrators.

**Was fühlen Tiere?
(unveröffentlicht 2001)**

*Neue Entdeckungen von
Zoologen zeigen:
Das Seelenleben von Tieren
ist komplexer als bislang
angenommen.*

**What do animals feel?
(unpublished 2001)**

*Zoologists have discovered
that the animal soul is more
complex than previously
thought.*

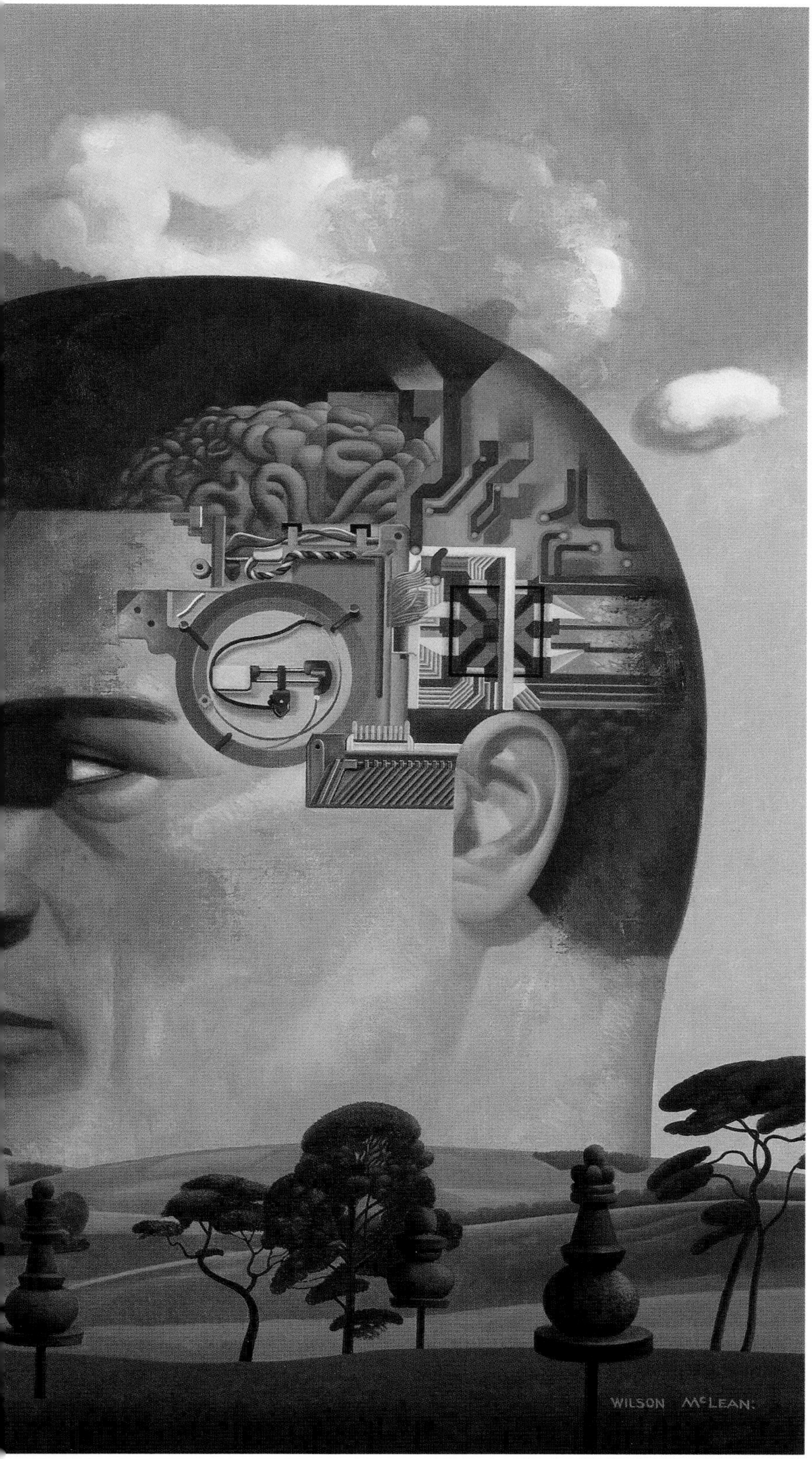

**Mensch gegen Maschine
(unveröffentlicht 1997)**

*Schachweltmeister
Garri Kasparow tritt
gegen den Super-Rechner
„Deep Blue" an.
Wie intelligent kann ein
Computer sein?*

**Man vs. machine
(unpublished 1997)**

*Chess world champion
Garry Kasparov
is competing against the
mega-computer "Deep
Blue". How intelligent can
a computer be?*

259

O Italien!
(unveröffentlicht 2003)

*Sommertheater 2003:
Die Liebe der Deutschen
zu Italien leidet unter
giftigen Äußerungen eines
Tourismus-Staatssekretärs
in Rom. Kanzler Schröder
sagt seine Urlaubsreise ab.*

O Italy!
(unpublished 2003)

*Summer theater 2003:
The Germans' love for Italy
is dampened by nasty
remarks from a state
secretary in charge of
tourism in Rome. Chancellor
Gerhard Schröder calls
off his vacation in Italy.*

Neue Heimat Süd
(unveröffentlicht 2001)

*Immer mehr Deutsche
wandern aus und werden
im Süden Europas sesshaft.*

Moving south
(unpublished 2001)

*More and more Germans
are leaving Germany to
settle in southern Europe.*

MARCO VENTURA

Seine gesamte Familie ist der Kunst zugetan: Der Vater von Marco Ventura arbeitet als Kinderbuchautor und Illustrator, die Mutter ist ebenfalls Künstlerin, sein Bruder Andrea ist ein bekannter Illustrator, ein anderer Bruder Fotograf. Marco Ventura wurde 1963 in Mailand geboren, wo er mit seiner Frau (Illustratorin) und seinen drei Kindern lebt. Er studierte an der Accademia di Belle Arti di Brera in Mailand sowie an der School of Visual Arts in New York. Nach Abschluss seiner Ausbildung kehrte Ventura nach Mailand zurück, wo er vier Jahre lang in einem Grafik-Design-Studio arbeitete. Seit 1989 ist er freiberuflich tätig für Zeitschriften wie „Atlantic Monthly", „Time", und DER SPIEGEL sowie für Verlage wie dtv und Penguin Putnam. Außerdem gestaltete Ventura mehrere Briefmarken für die britische Royal Mail. Mehrfach wurden seine Arbeiten ausgezeichnet, etwa mit Silbermedaillen der American Society of Illustrators und des Italienischen Art Directors Club.

Marco Ventura comes from an artistic family: His father is a children's book author and illustrator, his mother an artist, his brother Andrea a well-known illustrator and another brother is a photographer. Marco Ventura was born in Milan, Italy, in 1963 and still lives there with his wife (also an illustrator) and their three children. He studied at the Accademia di Belle Arti di Brera in Milan as well as at the School of Visual Arts in New York. After completing his training, Ventura returned to Milan, where he spent four years working in a graphic design studio. Since 1989, he has been working as a freelance illustrator for such magazines as "Atlantic Monthly", "Time" and DER SPIEGEL, and for pub-

lishing houses like dtv and Penguin Putnam. In addition, Ventura has designed several stamps for the British Royal Mail. He has received several awards, including silver medals from the American Society of Illustrators and the Italian Art Directors Club.

Register
Index

Boris Artzybasheff
32. Närrische Streiche der Barmherzigkeit, 1956, Gouache auf Karton, Leihgabe der Syracuse University Art Collection, USA, 30,5 x 25,4 cm
34. Kopf aus dem Sand, 1957, Gouache auf Karton, Leihgabe der Syracuse University Art Collection, USA, 29,5 x 24,8 cm
35. Die Seele ist ein Eisberg, 1959, Skizze, Bleistift auf Transparent-Zeichenpapier, Leihgabe der Syracuse University Art Collection, USA, 32,1 x 26,7 cm

Bernard Buffet
37. Kanzler Erhard, 1963, Öl auf Leinwand, Leihgabe von Leo Brawand, 89 x 72 cm

Hermann Degkwitz
39. Maos letztes Gefecht, 1967, Aquarell, 38,8 x 30,8 cm
40. Charles de Gaulle, 1967, Aquarell, 39 x 31,1 cm
40. CDU-Parteitag, 1967, Aquarell, 37,8 x 31 cm
41. Rettung durch neuen Kurs?, 1967, Aquarell, 40,6 x 32,7 cm
41. Moskaus größter Spion, 1968, Aquarell, 38 x 31 cm
42. Karl Marx, 1968, Aquarell, 37,8 x 30,9 cm
43. Moskaus Bild der Deutschen, 1969, Aquarell, 37,8 x 30,8 cm
44. Papst in Bedrängnis, 1969, Aquarell, 37,9 x 30,8 cm
44. Amerikas Militärmaschine, 1969, Aquarell, 39,8 x 32,4 cm
45. Die DDR nach Ulbricht, 1971, Aquarell, 38 x 31 cm
46. China, 1974, Aquarell, 37,8 x 31 cm
47. Kanzler in der Krise (unveröffentlicht), 1973, Aquarell, 37,8 x 31 cm
48. Der Höhenflug von Genf, 1985, Aquarell, 50,9 x 36,5 cm
49. Friedrich, 1986, Aquarell, 47,4 x 39,8 cm

Vicco von Bülow/Loriot
50. Wahl-Krampf um ein Wort, 1976, Feder auf Karton, 15 x 15 cm

Ursula Arriens
53. Sieg der Roten?, 1978, Tempera-Grundierung und Farbstift auf Karton, 66,1 x 52,4 cm
54. Chaos im Iran, 1979, Tempera-Grundierung und Farbstift auf Karton, 27,9 x 21,2 cm
55. 100 Jahre Stalin, 1979, Tempera-Grundierung und Farbstift auf Karton, 46,6 x 38,9 cm
56. Kommunismus reparabel?, 1980, Tempera-Grundierung und Farbstift auf Karton, 27,8 x 21,2 cm
56. Kanzlers letzter Einsatz, 1981, Tempera-Grundierung und Farbstift auf Karton, 31,7 x 23,9 cm
57. Thatcher gegen Europa, 1984, Tempera-Grundierung und Farbstift auf Karton, 31,2 x 22,7 cm
58. Wer ist der Dr. Vogel?, 1983, Tempera-Grundierung und Farbstift auf Karton, 29,8 x 21,9 cm
59. Herbert Wehner (unveröffentlicht), 1983, Tempera-Grundierung und Farbstift auf Karton, 48,2 x 39,3 cm

Hans-Georg Rauch
60. Castro's Cuba: Muster ohne Wert, 1980, Feder auf Karton, 22,6 x 19,7 cm

Michael M. Prechtl
62. Der Papst in Luthers Land, 1980, Feder in Sepia, Aquarell, Karton, 32 x 20,4 cm
65. Täter Hitler/Denker Nietzsche, 1981, Feder in Sepia, Aquarell, Karton, 28 x 21,4 cm
66. Zweifel an Freud, 1984, Feder in Sepia, Aquarell, Karton, 34 x 24 cm
67. Bayern-König Ludwig II., 1986, Feder in Sepia, Aquarell, Karton, 32 x 23 cm
67. Liebe und Verbrechen, 1990, Feder in Sepia, Aquarell, Karton, 30 x 24 cm
68. Denk ich an Deutschland…, 1997, Feder in Sepia, Aquarell, Karton, 34 x 24 cm
69. Der Dichter und der Schwefelgelbe, 1998, Feder in Sepia, Aquarell, Papier, 38,8 x 28,7 cm

Jean Solé
70. Revolution im Sowjet-Block, 1981, Feder und Pinsel auf Karton, 31,2 x 27,7 cm

Tilman Michalski
72. Die Angst der Deutschen, 1982, Mischtechnik auf Karton, 33,7 x 27,5 cm
74. Vereint, aber fremd, 1990, Michtechnik auf Karton, 29,3 x 26,2 cm
74. Deutsche gegen Deutsche, 1992, Mischtechnik auf Karton, 43,7 x 29,5 cm
75. Beamte weg?, 1991, Mischtechnik auf Karton, 40,9 x 31,1 cm
76. Weltmacht Deutschland (unveröffentlicht), 1993, Mischtechnik auf Karton, 40,1 x 30,1 cm
77. Vogel oder Kohl? (unveröffentlicht), 1983, Mischtechnik auf Karton, 29 x 24 cm

Horst Haitzinger
79. Was ist dran am Aufschwung?, 1983, Aquarell, 43,9 x 31,2 cm

Dieter Wiesmüller
80. Überall ist Seveso, 1983, Tempera auf Karton, 50,8 x 39,9 cm
82. Tempo 100, 1984, Tempera auf Karton, 35,9 x 28 cm
83. Reizthema Abtreibung, 1991, Tempera auf Karton, 47 x 34,5 cm
84. Ein Weltreich zerbricht, 1991, Tempera auf Karton, 46,8 x 37,5 cm
86. Deutsche in den Krieg?, 1993, Tempera auf Karton, 50,1 x 37,7 cm
87. Wer kriegt was?, 2000, Tempera auf Karton, 50 x 39,2 cm
88. Anschlag auf TWA-Jumbo (unveröffentlicht), 1996, Acryl auf Karton, 42 x 26,1 cm
89. Lauschangriff (unveröffentlicht), 1990, Tempera auf Karton, 40,7 x 31,9 cm
90. Olympische Spiele (unveröffentlicht), 1993, Tempera auf Karton, 48 x 37,9 cm
91. Russland läuft Amok (unveröffentlicht), 1996, Tempera auf Karton, 44,7 x 31,6 cm

Alfons Kiefer
93. Gewalt gegen Eltern, 1983, Acryl auf Karton, 51 x 42,9 cm
94. Der Steuer-Bluff, 1987, Acryl auf Karton, 60 x 49,3 cm
95. Vorsicht! Versicherung, 1994, Acryl auf Karton, 72,8 x 48,8 cm
96. Wem gehört Mallorca?, 1999, Acryl auf Karton, 99,7 x 80,2 cm
97. Die Aufklärer: Wer lügt?, 2000, Acryl auf Karton, 71,8 x 60 cm
98. Droge Macht, 2001, Acryl auf Karton, 64,5 x 45,6 cm
99. Der letzte Deutsche, 2004, Acryl auf Karton, 52,7 x 33,8 cm
100. Das Duell (unveröffentlicht), 2002, Acryl auf Karton, 89,7 x 75 cm
101. Der Pate (unveröffentlicht), 2003, Acryl auf Karton, 50,1 x 33,8 cm

Mathias Waske
103. Maria, 1983, Öl auf Holz, 79,5 x 57,5 cm
103. Michail Gorbatschow (unveröffentlicht), 1991, Öl auf Holz, 63,5 x 45,4 cm

Rita Mühlbauer
105. Anthroposophen in Deutschland, 1984, Mischtechnik auf Karton, 30,1 x 22,8 cm
105. Bauen mit der Natur, 1984, Mischtechnik auf Karton, 27,1 x 21,2 cm

Peter Schössow
106. Verlotterte Republik, 1993, Bleistift, Buntstift, Mischtechnik auf Karton, 28,9 x 25 cm
108. Gaukler oder Heiler, 1994, Bleistift, Buntstift, Mischtechnik auf farbigem Papier, 32,7 x 26,9 cm
109. Banken im Gewinnrausch: Das große Geld (unveröffentlicht), 1986, Airbrush, Tusche, Mischtechnik auf Karton, 25 x 21 cm
109. Brauchen wir Eliten? (unveröffentlicht), 1994, Airbrush, Tusche, Mischtechnik auf Karton, 27,4 x 23,5 cm

Friedrich de Boer
110. Die sanfte Heilkunst, 1985, Mischtechnik auf Karton, 72,8 x 49,8 cm

Hans Ulrich Osterwalder
113. Aids, 1986, Airbrush, Acryl auf Leinen, 99,7 x 69,7 cm

Dewa Waworka
114. Kohls gefährlicher Gehilfe, 1986, Acryl auf Hartfaser, 38,3 x 35,3 cm, Leihgabe von Michael Hartmann
116. Mission in Moskau, 1987, Acryl auf Hartfaser, 38,8 x 28,8 cm, Leihgabe von Michael Hartmann
117. RAF – Herbst des Terrors, 1997, Acryl auf Hartfaser, 40,1 x 30,1 cm
118. Der verlogene Wahlkampf, 1998, Acryl auf Hartfaser, 40,1 x 30,1 cm
119. Ein Mann sieht rot, 1999, Acryl auf Hartfaser, 38,1 x 29,9 cm
120. Marlene, 2000, Acryl auf Hartfaser, 41,4 x 30 cm
121. Der Bruch, 2000, Acryl auf Hartfaser, 40 x 30,1 cm
122. Der künstliche Kindersegen, 2002, Acryl auf Hartfaser, 39,9 x 30 cm
123. Generation Ich, 2000, Acryl auf Hartfaser, 40,1 x 30 cm
123. Moloch Medizin (unveröffentlicht), 1999, Acryl auf Hartfaser, 40,2 x 30,2 cm

Peter Krämer
125. Die Republik wird schwarz, 1987, Airbrush, 67,1 x 66,9 cm
126. Der Gen-Fraß, 1993, Airbrush, 65,7 x 50 cm
127. Das Stromkartell (unveröffentlicht), 1995, digital, 60 x 44 cm

Marie Marcks
128. Deutsch: Ächz, Würg, 1984, Buntstift auf Papier, 33,5 x 29,5 cm
130. Tollhaus Schule, 1988, Feder auf Papier, 22,8 x 22,1 cm
131. Frauen – Opfer der Einheit (unveröffentlicht), 1990, Aquarell, 29,9 x 19,9 cm

Kinuko Craft
133. Japan intim, 1988, Gouache über Federzeichnung auf Papier, 50,2 x 40,9 cm, Leihgabe von Rainer Wörtmann

Uwe Brandi
134. Gefahr für den Wohlstand?, 1990, Feder auf Karton, 25,9 x 22,9 cm

Dietrich Ebert
136. Die erstarrte Republik (unveröffentlicht), 1996, kolorierte Zeichnung, 40,4 x 30,3 cm
136. Dr. Arbeitslos, 1993, kolorierte Zeichnung, 24,5 x 33,8 cm

Nils Fliegner
139. Der Osten is' stark, 1994, Collage, 41,9 x 29,7
139. Sind deutsche Schüler doof?, 2001, digital, 43,3 x 31,9 cm

Silke Bachmann
140. Die roten Mörder (unveröffentlicht), 1998, Öl auf Leinwand, 80 x 60 cm
140. Feldzug der Moralisten, 1995, Öl auf Leinwand, 49,7 x 40,2 cm

Ludvik Glazer-Naudé
143. Wer ist Ich?, 1996, Acryl auf Hartfaser, 60,5 x 49 cm
144. Der göttliche Teufel, 1996, Acryl auf Hartfaser, 70,3 x 60,3 cm
146. Zeit: Die große Illusion, 1998, Acryl auf Hartfaser, 100 x 70 cm
147. Die Psycho-Falle, 1998, Acryl auf Hartfaser, 70,8 x 50,8 cm
148. Gottes Urknall, 1998, Acryl auf Hartfaser, 70 x 100 cm
149. Casanova (unveröffentlicht), 1998, Acryl auf Hartfaser, 70 x 49,6 cm

Tom Jütz
150. Nichts geht mehr, 1997, Airbrush, Mischtechnik
auf Karton, 39,6 x 27,7 cm
151. Absturz Ost, 1996, Acryl auf Leinwand,
62,7 x 55,1 cm

Braldt Bralds
153. Mythos Ché Guevara, 1996, Öl auf Hartfaser,
35,3 x 27,7 cm
154. Mephisto Goethe, 1999, Öl auf Hartfaser,
47,1 x 38,7 cm
155. Das Gehirn des Jahrhunderts, 1999, Öl auf Hartfaser,
40,4 x 34,3 cm
155. Bruder Affe, 2000, Öl auf Hartfaser, 38 x 32,4 cm
156. Die Manns, 2003, Öl auf Leinwand, 39,5 x 31,5 cm
157. Mordfall Jesus Christus (unveröffentlicht), 2004,
Öl auf Hartfaser, 51,8 x 44,8 cm

Mark Entwisle
159. Im Keller, 1997, Aquarell, 38 x 28,3 cm
160. Im Keller, 1997, Aquarell, o.l. 38,1 x 29,4 cm,
o. r. 38,1 x 28,4 cm, u. l. 38,1 x 28,2 cm,
u. r. 38,1 x 28,4 cm
161. Im Keller, 1997, Aquarell, o. 38,2 x 27,4 cm,
u. 28,1 x 39,2 cm

Tim O'Brien
163. Abenteuer Euro, 1997, Öl auf Karton, 40,6 x 30,5 cm
164. Aufräumen wie in New York?, 1997, Öl auf Karton,
38 x 25,5 cm
165. Abschied von der Mark, 1998, Öl auf Karton,
23,7 x 29,2 cm
166. Die Kirche und der Holocaust (unveröffentlicht),
1997, Öl auf Karton, 41,5 x 31,9 cm
166. Nazi-Geld in der Schweiz (unveröffentlicht), 1997,
Öl auf Karton, 34,8 x 26,7 cm
167. Die Party ist aus (unveröffentlicht), 2001, Öl auf
Karton, 40,6 x 33,4 cm
167. Weicher Euro (unveröffentlicht), 2002, Öl auf
Karton, 37,8 x 31,1 cm

Kazuhiko Sano
169. Homo erectus (unveröffentlicht), 2003,
Acryl auf Karton, 52,5 x 43 cm
169. Mensch gegen Maschine, 1997, Acryl auf Karton,
50,6 x 41,9 cm

Marvin Mattelson
170. Jesus, allein zu Haus, 1997, Öl auf Karton,
40,5 x 30,5 cm
172. Buddhismus, 1998, Öl auf Karton, 40,5 x 31,3 cm
173. Im Land der Lügen, 2000, Öl auf Karton,
40,9 x 35,2 cm

Guy Billout
175. 2 vor 2000, 1998, Airbrush und Feder auf Karton,
32,9 x 25,2 cm
175. Die Weltformel (unveröffentlicht), 1999, Airbrush
und Feder auf Karton, 29,2 x 21,6 cm

Robert Giusti
176. Der göttliche Funke, 1998, Acryl auf Karton,
30,2 x 22,6 cm
178. Der Krieg der ersten Menschen, 2000, Acryl auf
Karton, 39,3 x 22,6 cm
179. Amazonas (unveröffentlicht), 2001, Acryl auf Karton,
35,3 x 27,7 cm

Dubosarskij & Vinogradov
181. Abschied vom Gestern, 1998, Öl auf Leinwand,
200 x 165 cm

Dynamic Duo
183. Die kleinen Monster, 1998, digital, 38,1 x 26 cm
184. Ist Erziehung sinnlos?, 1998, digital, 35,6 x 29,4 cm
185. Das Zappelphilipp-Syndrom, 2002, digital,
29,3 x 35,6 cm

Nancy Stahl
186. Japan, 1998, digital, 38,1 x 30,5 cm
188. Was ist soziale Gerechtigkeit?, 1999, digital,
38,1 x 30,3 cm

190. Aufbruch ins Euro-Land, 1999, digital, 38,6 x 30,5 cm
191. Ist Europa noch zu retten?, 1999, digital, 38,4 x 30,5 cm

Jean-Pierre Kunkel
192. Rasender Stillstand, 1998, Airbrush, Mischtechnik
auf Karton, 50,9 x 41,9 cm
194. Der Prinz, der Schatz und die Nazis, 1999, Airbrush,
Mischtechnik auf Karton, 57,6 x 50,2 cm
195. Krieg ohne Sieg, 1999, Airbrush, Mischtechnik
auf Karton, 39,3 x 30 cm
196. Abschied mit Schimpf und Schande, 1999, Airbrush,
Mischtechnik auf Karton, 48 x 38,1 cm
197. Die Entmachtung der Eltern, 2001, Airbrush,
Mischtechnik auf Karton, 48,8 x 35,7 cm
198. Ernstfall für Rot-Grün, 2001, Airbrush,
Mischtechnik auf Karton, 50,9 x 38,6 cm
199. Die Bush-Krieger, 2002, Airbrush, Mischtechnik
auf Karton, 50,1 x 38,8 cm
200. Was man lesen muss, 2001, Airbrush, Mischtechnik
auf Karton, 50,8 x 41,9 cm
201. Putin und die Milliardäre (unveröffentlicht), 2003,
Airbrush, Mischtechnik auf Karton, 49,7 x 37,2 cm
201. Lafontaine und Gysi (unveröffentlicht), 2002,
Airbrush, Mischtechnik auf Karton, 45,4 x 35,1 cm

Rafal Olbinski
202. Das Ost-West-Gefühl, 1999, Acryl auf Leinwand,
43,2 x 34,2 cm
204. New Berlin, 1999, Acryl auf Leinwand, 50,3 x 36,5 cm,
Leihgabe von Gerald D. Wagner, New York City
205. Was kann Psycho-Therapie?, 2000, Acryl auf
Leinwand, 32,2 x 49,5 cm
1. Entwurf, Acryl auf Leinwand, 55,4 x 40,2 cm
206. Das Ende des Universums, 2002, Acryl auf
Leinwand, 46,2 x 34,8 cm
207. Die blockierte Republik, 2002, Acryl auf Leinwand,
50,3 x 40,5 cm
208. Musik, 2003, Acryl auf Leinwand, 41,9 x 31,1 cm
209. Wer arbeitet, ist der Dumme, 2003, Acryl auf
Leinwand, 36,7 x 30,9 cm
210. Das neue Europa, 2004, Acryl auf Leinwand,
45,5 x 35,7 cm
211. Dem Frieden (k)eine Chance? (unveröffentlicht),
1999, Acryl auf Leinwand, 99,1 x 71,9 cm
211. Putin und die Milliardäre (unveröffentlicht), 2003,
Acryl auf Leinwand, 41,1 x 32,1 cm

Werner Bandel
213. Mythos Atlantis, 1998, Aquarell, 47,9 x 39,9 cm
213. Wie Glaube entsteht (unveröffentlicht), 2002,
Aquarell, 39,5 x 31,2 cm

Robert Rodriguez
215. Wo ist die Moral?, 1999, Acryl, digital, 42 x 29,7 cm
216. Der gedachte Gott, 2002, Acryl, digital, 42 x 29,7 cm
217. Wohin steuert Amerika?, 2000, Acryl, digital,
42 x 29,7 cm

John MacDonald
219. Die www.Welt, 2000, Scratchboard, digital,
38,7 x 32,9 cm
220. Die teure Billig-Uni, 2004, Scratchboard, digital,
38,7 x 28 cm
221. Die Party ist aus (unveröffentlicht), 2001,
Scratchboard, digital, 40,7 x 29,9 cm

Gregory Bridges
223. Unternehmen Größenwahn, 2000, Airbrush,
Mischtechnik auf Karton, 61,1 x 51 cm
224. Das Universum im Kopf, 2001, Airbrush,
Mischtechnik auf Karton, 63,8 x 39,5 cm
225. Hightech-Welt 2001, 2001, Airbrush, Mischtechnik
auf Karton, 63,8 x 39,5 cm

Chris F. Payne
227. Die verwöhnten Kleinen, 2000, Acryl, Farbstift,
Wasserfarbe, Öl, Tusche, Pastell auf Zeichenkarton,
38,7 x 30 cm
228. Klassenkrampf, 2003, Acryl, Farbstift, Wasserfarbe,
Öl, Tusche, Pastell auf Zeichenkarton,
40,2 x 32,2 cm

229. Abgehauen (unveröffentlicht), 2001, Acryl, Farbstift,
Wasserfarbe, Öl, Tusche, Pastell auf Zeichenkarton,
42,3 x 31,4 cm
230. Beute Kind (unveröffentlicht), 2002, Acryl, Farbstift,
Wasserfarbe, Öl, Tusche, Pastell auf Zeichenkarton,
41 x 31 cm
231. Mobilmania (unveröffentlicht), 2004, Acryl, Farbstift,
Wasserfarbe, Öl, Tusche, Pastell auf
Zeichenkarton, 40 x 32,4 cm

Hannes Binder
233. Dumm gelaufen, 2002, Scratchboard, 30,3 x 25 cm

Roberto Parada
234. Falsches Spiel mit echten Mördern (unveröffentlicht),
2003, Öl auf Leinwand, 60,7 x 45,9 cm
234. Die Droge Wichtigkeit, 2002, Öl auf Leinwand,
60,6 x 45,4 cm

Rob Brooks
237. Radikal-Kur gegen Arbeitslosigkeit, 2002, Öl auf
Leinwand, 60,8 x 48,4 cm

Michael Pleesz
239. Genosse Schröder, 2002, digital, 40,8 x 31 cm
239. Schlaue Mädchen, dumme Jungen (unveröffentlicht),
2004, digital, 42 x 29,6 cm

John Harwood
241. Operation Dosenpfand, 2003, digital, 41,9 x 29,8 cm

Sandra Shap
242. Erfundene Krankheiten, 2003, digital, 35,6 x 27,9 cm

Michael Deas
244. Das Projekt Aufklärung, 2004, Öl auf Hartfaser,
76,1 x 58,3 cm

Daniel Adel
247. Wird Amerika wieder demokratisch?, 2004, Öl auf
Hartfaser, 60,8 x 45,5 cm

Thomas Fluharty
248. Schlaue Mädchen, dumme Jungen, 2004, Acryl
auf Karton, 43 x 39,2 cm
248. Der kleine Sheriff (unveröffentlicht), 2001, Acryl auf
Karton, 38,7 x 27,7 cm

Robert Hunt
250. Der Anfang war das Wort (unveröffentlicht), 2002,
Öl auf Karton, 55,9 x 51,2 cm
250. Die eingebildete Weltmacht (unveröffentlicht), 2003,
Öl auf Karton, 76,2 x 56,5 cm

Gary Kelley
252. Herr der Gene (unveröffentlicht), 2002, Pastell auf
Karton, 46,4 x 36,4 cm

Liz Lomax
255. Mobilmania (unveröffentlicht), 2004,
3-D-Objekt

John Martin
257. Was man lesen muss (unveröffentlicht), 2001,
Acryl auf Karton, 46,4 x 31,4 cm

Wilson McLean
259. Mensch gegen Maschine (unveröffentlicht), 1997,
Öl auf Leinwand, 55,6 x 45,9 cm
259. Was fühlen Tiere? (unveröffentlicht), 2001,
Öl auf Leinwand, 37,9 x 30,3 cm

Marco Ventura
260. O Italien! (unveröffentlicht), 2003, Öl auf Karton,
32,9 x 25 cm
260. Neue Heimat Süd (unveröffentlicht), 2001,
Öl auf Karton, 30,6 x 24,4 cm

Der SPIEGEL-Verlag dankt für die freundliche Unterstützung von:
SPIEGEL publishing house would like to extend its thanks for the kind
support of:

Adobe